The Lexington Automobile

ALSO BY RICHARD A. STANLEY

*Custom Built by McFarlan: A History of the Carriage
and Automobile Manufacturer, 1856–1928*
(McFarland, 2012)

The Lexington Automobile

A Complete History

RICHARD A. STANLEY

McFarland & Company, Inc., Publishers
Jefferson, North Carolina, and London

The present work is a reprint of the illustrated case bound edition of The Lexington Automobile: A Complete History, *first published in 2007 by McFarland.*

Library of Congress Cataloguing-in-Publication Data

Stanley, Richard A., 1936–
The Lexington automobile : a complete history / Richard A. Stanley.
    p.   cm.
Includes bibliographical references and index.

ISBN 978-0-7864-6934-5
softcover : acid free paper ∞

1. Lexington automobile—History.   I. Title.
TL215.L48S73   2012   338.7'6292220973—dc22   2006034610

British Library cataloguing data are available

© 2007 Richard A. Stanley. All rights reserved

No part of this book may be reproduced or transmitted in any form or by any means, electronic or mechanical, including photocopying or recording, or by any information storage and retrieval system, without permission in writing from the publisher.

Edited by Steve Wilson

On the cover: "Trail Blazer" ad by E. Pierre Wainwright
(courtesy of Suzanne Wainwright Evans)

Manufactured in the United States of America

McFarland & Company, Inc., Publishers
Box 611, Jefferson, North Carolina 28640
www.mcfarlandpub.com

To the memory of my late brother,
Marvin C. Stanley,
who was helpful in obtaining materials for this book.

He and his wife, Dottie, traveled to Detroit with my wife and me to visit the Detroit Public Library. I valued his opinions on mechanical terms and descriptions. He even used his mechanical know-how to get my 1921 Lexington running. He was a wonderful example for me in his service to God and to fellow man. I never dreamed that he would not be here to see this book in print, but he passed away unexpectedly September 23, 2006, in Terre Haute, Indiana.

Acknowledgments

Preparing this book for publication has truly been a labor of love. I have been a "car nut" since childhood, and have collected literature and information on automobiles since the close of World War II. I started visiting dealerships for literature when my family lived in Des Moines, Iowa, but continued when my dad changed jobs and moved to Terre Haute, Indiana. When I struck out on my own, it was a teaching job that brought me to Connersville, Indiana, where I learned about some of the industries that had bloomed and later withered in this community.

Many people have willingly offered material and assistance in preparing this book. First, and most important, has been the support and encouragement given by my wife, Carol. It was certainly a labor of true love for her to be involved as she is not terribly interested in automobiles, but she still spent hours looking at microfilm and checking spelling, grammar and punctuation. My family has helped with my limited computer skills and has given support. They are Diane, in Richmond, Indiana, Lynn and Mike Engle in Xenia, Ohio, Alan and Charlene and Andrew and Anne Stanley in Connersville.

Others who have provided materials or support are as follows:

Connersville, IN: Connie Lake, Paulette Hayes, Melissa Callahan and the staff of the Fayette County Public Library; Jim Wicker and the volunteers with the Fayette County Historical Museum; Ann Frost, Fayette County Recorder; Patrick Keller from the *Connersville News Examiner*; Cindy Nichols, Linda Siler and the staff at Commercial Printing; Jim Vermillion; Wayne Goetz; Mike Sparks; Bob Sparks; Jim Robinson; Shirley McCoy; John Blommel; Robert F. Williams; Pat Holmes and John Johnson. Marion, IN: Louis Ebert. Liberty, IN: Robert Barnard, Eldon and Audrey Brown. Boston, IN: William Tindall. Slatington, PA: Suzanne Wainwright Evans. Iola, WI: Keith Mathiowetz. Indianapolis, IN: Eric vonGrimmenstein, Donald Davidson of the Indianapolis Motor Speedway Museum, Jane Walker, John S. Ansted. Terre Haute, IN: Marvin and Dorothy Stanley. Detroit, MI: Kenneth Lane, the staff of the National Automotive History Collection, Detroit Public Library. Xenia, OH: Ben Thompson. Berlin, PA: R. Donald Williams. Louisville, KY: Wesley Schickli. Lexington, KY, area: Gene and Ann Towles, Grant Baker, David Estes, David Bottom, Bob Mason, William Ambrose, Jan Marshall and the staff of the Kentucky Room of the Lexington Public Library, Phyllis Rogers of the Keenland Racetrack Library. Nicholasville, KY: Bill Baker, Ray Clark. Georgetown, KY: John Toncray, the staff of the Georgetown–Scott County Museum. Paris, KY: James Poe. Barnstable, MA: Sturgis St. Peter. Clarksburg, MD: Bernard Wolfson. Cincinnati, OH: Ruth Bauer, Jerry Corbett, Jay Kolb. Dublin, OH: Ron and Peg Margello. Walton Hills, OH: James H. Davis. Youngsville, LA: Todd Goudeau. VA: Oscar Borufsen. Ft. Myers, FL: John J. Mawhinney. Ojai, CA: Raymond D. Gordon. Gardnerville, NV: Ted Bacon. San

Rafael, CA: Mike Gibbens. Karlsdad, Sweden: Igemar Olsson, Matts Heder, Jan Rune. Chatswood, Australia: David Manson, New Zealand: Arnold Koppens. I also extend my sincere heartfelt appreciation to any whom I may have omitted. This book would not have been possible without the information offered from so many willing persons.

   I have been diligent in my research and have made every effort to be accurate in my writing. Any errors in spelling or content which have crept into the text are certainly unintentional. I apologize now for any such errors.

Contents

Acknowledgments	vii
Preface	1
1. Birth of a Thoroughbred in the Bluegrass State	5
2. The Lexington Becomes a Hoosier	40
3. A New Name is Born	67
4. The War Years	96
5. Lexington Goes to the Races	121
6. A New Corporation and Continued Expansion	148
7. Loss of Credit and Credibility	179
8. Lexington Lives On	202
9. A Gallery of Surviving Lexingtons	207
Appendix: Lexington Models	233
Notes	235
Bibliography	241
Index	251

Preface

In the years since the first motorized carriages chugged out into the world of horses, more than five thousand different makes of automobiles have fueled the fancy of the American public and, indeed, of all the world. Many of these companies were obscure establishments that cobbled together a few machines but still made the roster of automobiles once produced in this country. Hundreds of volumes have been written about the various marques, but the concentration has naturally been on the better-known names.

When I moved to Connersville, Indiana, about 45 years ago, I soon learned that it had once been a center of automobile production and parts manufacturing. The community rightfully took a great deal of pride in pointing to the Auburns of the mid-thirties and earlier, and especially the Cord 810 and 812 as products of this southeastern Indiana city. Also mentioned as local products were unknowns such as the Central, the Van Auken Electric, the Empire and the Lexington. The Auburn and the Cord, as true American classics, have received appropriate attention from historians, but the lesser known makes have little to show for their existence.

The very earliest attempts at building automobiles in Connersville were not very successful. A 1917 Fayette County history by Frederic I. Barrows tells of the first known self propelled vehicle built locally. It seems that in the 1870s, Harvin Tryon built a steam wagon for the purpose of taking a trip to his old home in Georgia. Many thought him to be of unsound mind as he loaded his wagon and headed south. All went well until he attempted to ford a stream in southern Kentucky and got into quicksand, whereupon the wagon sank. When water reached the boiler an explosion occurred and Fayette County's first motorized vehicle passed into oblivion. What was probably the second attempt was the Central car, built by Central Manufacturing Company in 1905. The building where the vehicle was being assembled burned and destroyed the car before it was ever driven.

The automobile industry took off after that and played a significant role in the development of Connersville. Various automobiles were manufactured here including Ansted, 1921–1922 and 1926; Auburn, 1929–1936; Cord (810 and 812), 1936–1937; Empire, 1912–1915; GMC (army truck chassis), 1918–1919; Howard, 1913–1914; Lexington, 1910–1927; McFarlan, 1909–1928; and a small rear-engine delivery van, Package-Car, 1939–1941. There have also been numerous parts manufacturers over the years; notably the Indiana Lamp Company and Central Manufacturing Company, which later became part of Auburn Central. Here the bodies for the 1940 Packard Darrin were made and nearly 500,000 Jeep bodies and trailers for Jeeps were manufactured during World War II. The Tractor-Train Company of Indiana, which later became Lincoln Manufacturing Company; Wainwright Engineering, which sold out to McQuay Norris; Stant Manufacturing, which is still in operation; and Rex Manufacturing, which later became Philco-Ford and is now Visteon Corporation, are some of the better known firms.

Although not much had been written about the Lexington, Fayette County historian Henry Blommel laid the groundwork. Henry grew up in Connersville and studied local industry, becoming the recognized authority on locally made products. He wrote the booklet *Indiana's Little Detroit 1846–1964* that listed the better-known industries giving highlights of their existence. He also authored an article, "The Mighty Minute Man," about the Lexington Motor Company that appeared in the Nov./Dec. 1969 issue of *Antique Automobile*. More recently, a book entitled *Lexington Motor Car* was written and published by William M. Ambrose of Lexington, Kentucky. This work concentrates on the company's first couple of years while it was located in Kentucky.

As I heard from time to time various stories and tall tales about what a great performance car the Lexington had been, I wished there was more information readily available on this Connersville product. But I hadn't given serious consideration to doing anything about it until I was asked to help with a research project for the Fayette County Public Library. While reviewing newspapers on microfilm, identifying articles related to local automobile industries, I was amazed at the number of items relating to the Lexington Motor Company. After deciding to write a book, I made a second viewing of Connersville newspapers on microfilm making a copy of every article related to the company or persons connected with it. I was privileged to have conversations with some of the area's older citizens who willingly shared stories, opinions and photos. My wife and I also made trips to Lexington, Kentucky, and spent a number of hours in the Kentucky Room at the Lexington Public Library searching microfilm and copying articles. We also visited the Keenland Race Track Library and learned that the correct spelling of the early financier whose name is generally seen as Kinsey Stone is actually Kinzea Stone. On other trips to central Kentucky, we found valuable information and photos at the Georgetown–Scott County Museum and at Kenston, the mansion once occupied by Stone and his family. This beautiful home, including a lot of the original, ornate furnishings, is still being maintained in a stately manner. Additional research was done at the National Automotive History Collection in the Detroit Public Library, the Auburn-Cord-Duesenberg Museum at Auburn, Indiana, and at the Dayton Public Library. Everyone was most helpful and seemed pleased to be able to contribute to the cause. I had also collected several pieces of original literature and advertising through the years that provided important technical information.

The Lexington story is just one minuscule part of the industrial revolution that was given a tremendous boost by the advent of the self-propelled automobile. Although the industrial revolution was changing life across this vast nation decades before the automobile made its debut, the factories that produced these four-wheeled chariots plus the thousands of suppliers that provided parts, fuel and repairs have had an impact on the lives of individuals and communities beyond comprehension. Even during the earlier years, there was competition between towns to land one or more of the factories. It is common knowledge today that local communities and even states compete for new industry with various offers of financial assistance. It was a surprise to me to learn that even a century ago incentives were offered to get factories to locate in a specific town. When the first Lexington factory was built, the local commercial club, made up of businessmen and community leaders in central Kentucky, paid for the land upon which the plant was built. Within a few months after this building had been put into operation, feelers were being put out to other cities for a package that would encourage relocation. Initially, the home city was caught asleep, not recognizing the need for additional space or the danger of losing their new factory until it was too late. In Indiana, three cities in particular competed for this prize with the Connersville Commercial Club winning the contest by raising enough money to build a two-story brick building that included an up-to-date modern convenience in the form of an electric elevator large enough to move heavy equipment to the second floor. Additional perks given the company included free water and exemption from local taxes for five years. Almost certainly, many other communities would have matched or surpassed the offer had not family ties also entered into the picture. Even in those days, whom you knew was just as important as what you had to offer, so the first motor car manufacturer to locate south of the Ohio River moved from a thriving city to a much smaller but aggressive up-start industrial town. The industrial revolution had taken hold of communities large and small throughout America.

The intent of this book is to document as nearly as possible the Lexington and related automobiles, Howard and Ansted, by year and model, giving technical information and illustrations showing features. As far as I have been able to determine, no company records survive. There were numerous reports in newspapers, however, indicating the fat years and the lean ones, and sometimes there are clues as to why finances were what they were. Lexington was a leader in the use of color in magazine advertising and factory issued literature. They also used advertising to quietly support certain issues such as women's suffrage. Automobile trade magazines were good sources of technical information and innovative ideas that the company promoted. The finished product would not have happened without numerous persons who had a vision of being a leader in industry, of producing a better vehicle, or of making profits, or maybe to be able to save what someone else had started. The enthusiasm and desire of these numerous persons seemed to be just as strong with Kentuckians who started the operation as with Hoosiers who took up the banner and carried it on.

1

Birth of a Thoroughbred in the Bluegrass State

The year 1908 was enormously important in the history of the American automobile industry. There were approximately 63,500 cars produced that year, some of which still resembled horseless carriages of nearly a decade before. A few of the new names that arrived on the market that year were Bendix, Chalmers-Detroit, Davis, De Tamble, E-M-F, Garford, Palmer-Singer, Sears and Zimmerman. Among the well known makes already established were Buick, Cadillac, Ford, Franklin, Locomobile, Maxwell, Oldsmobile, Packard, Rambler, Reo and Stanley. Probably the most important events affecting the automobile industry that year were the founding of General Motors by William C. Durant and the introduction of the Model T by Henry Ford, both of which would have a profound effect on American industry and culture. Far less remembered would be the founding of the Lexington Motor Car Company in early December of 1908.

In Central Kentucky, and throughout the country, interest in this new form of transportation ran strong. Countless persons were experimenting with engines, installing them in buggies or homemade contrivances to achieve horseless motive power. One such tinkerer, John C. Moore, was born in 1869 near Oxford in Scott County, Kentucky.[1] He was raised in an atmosphere where good horses were a prized possession, but he was intrigued by the new types of transportation that were all the rage, getting attention in magazines and newspapers. Bicycles had become a popular means of personal conveyance and bicycle racing was a popular sport with the young folks. Moore entered a bicycle race in 1893 competing against Max Wilson, Clarence Graves, and George Cox, all from Scott County. The race was from Winchester to Lexington over muddy roads. Moore came in second with a time of fifty-eight minutes and thirty-two seconds.[2] A machinist by trade, in 1899 Moore put together his own experimental vehicle with the major component parts being a wagon and a gasoline engine.[3] This contraption was driven on the streets of Newtown and possibly Lexington, much to the amusement and ire of local residents.[4] Another vehicle was completed in 1901; then in 1907, while an employee of the Blue Grass Automobile Company of Lexington, he designed and built what he considered to be "a real automobile."[5] It was Moore and his automobile that stimulated enough interest among curious onlookers and investors to establish a company to manufacture a car in Central Kentucky where horses reigned.

So it was that the Lexington Motor Car Company was incorporated in Lexington, Kentucky. On December 2, 1908, papers were filed with Theo Lewis, Clerk of the County Court of Fayette County, by the Lexington Motor Car Company.[6] The

STATE OF KENTUCKY
OFFICE AUDITOR PUBLIC ACCOUNTS
FRANKFORT

HON. BEN L. BRUNER, Secretary of State,
Frankfort, Ky.

Dear Sir:

Notice is hereby given that the *Lexington Motor Car Co.* has this day paid into the State Treasury the sum of $ *50—*, being the organization tax of one-tenth of one per cent. of its authorized capital, imposed by law on all corporations organized in the Commonwealth pursuant to the laws thereof.

Given under my hand as Auditor Public Accounts this *15* of *Dec*, 190*8*.

F. P. JAMES,
Auditor.
By *Coon*

Return Check $ *3 oc*

Above and opposite: Articles of Incorporation were filed with the Kentucky Secretary of State acknowledging the new Lexington Motor Car Company. *Courtesy Kentucky Secretary of State.*

company was authorized to transact any business connected with automobiles such as buying, selling, renting, manufacturing, repairing, maintaining a garage or other such business.[7] The company office was established in the Hernando Building. Another announcement of the planned automobile production was made December 4 stating that drawings for the car were already being made and that a location for the plant would soon be determined and machinery ordered.[8] In a board meeting held December 7, Dr. Francis F. Bryan was elected president of the company and Kinzea Stone agreed to take the position of vice-president. On December 15, the articles of incorporation were filed with the Secretary of State, establishing the conditions under which the company would be operating and specifying that the corporation could be in existence for a period of up to 50 years and that the $50,000 in capital stock would be divided into 500 shares at $100 each. The names and place of residence of the initial stockholders were listed as follows:

The new corporation could commence business as soon as 50 percent or more of the capital stock was subscribed.[9] A short time later, Kinzea Stone purchased an additional 270 shares. He was then the majority shareholder.

Names	Residence	Shares
Kinzea Stone	Georgetown, Ky.	25
F. F. Bryan	Georgetown, Ky.	48
Benjamin Stone	Georgetown, Ky.	10
John Osborn	Georgetown, Ky.	10
J. P. Jackson	Georgetown, Ky.	10
L. H. McGraw	Georgetown, Ky.	5
V. A. Bradley	Georgetown, Ky.	5
Charles O'Neill	Georgetown, Ky.	5
J. C. Moore	Lexington, KY	31
G. D. Wilson	Lexington, KY	10
V. K. Dodge	Lexington, KY	10
F. O. Young	Lexington, KY	5

Kinzea Stone seems to be an unlikely participant in this kind of venture, let alone the major shareholder, because he was known for being a successful racehorse promoter. Born in 1850 in Bourbon County, Kentucky,[10] Stone entered the grocery trade with his brother. Then, at age 22, he struck out on his own, moving to George-

be subject to the payment of its corporate debts.

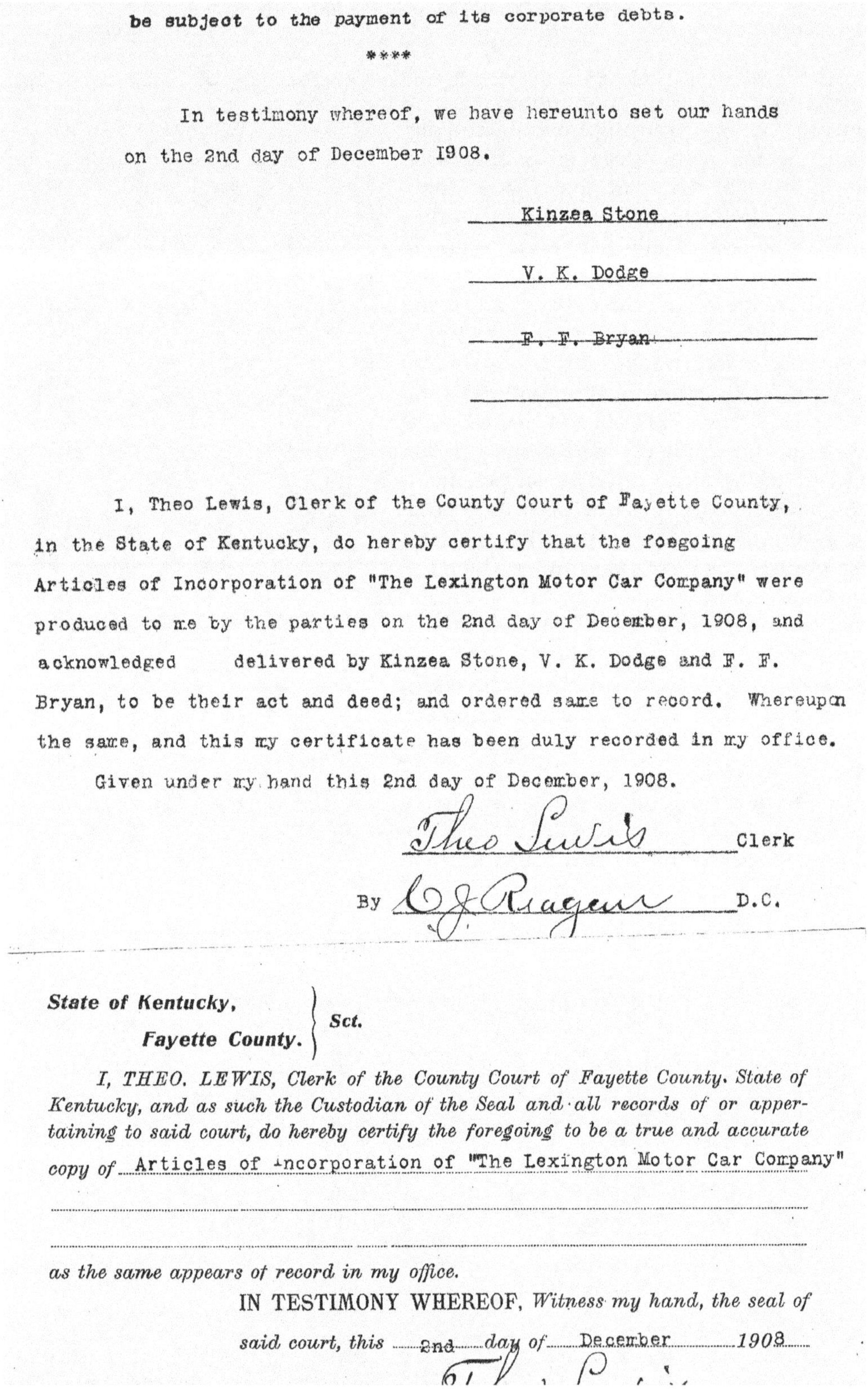

****

In testimony whereof, we have hereunto set our hands on the 2nd day of December 1908.

Kinzea Stone

V. K. Dodge

~~F. F. Bryan~~

I, Theo Lewis, Clerk of the County Court of Fayette County, in the State of Kentucky, do hereby certify that the foregoing Articles of Incorporation of "The Lexington Motor Car Company" were produced to me by the parties on the 2nd day of December, 1908, and acknowledged delivered by Kinzea Stone, V. K. Dodge and F. F. Bryan, to be their act and deed; and ordered same to record. Whereupon the same, and this my certificate has been duly recorded in my office.

Given under my hand this 2nd day of December, 1908.

Theo Lewis Clerk

By *C J Reagan* D.C.

State of Kentucky,
Fayette County. } Sct.

I, THEO. LEWIS, Clerk of the County Court of Fayette County, State of Kentucky, and as such the Custodian of the Seal and all records of or appertaining to said court, do hereby certify the foregoing to be a true and accurate copy of Articles of Incorporation of "The Lexington Motor Car Company"

as the same appears of record in my office.
IN TESTIMONY WHEREOF, Witness my hand, the seal of said court, this 2nd day of December 1908

Fayette County, Kentucky, was to be the first home of the Lexington Motor Car Co. *Courtesy Kentucky Secretary of State.*

Kenston, built in 1892 on a hill overlooking Georgetown, Kentucky, was the residence of Kinzea Stone. *Photograph by the author.*

town where he continued in the same type of business. In 1892 he built Kenston, a pretentious mansion that is still impressive, on a hill overlooking the business district of Georgetown. Stone was especially successful with breeding and racing horses, being co-owner of Kingman, who won victories at both the Kentucky and Latonia derbies in 1891 while ridden by Isaac Murphy. In his later years, Stone was part owner of Sweep, a stallion that sired 46 stakes winners. In addition to his successes with horses, Stone was mayor of Georgetown from 1914 to 1918. He also owned the Maud S. Tobacco factory, cotton and sugar cane land in Cuba, phosphate lands in Florida and oil holdings in Kansas.[11] It was his ability to earn on his investments that brought Stone into the automobile business.

No time was wasted putting things into motion. The building site for the Lexington Motor Car Company was being paid for by the Lexington Commercial Club, and a committee from that group assisted in securing the location. The committee was composed of Commercial Club President E. D. Bassett, J. W. Porter, John Skain, E. B. Ellis, H. K. McAdams, and Secretary John G. Cramer.[12] At least two locations for the factory were considered: an unoccupied property just west of the Catholic cemetery on West Main Street and a building occupied by the Mammoth Skating Rink on Fourth Street near downtown. There is no indication as to whether any of the committee members had an interest in either property, but two and one half acres of property was purchased from Patrick Sharkey on or about December 15.[13] The property had 427 feet fronting on Leestown Pike (also known as West Main) at the intersection of the Queen and Crescent Railroad and the end of the Belt Line. The Belt Line was the local trolley line that offered transportation for work-

This Lexington limousine was purchased by Kinzea Stone and fitted with special wheels he designed. *Courtesy the Stone collection.*

ers. No sooner had the agreement been reached to purchase the Sharkey property than an effort was made to interest company officials in trading their unoccupied land plus some additional payment for the Mammoth Skating Rink. A committee appointed by the officers of the newly formed company inspected the large building and also visited the Sharkey property. The Fourth Street property was regarded as desirable because it already contained a building that, with a few changes, would suit the needs of the company. Another feature in its favor was the fact that considerable money and time could be saved because a building would not have to be built, enabling production to begin sooner.[14] After inspecting both properties, Dr. Bryan, president of the Lexington Motor Car Company, announced that the Fourth Street location was not suited to their purpose because it was too far away from the railroad so receiving goods and shipping finished products would not be convenient.[15]

The plans for the new factory were unusual in that the building was designed in the form of a cross. Each wing of the cross was to be 152 feet long by 40 feet wide. Plans were to have the building completed by March 1, 1909.[16] The fact that a factory to build automobiles was being planned brought excitement because it would be the first of its kind in Kentucky. By mid–January the contract for the single story brick building had been let to local contractor Frank Corbin. Work began immediately on grading for a railroad siding and preparing for the foundation for the new building. The weather was exceptionally cooperative with warmer temperatures some days than would usually be expected. On January 22, a balmy 66 degrees was recorded, breaking the old mark for that date, but then it was discovered that, due to an error in surveying, the construction was about fifteen feet over on the Chesapeake and Ohio Railway right of way. Railway General Agent Andrew Mitchell brought the matter to the attention of company president Dr. Bryan and all work was stopped for a few days until the controversy was settled and building plans could be altered to eliminate the encroachment.[17] The end result was that the building became rectangular in shape, no longer in the form of a cross, and may not have been as spacious as had originally been planned.

At a board meeting held January 12, 1909, the name for the new automobile was selected. After much discussion of the most appropriate name, the stockholders decided on the name Lexington, intending to take advantage of the reputation that the city had already established.[18] This act showed a great deal of pride held by these gentlemen for this Central Kentucky city. None of their own names was to adorn the front of the radiator as often happened when choosing a name for a vehicle. By late January the company office was moved from the Hernando Building to the Trust Building, where offices had been handsomely furnished to accommodate company officials.[19]

A portrait photograph of Preston Kinzea Stone. *Courtesy the Stone Collection.*

New personnel had been hired to get ready for production. Fred N. Coats was brought in from Dayton, Ohio, as plant manager and to be in charge of sales. He brought actual experience, having worked for the Dayton Motor Car Company, makers of the Stoddard-Dayton automobile, for a number of years. He also had con-

Stone's signature, showing the correct spelling of his name.

tacts with experienced upholsterers and painters who would be needed when operations actually started. John C. Moore was to be in charge of the mechanical department, selecting the components that were to make up the finished product. On January 13, Moore and Coats boarded a train for the North to contract with companies who would supply parts to include engines, tires, axles, bodies, bearings and so on.[20] Stops on their trip were almost certainly Connersville and Logansport, Indiana, and Canton and Akron, Ohio. Connersville had companies that manufactured springs and car bodies, Indianapolis had the Prest-O-Light factory for lights, Logansport was the headquarters for the Rutenber Engine factory, Akron had tires,

Top: Kinzea Stone and his family with his Lexington Limousine dressed up for a Georgetown parade. The building in the background is now the Georgetown College president's house. *Bottom:* A parade at Georgetown, Kentucky; Kinzea Stone is standing at the far right. The car is a Lexington touring owned by Stone. *Courtesy the Georgetown–Scott County Museum, Georgetown, Kentucky.*

Inside the West Main Street assembly plant in Lexington, Kentucky. *Malick's Art Studio, Lexington, Kentucky.*

and Canton was home to the Timken Roller Bearing Axle Company. Although Moore was the recognized designer of the new marque, Coats' previous experience in car manufacturing and familiarity with suppliers had an obvious influence in choosing the same engine make and a very similar design for the radiator as was used by Stoddard-Dayton.

The next month, Fred Coats again went north, this time with Dr. Bryan, to attend the National Automobile Show that was held in Chicago. This show was reported to have been the largest automobile show in the country because it included both licensed and unlicensed manufacturers.[21] In New York City, there had been two separate shows; one for companies that had been licensed under the Selden patent, and another for unlicensed companies that had refused to pay the patent royalties. This confusing part of automobile history came about when patent number 549,160 was granted to George B. Selden in 1895, for a gasoline-powered carriage. In order to collect royalties from automobile producers, the Association of Licensed Automobile Manufacturers was formed in 1900. The A.L.A.M. coerced many companies to join their group and pay a percentage of their sales to the organization or face court action. There were indications that all carmakers would eventually give in and pay up, but Henry Ford refused to do so. After a long battle he defeated the A.L.A.M. in 1911, convincing an appeals court that the patent applied

The first Lexington built was purchased by Sidney D. Clay of Paris, Kentucky. The West Main Street factory is in the background. *Courtesy the Stone collection.*

only to two-cycle engines, whereas the industry was using almost exclusively the four-cycle type.[22] The Lexington Motor Car Company never became licensed with the A.L.A.M. and was not pressured to do so since the association was busy litigating larger companies. By 1912, the A.L.A.M. was no longer a viable force and New York City hosted only one major car show.

The two cars that really gained Coats and Bryan's admiration at the Chicago show were the Thomas Flyer that had carried the American flag around the world in the New York to Paris race, and the Locomobile that had won the Vanderbilt Cup the previous fall. That was the first time the cup had been won by an American racer.[23] The challenge of winning in competitive events had made its mark, and Coats had boasted that there would be several Lexingtons in the upcoming Glidden Tour.[24]

Back in Kentucky, construction at the plant progressed rapidly, so that by early February, the concrete floor was being put down and the roofing was progressing. The floor was given a green finish to harmonize with the "mission furnishing" of the offices. The health and convenience of employees was taken into account with ventilation and lighting provided by the many windows, and hot water was piped to the washroom from the water cooling apparatus of a gas engine.[25] By March 2 machinery was being installed and the company offices had been moved from the Trust Building to the new factory.[26] Several rail car loads of parts and supplies that had been ordered earlier in the year were arriving and being made ready to begin the assembly process.[27] The expectation was that approximately twenty-five men would be needed to work in the factory for this company that was the first of very few automobile manufacturers to locate south of the Ohio River.[28]

The Lexington was an assembled car, meaning that the company did not manufacture individual parts, but "brought together an accumulation of tried and

1—Birth of a Thoroughbred in the Bluegrass State 15

Top: The office of Fred N. Coats, manager of the company. *Bottom:* The office of Lexington designer J. C. Moore and Harry S. Johnson, purchasing agent. *Courtesy David Estes.*

The office of company president Dr. F. F. Bryan and his secretary G. D. Wilson, Jr. Bryan resigned as president in September 1909. *Courtesy David Estes.*

proven parts" that were put together to become a finished product.[29] Lexington would be considered an assembled car throughout its history; however, in later years they were closely allied with supplier factories under one family's ownership so that the "assembled" designation could well be challenged. Among the component parts that became a Lexington were bodies "in the white" by Central Manufacturing.[30] The bodies were shipped unfinished so the customer could choose the paint color and upholstering material. Painting and upholstering were done at the Lexington plant. The brass plated radiator shell, headlights and various smaller trim parts added sparkle to the variety of colors offered. Fuel for the headlights was provided by acetylene gas from a brass tank mounted on the running board. Brass sidelights and tail lamps used kerosene to provide light. The standard five-passenger touring body could be ordered with two additional seats to accommodate seven passengers. The steering wheel and dashboard were made from Circassian walnut and were highly polished.

The heart of the car was the four cylinder 40–45 horsepower water cooled 4 cycle Rutenber gasoline engine with 4¼ inch bore and 5 inch stroke giving a displacement of 283.7 cubic inches.[31] The engine had double ignition, and a vertical shaft in front powered the oil pump, magneto and the timer. Individual castings for each cylinder permitted repair or removal of any one of the four pistons without affecting the others so there was no engine block. The lower part of the engine was enclosed by a two-piece crankcase, the bottom part being the oil pan and the top part supporting the five bearing crankshaft. The flywheel was of large diameter and heavy, but its momentum, when running, provided smoothness of operation. The driveline included a leather-faced cone clutch with cork inserts, three-speed selective gear-set with H quadrant and the shift lever to the right of the driver mounted on the outside of the body along with the hand brake. As with most cars of that day, the driver sat on the right hand side of the car, the steering wheel being positioned so that the operator had a clear view of the edge of the road so as not to get too close to the side ditch that was likely to be muddy. A Timken floating rear axle was used. With this type of axle, the weight of the car was carried by the axle housing and not by the shafts that turn the wheels. Large Schwarz wheels carrying 36 inch × 4 inch Goodrich tires on Goodyear universal rims gave necessary ground clearance for muddy roads that were all too common. Each front wheel had ten spokes with twelve for each rear wheel. Brake drums were fastened to the rear wheels with a bolt through each spoke. The drums did double duty with the hand brake applying pressure to the outside of the drum whereas the foot brake controlled internal expanding binders. The front axle, also Timken, was of I beam design carrying the front wheels on tapered roller bearings. The main frame was of pressed channel steel with a sub-frame upon which the engine and transmission were hung. Both front and rear springs were semi-elliptic with the front being 40 inches and the rear 52 inches long.[32]

The Rutenber engine was one of several popular powerplants of the day and the company claimed to be the first in the United States to manufacture four cylinder motors.[33] Its founder, Edwin A. Rutenber, was born in Sadorus, Illinois, in 1876. After learning the machinist's trade as a youth, he began experimenting with gasoline engines. His first successful attempt at engine building resulted in a single-cylinder unit built about 1892, but he had built a four-cylinder motor by 1898. Beginning in late 1901, the Rutenber four-cylinder engine was being produced in Chicago and was marketed for automotive, marine and stationary use. By the middle of the next year the company, needing more space, relocated in Logansport, Indiana, in a building adjacent to the Logansport Foundry Company. Rutenber arranged for the neighboring foundry to make castings for their motors. Within a few months, the two companies combined to form the Western Motor Company. By 1909 the company again needed more space and was induced to locate a branch plant in Marion, Indiana.[34] Therefore, when Fred Coats and John Moore traveled north to purchase parts for the new Kentucky produced automobile, they would have placed the order at Logansport, but when Lexington production actually got rolling, Rutenber engines were coming from Marion. By 1912, the Western Motor Company claimed to have approximately 450 men employed between the Marion and Logansport plants, and was supplying Rutenber engines for thirteen different automobile companies including Auburn, Lexington, Luverne, Nyberg and Wescott.[35]

On Saturday afternoon, April 3, 1909, the first Lexington was shown on the streets and was viewed by many admirers. The car was a five or seven-passenger touring with "enough power for any road and speed enough for any occasion" and listed at $2,500.[36] After some good natured competition to see who would get the first car, it was purchased by Sidney D. Clay of Paris, Kentucky. According to Dr. Bryan, company president, the company was by this time fully equipped for manufacturing its finished product and they expected to turn out five automobiles a week.[37] Majority stockholder Kinzea Stone purchased the second car produced, a touring car.[38] Less than a year later, he purchased a new white limousine, built on custom order.[39] He also had at least one truck built for use in his grocery and dry goods

Rutenberg motors were first made at Logansport, Indiana, but production had been moved to Marion, Indiana, by the time Lexington cars were being assembled. *Ad from* Automobile, *Jan. 14, 1909.*

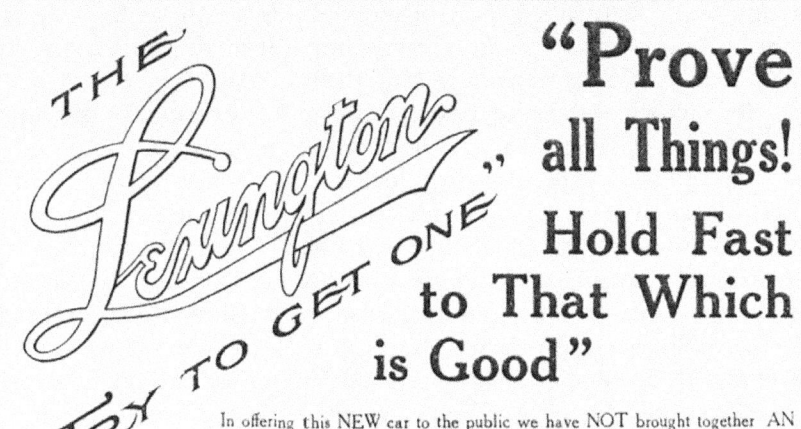

The introductory advertisement for Lexington appeared in the May 1, 1909, *Cycle and Automobile Trade Journal*, a well known automotive trade magazine.

businesses. Kinzea always referred to the automobile as "that machine." He did not drive, but instead employed a chauffeur. In July of 1910, Kinzea took a trip to Chicago in his Lexington limousine to see his sister who was known as Aunt Betty Bell. His wife was never comfortable riding in a car, but still made the lengthy trip, which would have been a significant undertaking in those days.[40]

The introductory notices for Lexington listed three models; the Model A, five or seven-passenger touring, Model B, four-passenger light touring, and Model C, two-passenger roadster with a rumble seat or "mother-in-law seat," all priced at $2,500. Wheelbase of all models was 120 inches with 56 inch tread (or track).

By the time the Lexington Motor Company had been producing cars for a little over two months, arrangements were made for the Commercial Club to tour the plant and see how their money had been used.[41] On June 11 the guests were transported from the depot on South Broadway to the Lexington plant by a special train provided by the Queen and Crescent Railroad. There, the club members were given a "glad hand tour and were royally entertained."[42] They were able to witness more than sixty men assembling nineteen cars that were in various stages of completion. Every phase of the work of building a car, from painting the frame to doing the finishing touches, was being done. After the tour, a Dutch lunch was served before the group returned to the city. The guests were told of the need to enlarge the building because of the growing business. Lexington was currently turning out five cars per week, but hoped to increase the volume somewhat.[43] The company that started out expecting to employ twenty-five men already had sixty employees and would be adding more as orders were received.

The Lexington name selection must have been a good one, because even for this entirely new marque, orders were coming in from far and near. In mid–April, photographs of the new touring car were sent to New York City and other eastern cities for advertising purposes.[44] In June, two cars were shipped to the Deright Auto Company in Omaha, Nebraska, two to the Haynes Auto Company of Minneapolis, two to the Houghton & Bell Company of Richmond, Indiana, and a big touring to the Collins Auto Company of San Antonio, Texas. The really substantial order had come from the Nock Auto Company of Providence, Rhode Island, for twenty-five cars.[45]

One way that automobile manufacturers had of building a name for themselves was through competition in various contests. A particular contest that attracted the attention of company officials early on was a hill climb competition at Chattanooga, Tennessee, sponsored by the Lookout Mountain Automobile Club. The event was to be held April 22–24 and it was announced that a Lexington would be among the competitors. The intent was to showcase the new make in an event that would draw national recognition and would probably attract upwards of one thousand auto enthusiasts.[46] Soon after the initial announcement had been made, though, the company reversed its position saying the earlier statement had been made without authority and that the expert men that would be required for participation in the hill climb contest could not be spared at that time.[47] All hands were needed to get production under way and there was also a lack of available vehicles as finished cars were just beginning to trickle out of the factory.

Another event was promoted by the Phoenix Motor Car Company, the local dealer for the Lexington, along with support from the factory. In large ads, they announced that $100 in gold had been deposited in the Phoenix National Bank and would be given to the winner of a fifty mile race.[48] The competition, originally

This newspaper ad in *The Lexington Herald*, May 5, 1909, announced a race sponsored by Phoenix Motor Car Co., the local Lexington dealer, with $100 in gold given to the winner.

Automobile races were used to promote products and prove reliability. Lexington entered this race long on optimism and short on experience. The Lexington Herald, *May 9, 1909.*

scheduled for May 29, was held on June 5, at the Kentucky Trotting Horse Breeders' Association track. In the process of planning the race, company officials learned that the American Automobile Association had adopted a rule requiring that all contests be subject to the rules of the association if the car owners desired to be eligible to enter any events sanctioned by the organization. It was thought that participants would be "practically black listed" for entering non-sanctioned events. Therefore, the contest was conducted under the auspices of the Blue Grass Motor Club, the local branch of the American Automobile Association.[49] The Lexington Motor Car Company, to prove their confidence in their new car, invited all cars regardless of price or grade, except racing cars or professional drivers, to enter the fifty mile event. There was no entry fee, but cars were to be stock and drivers had to be bona fide residents of the state of Kentucky.[50] The Lexington that competed was driven by Mr. William Hair and was raced without a hood. Whatever was gained by the additional ventilation and weight reduction was lost when dirt got into the carburetor requiring disassembly and cleaning. The gold prize money was won by a Packard from Cincinnati, but reports were that the local car had made a good showing as it still defeated a Mercedes. One Queen City resident who witnessed the race was so impressed with the Lexington that he applied for the agency rights in the Cincinnati territory.[51]

A really ambitious undertaking for the new manufacturer was their entering the Glidden Tour. This was an endurance contest, sponsored by the American Automobile Association, intended to promote cross-country tourism by demonstrating the reliability of the automobile. The 1909 tour started in Detroit on July 12 and ended in Kansas City, Missouri, on July 30, by way of Minneapolis and Denver, making a distance of approximately 2,650 miles. The contest was named after Charles J. Glidden of Glidden Paint fame, who was also an automobile enthusiast. All entries were to be stock production cars without modification. The contests were held from 1905 to 1913, but this was the first one to journey west of Chicago.[52] Contestants were competing in three categories in the 1909 event. Thirteen touring car entries vied for the Charles J. Glidden trophy, fourteen runabout entries, including Lexington, sought the Hower Cup to be presented by Chairman F. B. Hower, and three entries sought the Detroit prize. All participants traversed the same route.

The trip itinerary was as follows:

July 12, Detroit to Kalamazoo, Michigan (142 miles)
July 13, Kalamazoo to Chicago (173 miles)
July 14, Chicago to Madison, Wisconsin (175 miles)
July 15, Madison to La Crosse, Wisconsin (154 miles)
July 16, La Crosse to Minneapolis, Minnesota (200 miles)
July 17 and 18, layover at Minneapolis
July 19, Minneapolis to Mankato, Minnesota (132 miles)
July 20, Mankato to Fort Dodge, Iowa (181 miles)
July 21, Fort Dodge to Council Bluffs, Iowa (181 miles)
July 22, Council Bluff to Kearney, Nebraska (200 miles)
July 23, Kearney to Julesburg, Colorado (206 miles)
July 24, Julesburg to Denver, Colorado (200 miles)
July 25 and 26, layover at Denver
July 27, Denver to Hugo, Colorado (173 miles)
July 28, Hugo to Oakley, Kansas (165 miles)
July 29, Oakley to Salina, Kansas (199 miles)
July 30, Salina to Kansas City, Missouri (212 miles)[53]

The Lexington Motor Car Company entered this prestigious contest using a 40–45 horsepower Model A with J. C. Moore as the driver, Charles Blackburn as mechanic and Victor K. Dodge the observer. The mechanic had the responsibility of keeping the car in good operating condition. Much of his work was done after arrival in the evening or before departure in the morning. He kept the oil level up and filled the gas tank before each run, pouring the gasoline through a fine strainer or chamois to keep out water or particles of dirt. As an observer, Mr. Dodge would ride in other contestants' cars to watch for possible infractions. Cars would be penalized points for any adjustment or replacement of parts that was necessary or for arriving behind schedule.[54] The Lexington car left its home city on July 5th bound for Detroit by freight car, the men traveling by passenger train, left several days later.[55]

The following letter was received from Mr. Moore after his arrival in Detroit:

Detroit, July 9, 1909

Lexington Motor Car Company
  Gentleman:
  When we arrived here, after a night on the cushions, as we were not able to get a berth at all, we found the car at the depot. Charley and I proceeded to get it out at once and went over it thoroughly to get everything in the best shape possible. We then went out to try it, driving some 40-odd miles, and it is certainly a dandy. I can see no reason at all why it shouldn't do business in a business like manner. While the cars were lined up in front of the hotel this morning waiting to check in, we had a crowd around the car all the time—about four or five times as many as any other car here.
  People would walk off and we could hear them say, "That's a dandy," "That's a good looking car," etc. The boys made at least a half-dozen pictures of the car in several

Top: The steering wheel was on the right hand side of the car and the gear shift lever, hand brake, and horn were all located to the right of the driver on the outside of the body. *Bottom:* The first Lexington closed car was pictured in front of the West Main St. factory. This car was still running in 1922 and was being used regularly as a taxicab. Horseless Age, *March 1922.*

positions. I mean the press and official photographers. We have had to hang around all day waiting to check in and as yet have not done so, all cars having not yet arrived. It is rather funny to see the buggy men and hear them talk about what they can do. Some of them are running around on one cylinder part of the time, and part of the time on two. It does seem to me that if they can get through we ought to. At any rate Charley and I are going to Kansas City, if careful work will take us there. We understand it is a bad road and no car is expected to go through with a clean score.

Here's hoping for good luck.

J.C.M.[56]

At 10:00 a.m. on July 12, there was a grand sendoff from Hotel Pontchartrain to the fanfare of trumpets supplied by the Maxwell-Briscoe band, the booming of cannon and the waving of banners. Forty-two cars were released to go at one-minute intervals. The first car, driven by Pilot Dai Lewis, had the confetti that was sprinkled along the roadway to mark the route. This was especially important at every crossroad or turn since road markings were nonexistent. The second car out carried Chairman F. B. Hower; then there were a dozen official, press and general supply cars and trucks in addition to the contestants.[57] Some of the trucks carried cans of gasoline for refueling since many of the small towns that the tour went through would not have a plentiful supply in their local general store or machine shop where gasoline was sold. The trip to Kalamazoo provided a good "shake down experience" for most contestants. Except for the dust, good roads made the running easy The main problem of the day was that some of the cars would have tire trouble after hitting a patch of sand in the road. One car blew three tires and another one two. The only cars receiving penalty points were the McIntyre buggy for being late, the Chalmers-Detroit for having to fasten a fender with wire and a strap purchased along the way, and the number 104 Brush for having to replace the complete connecting rod and bearing.[58] The Brush was later withdrawn from competition.

The first week of travel was over generally good roads well into Wisconsin. From Madison on to Minneapolis was quite challenging, but most of the cars received

The Lexington Number 114 that competed in the 1909 Glidden Tour with J. C. Moore behind the wheel and Charles Blackburn the riding mechanic. *National Automotive History Collection, Detroit Public Library.*

few if any penalty points. The number 3 Chalmers-Detroit had more fender trouble and the Jewel crew had to tighten a hub flange. Moore sent a telegram upon arrival at Mankato, Minnesota, stating that he had arrived one hour and fifteen minutes ahead of schedule and had passed three cars in the ditch, but his score was still perfect.[59] A letter from Moore describing the journey from La Crosse to Minneapolis stated, "to drive a car and average twenty miles an hour is certainly the hardest test you can give one on such roads as we have had so far. Sand half to the axle most of the time. I am sore all over from shocks and jerks as the car follows the track in the sand." The Lexington still used only ten gallons of gas for the 177 miles traveled that day. Another problem occurred because the Rapid truck, part of the tour as a supply vehicle, had "turned upside down and blocked the whole tour for twenty minutes, until the boys turned it upright again."[60]

When the tourists reached Minneapolis, they were given one of the finest entertainments on record. Elaborate preparations had been made by the Minneapolis Automobile Club that included dinners, a boat ride on Lake Minnetonka, military reviews and a parade. A mammoth automobile parade was held on Saturday evening. There were 358 cars in the parade, with their lights lit, moving through the downtown streets, making them as light as day. About forty of the cars were elaborately decorated and prizes were given for those that were particularly fine.[61] Moore mentioned the event in his letter of July 17:

Lexington Motor Car Company　　　　　　　　　　　　　　　　　July 17, 1909
Lexington, Ky

Dear Sirs—Since leaving Detroit we have had some remarkable roads and fine weather. The run from Madison to La Crosse, 154 miles, was certainly the worst proposition I ever saw in my life. The very best that you could say of it is that it is road. A wagon perhaps passing over it a few times since Columbus discovered this country. We climbed over three mountains that were not actually safe for a man on horseback, so steep were the hills that every car had to use low gear and wish he had one lower—nothing short of dangerous.

You can imagine a hill so steep to go down that both my brakes would not hold the car. I locked the wheels and slid down over the water breaks, rocks and sand, until at one time I thought the car was gone, but managed to hold it straight in the road until I reached the bottom. I looked for it to go into a thousand pieces, however, landed safe in La Crosse on time, the last 42 miles made in one hour and five minutes over a road not fit to run over at a rate to exceed ten miles an hour.

A good big percent of the cars came through with perfect scores, and I understand that Hower was really mad about it, as the road was picked out that way in order to weed out many perfect score cars, but the boys fooled him just a little, and came in clean.

The Minneapolis club has put up quite a nice program for us. I understand they raised $8000 dollars with which to entertain the tourists and they are doing it nicely. Minneapolis is certainly a fine auto town.

Hoping everything is going nicely, I remain, Yours very truly.

　　　　　　　　　　　　　　　　　　　　　　　　　　　　John C. Moore[62]

Heading west and south out of Minneapolis, road conditions deteriorated so that, at times, it was difficult to determine that there was indeed any road at all. When the tour reached Council Bluffs, Iowa, they were at the approximate halfway point. The Lexington still had a perfect score, but about half of the cars had lost theirs. The touring cars that still had a perfect score were the White, Maxwell, Marmon, Thomas, two Premiers and two Pierces. The roadsters with perfect scores were the Chalmers, two Pierces, number 101 Moline and the Lexington. For the Detroit prize the American Simplex and Chalmers were still perfect.[63]

Across Nebraska and Colorado, the heavier soils of the Midwest gave way to sandy mixtures that easily trapped vehicles. A telegram dated July 23, from J. C. Moore, noted that from Kearney, Nebraska, to Julesburg, Colorado, roads were miserable. He had passed three cars that were "hung up" and ten of the tourists had to be towed through the sand. Moore had still arrived at Julesburg one hour and forty minutes ahead of schedule with a perfect score.[64] An excerpt of a letter Moore sent to the company dated July 24 described some of the trip from Julesburg to Denver: "We checked out of Julesburg this a. m. with nine of the big cars ahead of us; checked in at Denver behind the fourth car, having covered 206 miles without stopping the motor, except ten minutes in which to help pull a big Thomas 70 out of a hole where it had broken through a bridge in crossing a slough." The Lexington crew than patched the bridge enough to get over it and went on. The run that day was decidedly the worst one of the tour, sometimes in sand half up to the axle, so deep that the pan would drag. The next few minutes the car would be in slough up to the hubs. After driving more than 2,000 miles, the team from Kentucky had not had to replace a single tire and had experienced only one small puncture.[65] That feat, in itself, was quite unusual in a day when tire failures were a regular part of motoring.

At the end of the second week, the entourage had reached Denver, Colorado.

Approaching Kansas City, a cotter pin worked out, necessitating a stop to replace it and causing the loss of a perfect score. The Automobile, *August 5, 1909.*

For a period of six days they had been traveling over the worst roads while covering the longest distances. Arriving in Denver meant two days of relaxation and time to prepare for the remaining four days of touring. It also meant they had reached the farthest point west for this tour and would be turning south and east for the remainder of the trip.

The journey from Denver to Hugo was by way of Colorado Springs, skirting the foothills on the way south. At Palmer Lake, a reception committee of motorists met the tourists and escorted them to Colorado Springs where they were entertained and got a good view of the famous Pikes Peak.[66] J. C. Moore would become much more familiar with this impressive mountain more than a decade later in an event that Lexington dominated for a few years. From there, the route headed east, back across the plains. An excerpt from a dispatch to the *Cincinnati Enquirer* from Oakley, Kansas, noted, "The perfect score cars with two days still to run, are as follows; Touring cars—Marmon, two Pierces, two Premiers. Roadsters—Chalmers, Moline, Lexington and two Pierces. The Lexington is a new car made in Lexington, Ky., and its record so far has surprised the experts."[67]

The Lexington automobile and its driver, John C. Moore, had done such a fine job driving more than 2,600 miles while maintaining a perfect score. It must have been disheartening when, as Moore approached the final destination, a cotter pin worked out, necessitating a stop to fix it. This ended the perfect score for Lexington with a 2 point penalty.[68] On the final day's trip, the two pilot cars gave out and their occupants rode with Chairman Bowers, spreading confetti the rest of the way. At the state line, nearly 500 automobiles were waiting to greet the sunburned, mud-spattered tourists, and escort them into Missouri. Lexington's plant manager, Fred Coats, had traveled to Kansas City and met them upon their arrival.[69]

All of the contestants' cars were parked in the Kansas City Convention Hall where they were to be inspected by the technical committee to determine their overall condition after the grueling journey.

Top: The Stone family traveled to Chicago in July of 1910 to visit Kinzea's sister. Kinzea is second from left. *Bottom:* One or more trucks were built for Stone to use in his various enterprises. *Both photographs courtesy the Stone collection.*

A Lexington Model A touring in front of the Lancaster Hotel in Georgetown, Kentucky. *Courtesy the Stone collection.*

SUMMARY OF THE CARS PARTICIPATING IN THE 1909 GLIDDEN TOUR[70]

Glidden Trophy

No.	Make	Driver	Road Pts.	Technical Pts.	Total Pts.	Tires	Carburetor	Magneto
9	Pierce-Arrow	Winchester	0	0	0	Goodrich	Pierce	Bosch
2	Premier	Hammond	0	1.5	1.5	Goodrich	Schebler	Bosch
8	Pierce-Arrow	Dey	0	1.6	1.6	Goodrich	Pierce	Bosch
5	Marmon	Marmon	0	7.3	7.3	Diamond	Schebler	Bosch
4	Marmon	Wing	8	2.5	10.5	Diamond	Schebler	Bosch
6	Maxwell	Gager	8.5	4.6	13.1	Ajax	Maxwell	Splitdorf
1	Premier	Jay	0	16.9	16.9	Diamond	Schebler	Bosch
12	Midland	Hayes	4.3	31.3	35.6	Diamond	Kingston	Remy
14	White Steamer	Searies	19.3	26.2	45.5	Diamond	Kerosene	
7	Jewel	Bernhart	11.2	394.8	406.0	Diamond	Schebler	Bosch
10	Glide	Bartholomew	682.9	6.2	689.1	Goodyear	Schebler	Eisemann
11	Thomas	Buse	1,005.0	Withdrawn	1,005.0			
3	Chalmers-Detroit	Bolger	1,225.5	Withdrawn	1,225.5			

Detroit Prize

No.	Make	Driver	Road Pts.	Technical Pts.	Total Pts.	Tires	Carburetor	Magneto
52	Chalmers-Detroit	Bemb	6.0	17.8	23.8	Diamond	Mayer	Bosch
53	Premier	Waltman	26.1	8.2	34.3	Diamond	Schebler	Bosch
51	American-Simplex	Wood	1.4	50.8	52.2	Goodrich	American-Simplex	Bosch

Hower Cup

No.	Make	Driver	Road Pts.	Technical Pts.	Total Pts.	Tires	Carburetor	Magneto
108	Pierce-Arrow	Williams	0	0	0	Goodrich	Pierce	Bosch
101	Moline	Wicke	0	1.1	1.1	Goodrich	Schebler	Bosch

No.	Make	Driver	Road Pts.	Technical Pts.	Total Pts.	Tires	Carburetor	Magneto
114	Lexington	Moore	2.0	1.8	3.8	Goodrich	Schebler	Bosch
100	Moline	Van Dervoort	3.1	5.2	8.3	Goodrich	Schebler	Bosch
109	Pierce-Arrow	Schofield	0	10.2	10.2	Goodrich	Pierce	Bosch
107	Maxwell	Goldthwaite	35.4	8.2	43.6	Ajax	Maxwell	Splitdorf
102	Moline	Gregory	46.6	2.8	49.4	Goodrich	Schebler	Bosch
111	Jewel	Uhl	38.2	69.6	107.8	Goodrich	Stromberg	Bosch
112	Mason	Snyder	334.5	10.3	344.8	Diamond	Schebler	Splitdorf
103	Brush	Trinkle	1,005.6	Withdrawn	1,005.6			
106	Hupmobile	Nelson	1,358.0	Withdrawn	1,358.0			
110	McIntyre	Goodwin	1,452.7	Withdrawn	1,452.7			
104	Brush	Huss	2,251.6	Withdrawn	2,251.6			
105	Chalmers-Detroit	Machesky		Disqualified				

The Lexington, with J. C. Moore driving, placed third in the Hower Cup contest with only 3.8 penalty points against it. This was an outstanding accomplishment for a new make of automobile that had been on the market less than three months, and a driver who had never competed in a contest of this type before. The Glidden contestants returned to Kentucky within a couple of days with many stories to tell. Mr. Coats stayed with the car until it could be shipped home by rail.[71]

The Lexington Company exhibited each of the three models they were producing at the Blue Grass Fair along with the Glidden car with the mud still upon it, just as it was when it arrived in Kansas City.[72] Opening day of the fair was August 8, and a record crowd assembled to watch the auto parade that left downtown Lexington at 1:30 p.m. The leading car was a new Lexington with Governor Willson and Adjutant General P. P. Johnston as passengers; following was a Winton with members of the governor's staff; next came the Glidden Tour Lexington making the five mile run to the fair grounds.[73] In all, there were about 150 cars in the parade, everything from a one-cylinder runabout to the latest six-cylinder racer. They entered the fair grounds and were greeted by the enthusiastic crowd of onlookers. Governor Willson, after a complimentary speech, presented the Glidden participants with awards. J. C. Moore, driver, was presented with a handsome open faced gold watch; V. K. Dodge, observer, received a pair of gold cuff buttons, and Charles Blackburn, mechanic, was given ten dollars in gold.[74]

A local professor at State University, now the University of Kentucky, helped promote the new Kentucky product by conducting tests to determine how efficiently it operated. Professor F. Paul Anderson and a corps of student assistants used a series of rollers upon which the car's driving wheels were placed to measure traction and the efficiency of the gearing. The Lexington seven-passenger car, with the throttle nearly half open and the wheels turning at a rate of about 25 miles per hour, delivered 95 percent of the engine energy at the rear wheels. Company officials were present at the test and were quite pleased with the results. Professor Anderson also held a public demonstration using his apparatus erected by himself and his students. Owners and prospective buyers were invited to attend to see how the car was tested.[75] There was no mention as to whether or not the professor received compensation from the company for his efforts.

One unusual problem surfaced near the end of June when Deputy Sheriff J. C. Bosworth went to the factory to serve a subpoena to William Keefe, a Lexington employee. The deputy did not initially identify himself as an officer of the court and was refused admittance to the building. He returned the next day and presented the subpoena in the presence of Dr. Bryan and Fred Coats, but understood them both to declare that Mr. Keefe would no longer be employed there if he took time off work to testify in the civil suit. The end result was that Bryan and Coats had to spend a day in circuit court to answer charges issued by circuit judge Robert L. Stout, to show cause why they should not be punished for contempt of court. Both men claimed the whole thing was a complete misunderstanding and that they had perhaps been too hasty since they had been bothered a great deal with officers serving garnishments on employees.[76]

A dangerous incident occurred June 30 when two Lexingtons being loaded at the Queen & Crescent depot were damaged by fire. The cars were partially loaded and one man was draining the gasoline from the tank of a car when another man approached carrying a lantern. Fumes from the gasoline ignited causing a fierce blaze that was knocked down quickly using the fire fighting equipment on the yard engine. The box car received only slight damage, but the tops of both Lexingtons were heavily damaged.[77]

Top: An early production Model C roadster. *Bottom:* Plant manager Fred Coats with a partially assembled automobile, possibly used for testing. *Both photographs courtesy Wayne Goetz.*

A more serious accident occurred near the end of the year when John Coats, brother of plant manager Fred Coats, was painfully injured. John was in charge of the final assembly department and was assisting with soldering a gasoline tank when it exploded, burning Coats about his face and chest. He was removed to St. Joseph's Hospital for treatment of injuries that were painful but not critical.[78]

Lexington's outstanding performance in the Glidden Tour plus testimonials from owners added to demand for their cars and increased the need for more space at the already overcrowded company facility. Just when the seeds were planted to consider a move to a larger facility is not known. It may have happened when Fred Coats traveled north while on his way to Kansas City. He likely would have made

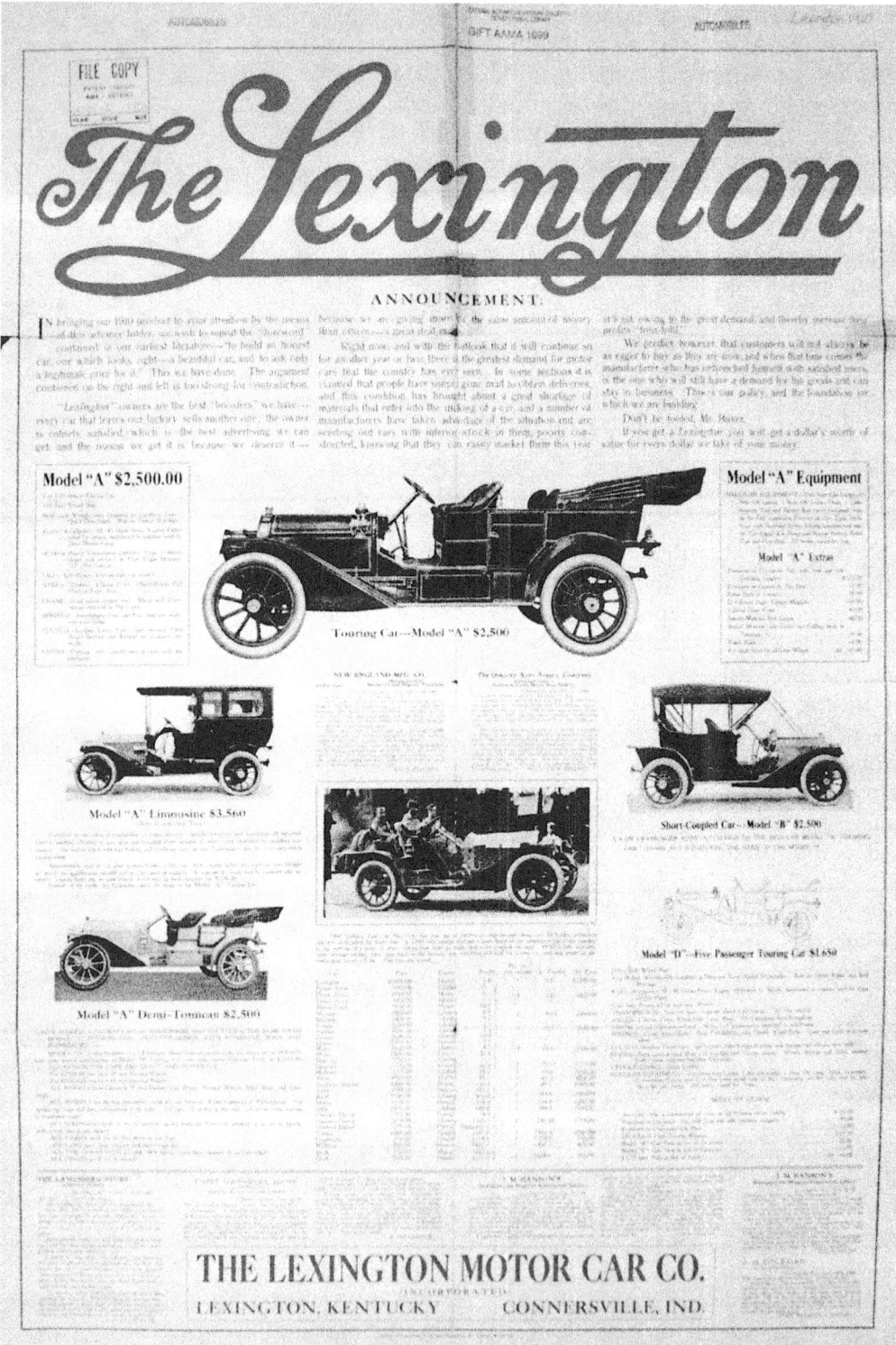

The move to Indiana was evident in this brochure that lists both Lexington and Connersville addresses.

contacts with various suppliers in Connersville and Marion, Indiana. By the end of August, there was speculation in Connersville that a certain Southern automobile plant was seeking a new location in the North. Both Connersville and Marion believed they had a good chance of hosting the move to their community.

As rumors spread of a possible move, shareholders became uneasy. In September, Dr. Bryan sold the 93 shares owned by himself and his family to Kinzea Stone.[79] At a meeting of the board of directors on September 20, Dr. Bryan's resignation from the position of president of the company was accepted.[80] By the time the October 8 Board of Directors meeting was held, the majority of stock was owned by E. D. Johnston of Connersville. Three of the board members had sold their holdings and had resigned from the board. New appointees replacing those who had resigned were E. D. Johnston and A. E. Leiter of Connersville plus H. D. Johnson of Lexington. Those remaining on the board were V. K. Dodge, F. N. Coats, G. D. Wilson, B. F. Stone and V. A. Bradley, all of Central Kentucky. The new officers that were elected were E. D. Johnston, president, A. E. Leiter, vice-president, F. N. Coats, secretary and general manager, G. D. Wilson, treasurer, and J. C. Moore, mechanical engineer. Another outcome of that meeting was the statement, "Resolved—that a new factory will be erected at the earliest possible practical moment for the purpose of building Lexington automobiles and that the building will be erected at Connersville, Indiana."[81] It was also acknowledged that when the plant was constructed on West Main, the Commercial Club had paid for the ground upon which the plant was built. One condition that accompanied the deed was that if the company was not in operation at the end of three years, they were to reimburse the Commercial Club $1,600 for the land. A member of the company gave his assurance that the money would be paid promptly if the factory were moved.[82]

Even with the new board members, there were two votes in opposition to moving. Those feelings were expressed in a statement released by disgruntled board members, which read in part, "Lexington people feel deeply about the loss of the big plant and were preparing to make a fight to retain it." By mid–October, in an attempt to keep the company in Lexington, Victor Dodge had begun negotiating to purchase controlling interest in the company from Edgar Johnston of Connersville. Johnston held a large block of stock owned by himself, A. E. Leiter and others. An option to purchase Connersville held stock for $75,000 was obtained under the leadership of Major Alexander G. Morgan. An option on Kentucky held stock was also obtained by the Hoosier board members.[83]

Newspaper articles were calling attention to the potential loss of the Lexington Motor Company, which was one of the community's largest manufacturing concerns. The company had produced a significant number of cars by this time and had orders that were being filled as circumstances allowed.[84] When a committee of local businessmen looked closely at the company records, they determined that conditions were far better than most supposed them to be. Plans were made to increase the capital stock to $100,000 and to hold 500 shares as a treasury fund.[85]

On November 4, a meeting was held at the Phoenix Hotel to try to raise $75,000 to pay $115 per share for the 340 shares of stock.[86] The amount included the money to be paid to Mr. Johnston plus a deposit to be made on contracts with the suppliers for motors and axles. Plans seemed to be in good order with men from Georgetown expected to put up the balance of the funds needed to close the deal. The Georgetown group was comprised of Victor Bradley, Kinzea Stone, who had recently

Lexington's display at the 1910 Chicago Automobile Show, which included both licensed and unlicensed manufacturers. Those that were licensed paid royalties to the ALAM acknowledging the Selden Patent. *National Automotive History Collection, Detroit Public Library.*

disposed of his stock in the company, John Osborne and Benjamin Stone, a brother of Kinzea. The local men involved were Charles Scott of the L & E Railroad Company, Younger Alexander, J. L. Watkins, G. D. Wilson and Victor Dodge.[87]

Both options for stock transfers expired at midnight on November 9 with no action having taken place on either side. In Connersville, the factory move was considered a done deal, and construction was begun on the new building. In Lexington, there was still a glimmer of hope of retaining the company. It was reported that the time for the option to close had been extended and that Mr. Johnston was expected to come to Lexington the next week, and in all probability, the deal would be closed at that time.[88]

While all of the maneuvering and speculation was continuing, the 1910 models had already been announced. They were basically a carryover from the first year of production, but more emphasis was now placed on building all three models and not just the model A that had dominated production up to that time. One statement from the 1910 literature explained the company philosophy. It noted, "We are not too original, but have endeavored (and successfully) to design a car embodying in it the best qualities of the best cars."[89] Lexington ads touted the "assembled" car to be the most desirable because the company could choose components with preferred features from many sources.

Touring Car—Model "A"

Roadster—Model "C"

Short-Coupled Car—Model "B"

Models for 1910 were announced in the fall of 1909: models A, B and C. Model D was introduced later.

Chassis

Chassis

Two views of the 1910 Lexington chassis.

The engine for 1910 continued to be the Rutenber 4¼ inch bore by 5 inch stroke. The Schwartz wheels had wide flat spokes that interlocked with each other for added strength. A heavy duty transmission with three speeds forward plus reverse was provided. One unusual feature was the use of a short shaft with double universal joints between the clutch and the transmission. This was supposed to eliminate vibrations from the powerplant. Bodies were made with solid wood bendings and were reinforced with wide sills. Models offered were the Model A Touring, Model B Short-Coupled Car and Model C Roadster, all for $2,500. Options included the Pantasote or cravenette top with side courting (curtains) at $125 for Models A and B or $75 for the Roadster; extra seats for the touring, $50; D-4 Bosch high-tension

The body in the white. Made of solid wood bendings thoroughly re-inforced inside, underneath the upholstering. Sills are very wide and heavy. All bodies come ironed for tops, regularly, and are painted and upholstered in the color that best suits each individual customer without extra charge. We feel that when a man pays $2,500 for a car, he ought to have pretty near what he wants.

The basic body structure of the 1910 car.

magneto, $150; folding windshield, $40; special upholstering from $10 to $40.[90] A late arrival was the new Model "D" that used a smaller 30–35 horsepower Rutenber RA engine. Even with its smaller engine, this car was a good hill climber as it weighed about 1,000 pounds less than the other Lexingtons. The new models were displayed at various automobile shows as the new year got under way.

All of the efforts made to keep the company located in the city of its origin failed and as fall moved into winter, plans were being made for the move north. The problems with limited space became more acute as production continued to grow, to the point that additional space was sought in the Lexington area for temporary use. In January of 1910, the company purchased or leased the Mammoth Skating Rink on Fourth Street from the Lexington Athletic and Amusement Company to use for painting, upholstering and finishing automobiles.[91] Unfinished bodies and a large stock of paint were moved from the plant on West Main. By late January, five carloads of materials that had been standing on the tracks for several days were unloaded and were transported to the Fourth Street facility.[92] This move was made during the time that the Connersville plant was under construction. The new facility was supposed to have been completed by mid–January, but its progress was much slower than expected, so production continued at Lexington well into the year.

Toward the last of January, two Lexingtons were shipped to Chicago where they were exhibited in the National Automobile show. The cars shown were examples of Lexington's large touring and small runabout. The company also intended to display a limousine, but, because of a large number of entries, the show management restricted each company to two entrants.[93] Earlier in the month, Fred Coats had a display of Lexingtons in the New York show and one boastful New York

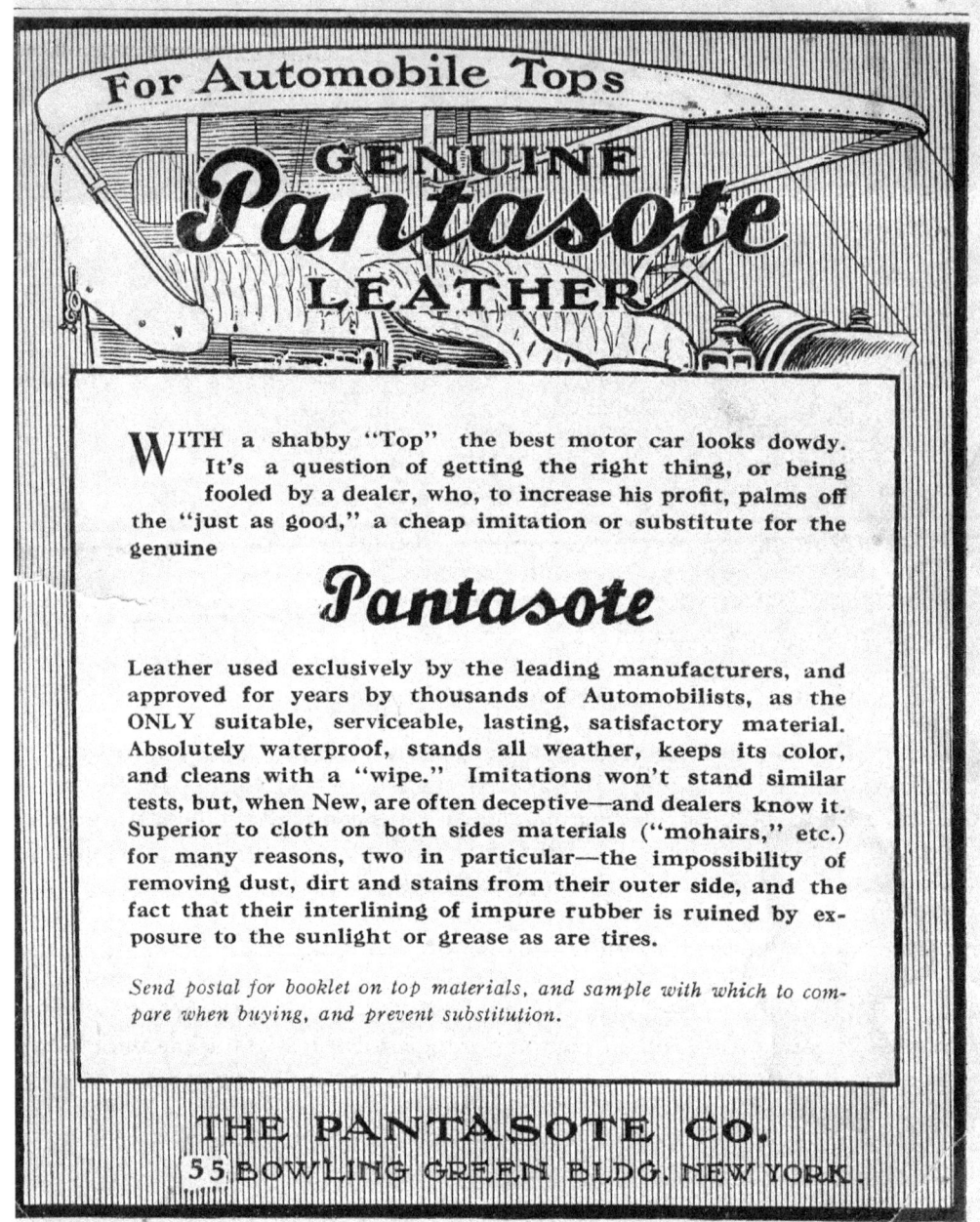

The Pantasote top was one of the many brand name products Lexington customers could recognize to assure top quality in their assembled motor car.

City dealer expressed his assurance that he could handle 75–100 cars during the year.[94]

The West Main Street location was vacated by mid–April, just one year after the first automobiles had been assembled in that building. The Fourth Street building continued working well into June. Two of the last vehicles to leave that facility were the cars that would be entered in the 1910 Glidden Tour. This young upstart company had already made some waves but would now leave its birthplace of Fayette County, Kentucky, for a new home in Fayette County, Indiana. The West Main Street factory building was sold and was used by various businesses over the next seventy years before it was razed about 1980. The present occupant of the property is the Palumbo Lumber Company.

2

The Lexington Becomes a Hoosier

The Lexington Motor Car Company had been formed less than a year when it decided to move to another location. What would cause a company that chose to honor the city of its origin by using the name Lexington to leave the building that had so recently been constructed through the efforts of the local commercial club? News accounts of the period give clues as to the reasons for the move.

The Evening News of Connersville, in its premier announcement of August 30, 1909, headlined "Southern Auto Plant Wants to Locate Here," stated that the company was having difficulty retaining workers in Lexington. The article continued, "North of the Ohio, factories of all kinds are plentiful and skilled workers are more pleased with conditions as they can move from one (factory) to another."[1] This statement seems satisfactory on its face, but it overlooks the important fact that a high percentage of Connersville area workers had actually emigrated from none other than the bluegrass state of Kentucky. They were good workers, but many of them returned to their home state whenever possible and often referred to Kentucky as "God's Country."

Another reason alluded to in that same newspaper article had to do with the proximity of parts suppliers. The bodies for the Lexington automobile were supplied by the Central Manufacturing Company of Connersville and many other parts used in the assembly of the automobile were available locally, including lights from the Indiana Lamp Co., springs and axles from the Ansted Spring and Axle Co., wheels from the Connersville Wheel Works, and upholstering from George R. Carter Leather Co.[2] Actually, nearly all of the parts that were assembled to make the Lexington automobile were manufactured in northern cities, so Lexington could significantly improve parts availability and lower transportation costs by locating nearer to the source of their manufacturers.

There were also space problems in the plant in Lexington, Kentucky. The need for a larger facility was brought to the attention of the Lexington Commercial Club a little over a month after production had started.[3] It became so critical that in January of 1910, the company leased a building on Fourth Street in downtown Lexington for painting, upholstering and finishing.[4] That move was made during the time when the new factory was under construction in Connersville and, in fact, was expected to have been completed by that date. The original facility, built less than a year earlier, was simply not large enough to handle the quantity of parts and the variety of operations required for automobile production.

A fourth factor may also have had a great deal of influence in the relocation to Connersville. The president of the Connersville Commercial Club, Arthur E. Leiter, is given great praise for his efforts in encouraging the move. Mr. Leiter was a prominent Connersville businessman who saw his own dry goods business grow as the city prospered, so he had good reason to want to see the company relocate. However, a more powerful pull may have come from family ties, as Mr. Leiter was a brother-in-law of Mr. Fred Coats. Arthur's wife's brother was the Lexington Motor Car Company secretary and general manager.[5]

Immediately after the initial announcement of the possibility of landing the Lexington factory, the Connersville press carried news items almost non-stop, often two or three times a week. An article in the Sept. 4, 1909, edition of *The Evening News* noted that a committee had already been formed to raise money "to land the Lexington Motor Car plant." Committee members were all Connersville men: J. E. McFarlan, W. B. Ansted, Dr. J. R. Mountain, and George R. Carter.[6] James McFarlan was from one of the finest families in town. His father owned the McFarlan Carriage Company that began producing the McFarlan automobile, even before Lexington was established in Connersville. William B. Ansted was a member of the most prominent local family and would later become a director of Lexington. Dr. Mountain was a well-known physician, and George R. Carter was owner of the Carter Leather Co., provider of upholstery materials. The newspaper also reported that "the company is asking no specific amount as bonus" and in the same article it stated, "It is probable that Connersville could get the plant for less money than some other towns because of the advantages of getting supplies."[7] The two other Indiana towns that turned out to be most competitive were Marion, where the Rutenber engine, used by Lexington at that time, was manufactured, and Muncie, Indiana.[8] Muncie is located midway between the other two cities, and the Warner Gear Company that was the source of Lexington's transmissions was located there. Both of the competing cities had transportation arteries as good as, if not better than, Connersville's, but neither of them had A. E. Leiter, whose brother-in-law, Fred Coats, as Lexington general manager, had the potential of influencing the negotiations on behalf of Connersville.

Arthur Leiter was born in 1873 and entered the mercantile business in Connersville in 1904. He became active in civic affairs early on and by 1909 was president of the Connersville Commercial Club where he was influential with the development of Connersville as an industrial center. Mr. Leiter remained active in his business until his death in 1947.[9]

The September 17, 1909, edition of *The Evening News* termed the "Lexington Plant Almost Assured."[10] Council was asked for some concessions including an $8,000 bonus to be paid the company and free water and tax exemption for a term of five years.[11] On October 1, it was announced that the company was surely landed.[12] The money required to pay the bonus had already been raised through contributions from local citizens, and a celebration was to be held at the Commercial Club that evening. On the following Monday, Oct. 4, plant manager Fred Coats and chief engineer J. C. Moore came to Connersville to select the building site. But as one hurdle was cleared, two more seemed to pop up. There was disagreement over the best location, so the company took two options to purchase land.[13] One person even offered to give a thousand dollars bonus if the plant was located in the place that he favored.[14] There was also a continuing effort in Kentucky to keep the plant from leaving. The uncertainties kept the company from starting construction until late in the fall. The factory would ultimately be located in what is now known as Edgewood, an area that was probably the nation's first industrial park.

This park was located at the northwest edge of the city on the west side of the

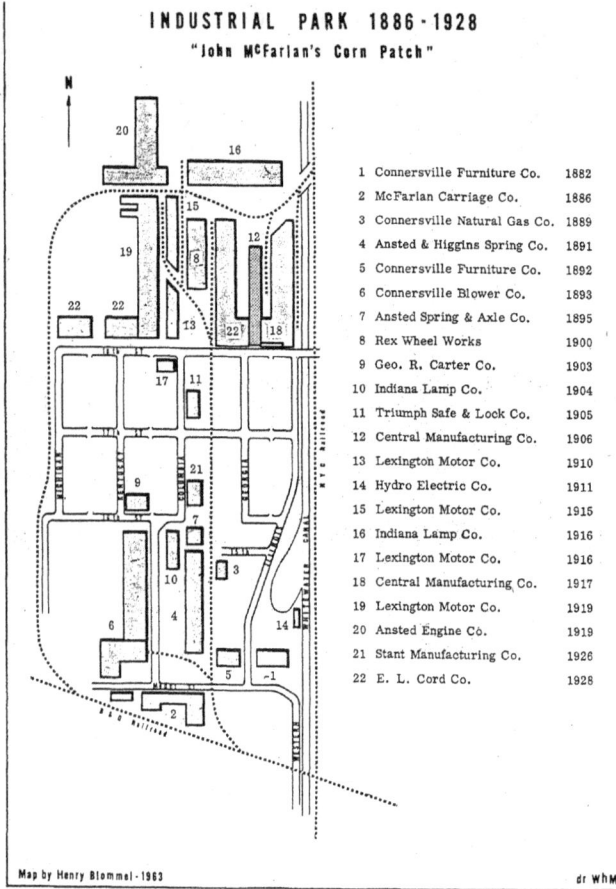

The nation's first industrial park was located in the northwest part of Connersville, west of the Whitewater Canal. It was developed by John McFarlan to attract parts suppliers for his carriage manufacturing concern. Connersville News-Examiner, *October 19, 1987.*

old Whitewater Canal. It was the brainchild of John B. McFarlan and was sometimes jokingly referred to as "John's corn patch" because it had been his farm field before the transformation. John had come to Connersville in 1856, purchased two small buggy manufacturing companies and began producing McFarlan Carriages. He catered to the more affluent clientele, offering high quality materials in a stylish means of conveyance. McFarlan's idea was to attract various other factories that would locate in the immediate area and could supply parts for his growing carriage industry. In 1886, he created the Connersville Land and Improvement Company for the purpose of developing a location for supplier factories to increase the flow of parts for his carriage trade. In addition to McFarlan's own factory, other suppliers that located nearby included the Ansted Spring and Axle Company, the Central Manufacturing Company for bodies, the Connersville Wheel Company and the George R. Carter Leather Company. John McFarlan thus developed what became the nation's first known industrial park.[15]

The Lexington plant location was to be in the northern part of the industrial park next to the already existing Connersville Wheel Works, north of what is now 18th Street.[16] Construction was to be supervised by company officials plus a committee from the Commercial Club. The contract for construction was let October 20, 1909, with Thomas H. Stoops as the builder. The structure was to be built of brick; its size was 50 feet by 300 feet and two stories high, giving an area of 30,000 square feet, with an electric elevator large enough to lift machinery to the upper level. The optimistic projection was that the building would be ready for occupancy by early January 1910. Payment for the building construction was made by the Commercial Club using the bonus money that had been collected from many community members.[17]

At the Board of Directors meeting held in Lexington on October 8, 1909, Connersville men were elected to the positions of company president and vice-president. E. D. Johnston assumed the top position and was also the majority stockholder, and A. E. Leiter became second in command.[18] The new president of Lexington Motor Car Company, Edgar Dwight Johnston, was born in Cedarville, Ohio, in 1861, where he spent his childhood. After attending public schools in his hometown and in Portsmouth, Ohio, Edgar studied music and voice in Cincinnati where he met his bride, Jane Roots, daughter of Connersville industrialist F. M. Roots. After coming to Connersville in 1885, he became well known as he advanced to the position of vice-president and later president of the P. H. and F. M. Roots Company, the developer of the Rotary Positive blower. He also became president of the Hydro-Electric Light and Power Company and the Hydraulic Company and was on the board of directors of the First National Bank. These concerns were all located in Connersville. He was regarded as a community leader in addition to being responsible for the employment of many men.[19]

The various attempts to keep the car company in Lexington left things in limbo at Connersville, so the actual brick and mortar work could not be started until it was certain just where the factory was going to be located. When both options for stock transfers expired at midnight on November 9, with no action having taken place, the Connersville building site was finally agreed upon on the next day.[20]

A contract between the Lexington Motor Car Company and the Connersville Commercial Club was signed on December 1. It stated that "in consideration of the subscriptions to the amount of $7970.00 by citizens of Connersville and Fayette County, said company agrees to move its plant, except for real estate and buildings, to the city of Connersville." The agreement also stated, "Said plant and business is to be operated for a period of not less than five (5) years as an automobile factory. If by reason of inevitable accident or financial failure the said company shall not operate its said plant in good faith for the entire period, then there shall be rebated to said Club pro rate share of such donation." Thus if the company were to fail before the five-year period was up, it was to repay a pro rated part of the money it had received for relocating. The agreement was signed by E. D. Johnston, president of Lexington, Fred N. Coats, secretary, E. V. Hawkins, president of the Connersville Commercial Club, and Geo (George) Ansted, secretary. The agreement was not recorded until December 14, 1912, possibly because the company was at that time having financial problems and was facing reorganization.[21]

Construction of the new factory building started Nov. 11. The contract with the Connersville Commercial Club was to determine how the bonus would be paid.[22] By the end of November the local newspaper reported that the brick was about four feet above the foundation. The news item continued boastfully, "At that rate, should fair weather continue, it might be possible to have the structure under roof by the first of the year."[23] An article in the December *Automobile* magazine claimed that the brick plant at Connersville was "well under way, the first story being nearly completed."[24]

Indiana winters are not always conducive to construction, and bitter cold weather during December slowed progress. By the end of the month, there had been a six-inch snowfall with zero degree temperatures and stiff winds causing significant drifting. For six weeks central Indiana was in the throes of uninterrupted winter, the severity being unusual for this area.[25] The below normal temperatures

Top: Some of the workers at the Connersville plant soon after the company relocated. *Courtesy Wayne Goetz. Bottom:* The new two-story Connersville factory soon after it was completed in 1910.

remained until mid–January, the date when the building was expected to be ready. Then there was a matter of materials not arriving on time. It was reported on January 21, 1910, that "a consignment of special size lumber for beams and joists for the new factory was lost in transit."[26] This meant that the building had not risen beyond the first story by late January. The February 7 *Evening News* stated, "A week of ordinary winter weather would enable workmen to get the building under roof."[27]

But February was snowy and cold with nearby Indianapolis setting a record for the month with 21 inches of the white stuff, a record that would stand until the year 2003. Materials finally arrived, the weather became more cooperative and the factory building took shape. Then, talk turned to when the move would take place.

Plant manager Fred Coats had relocated to Connersville by early April and was supervising construction progress. Reports were that the building was almost ready to move into; however, it was also noted that the concrete floor was not yet in. Expectations were that equipment would be moved as space was made ready and production would continue at both Kentucky plants while it was getting started here.[28]

Early estimates were that over a hundred men would be coming to Connersville with the Lexington plant. However, a survey made in mid–March found that if even half of the present workforce transferred to Connersville, there were only about a dozen houses vacant. Thus "there will necessarily be a lot of 'doubling up' or else tents will have to be brought into requisition."[29] The overcrowding may have been very temporary, as some of the men who came to Connersville may have had a brief stay. Eighty-nine-year-old Wayne Goetz of Connersville told the story of his father, Henry, coming to Connersville with the Lexington move. Wayne remembers his father saying that three-fourths of the workers from Kentucky got drunk the first night in their new locale and were promptly fired and sent back south.[30] If this happened, it was not recorded in the local newspapers. On April 18, the newspaper did report eight arrests for intoxication over the weekend, and Fayette County, Indiana, was "dry" at that time, meaning it was illegal to buy, sell, or consume alcoholic beverages. The same newspaper that reported the arrests also claimed that Lexington's West Main Street factory had been dismantled. Machinery from that location was either already in Connersville or was on its way, and they were requesting laborers to unload box cars.[31] The Fourth Street branch, the old skating rink, was still busy putting the finishing touches on cars that had already been built. It would remain in operation for several weeks. Henry Goetz had started working for Lexington when he was just out of high school and the plant was still in Kentucky. He continued to work for Lexington and was part of their "glory days" at Pikes Peak serving as a mechanic for the race team, and stayed with them until they went out of business.[32] By June of 1910, it was estimated that employment at the new factory had topped 100, and management was planning a 50 by 60 foot addition to the building. The company had more orders for cars than they were immediately able to fill.[33]

One local customer who was able to take delivery of a new seven-passenger touring car was Frank Ansted, an attorney who would become very much involved with this company. Mr. Ansted journeyed to Lexington to purchase his treasure, where he observed the work progressing at the Fourth Street finishing plant. Mr. Ansted's touring car was reported to have been finished in bright colors.[34] Offering a wide choice of colors was one of the attractions for which Lexington became known over the years.

As soon as the move was completed and production was underway, attention turned to upcoming competition. Successes of the previous year prompted the company to encourage participation in various performance and reliability runs again in 1910. The May 18 *Lexington Herald* reported the results of a Kansas City, Missouri, hill climb. In a slight overstatement the newspaper reported, "every noted make of automobile in the country is entered." The "Lexington Model D takes all honors of the day driven by Self." The article continued, "Cars we beat on Dodson Hill today are Apperson, National, Palmer-Ginger, Pennsylvania, Great Smith, Jackson Special, Great Western, Auburn, Parry Car and many others. Model D holds records for this hill."[35] Later that month a Lexington won the All-Connecticut Reliability Contest with a perfect score. The contest had run from May 23 to May 28 with 23 cars entered, including Franklin, National, Chalmers, Speedwell, Corbin and others.[36] A Lexington was awarded the Kansas Magazine Cup several months after that contest was held when the contest board of the American Automobile Association reversed its initial decision and awarded the trophy after the Lexington company appealed their original decision.[37]

Now attention turned toward the upcoming 1910 Glidden Tour, an endurance contest sponsored by the American Automobile Association that was to cover a distance of 2,850 miles over a period of about two weeks. Contestants were vying for the Charles J. Glidden Trophy for touring cars and the Chicago Trophy for runabouts. The Chicago Trophy was actually a huge bronze plaque that was offered by the Chicago Motor Club in honor of the city where the Glidden Tour would end on June 30. Both contests followed the same rules and ran over the same course. A Lexington had made an excellent showing in the previous year's tour, so this contest attracted special attention, both in Connersville, now the home of the Lexington automobile, and in Lexington, Kentucky, where the car still had an enthusiastic following. To add to the excitement, the first stop on the Glidden Tour, after starting at Cincinnati, would be in Lexington, Kentucky. This was a lunch stop to be held downtown at the Phoenix Hotel. The Lexington car dealership of that city, the Phoenix Motor Company, was located next door to the hotel. The owner, Victor K. Dodge, also a member of the Lexington Motor Company board of directors, was a member of the Glidden crew.[38] Two Lexingtons were entered in the 1910 Glidden Tour. In early June, the cars, both Model A roadsters, were shipped to Connersville from the Fourth Street plant in Lexington, where they had received their finishing touches.[39] They were then driven to Cincinnati after first being displayed on the streets of their new hometown where a crowd of several hundred looked the cars over. Number 103 was driven by J. C. Moore with Harry Johnson as his mechanic and Victor Dodge as an observer. E. O. Hayes piloted Number 110 with Herman Broedlin as mechanic and George Tebbs as observer.[40]

Two of the most interesting vehicles in that year's Glidden Tour were military cars, both Cadillac 30s, carrying Colt automatic 30-calibre guns that were mounted in the center of the car immediately in front of the driver. The guns were valued at $786 each and had a shooting capacity of 480 shots per minute, with a range of three thousand yards. The cars also carried tents, stoves, one day's rations and five thousand rounds of ammunition.[41] These cars were non-contestants, entered by the Northeastern Military Academy of Highland Park, Illinois. While it was considered safe to travel through the once turbulent Southwest frontier, it was thought that the young military students would receive a realistic demonstration of the conditions under which troops and stores would be transported over ordinary roads. Major Davidson, who was in charge of the military automobiles, claimed that the conditions under which they would be operating were exactly the same as those encountered in regular field service.[42]

The daily itinerary for the 1910 Glidden Tour was as follows:

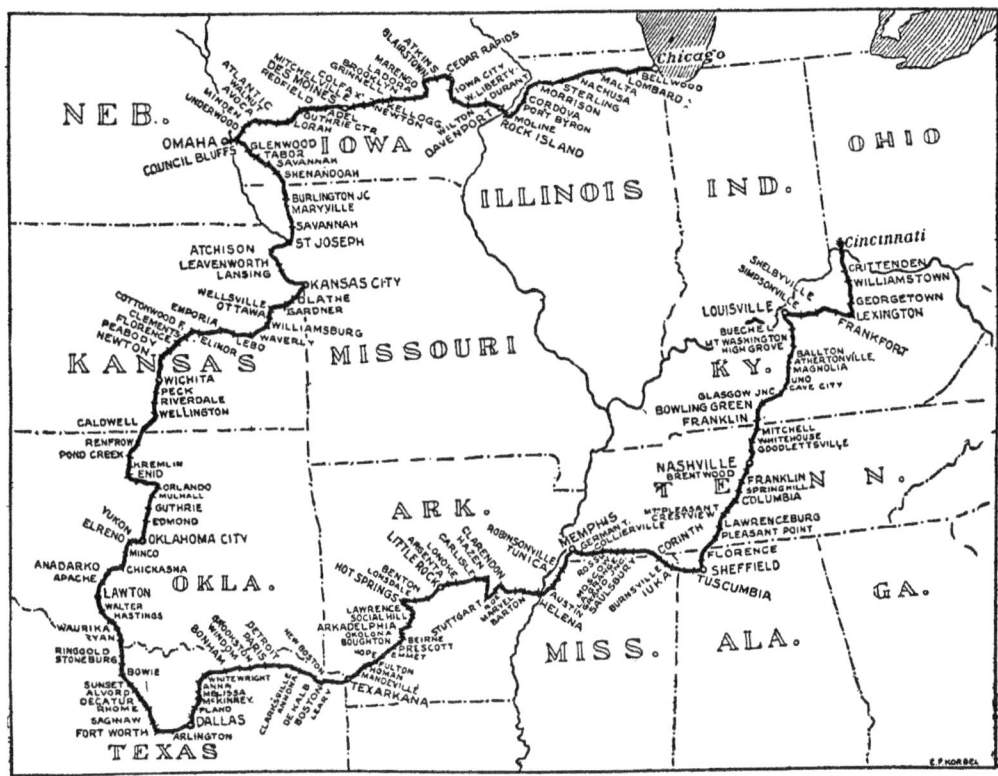

The route taken by the 1910 Glidden Tour started at Cincinnati and went through the Southwest, ending up in Chicago. The Automobile, *June 16, 1910.*

Date	Starting Point	Intermediate Stop	Finishing Point	Miles
June 14	Cincinnati, Ohio	Lexington	Louisville, Kentucky	162
June 15	Louisville	Bowling Green	Nashville, Tennessee	194
June 16	Nashville	Columbia	Sheffield, Alabama	120
June 17	Sheffield	Corinth, Tenn	Memphis, Tennessee	162
June 18	Memphis	Clarendon	Little Rock, Arkansas	208
June 19	Little Rock		Hot Springs, Arkansas	53
June 20	Hot Springs	Prescott	Texarkana, Arkansas	138
June 21	Texarkana	Paris, Texas	Dallas, Texas	217
June 22	Dallas	Terral	Lawton, Oklahoma	201
June 23	Lawton	Chickasha	Oklahoma City	145
June 24	Oklahoma City	Enid	Wichita, Kansas	216
June 25	Wichita	Emporia	Kansas City, Missouri	235
June 26	Layover in Kansas City			
June 27	Kansas City	Maryville	Omaha, Nebraska	242
June 28	Omaha	Guthrie Center	Des Moines, Iowa	159
June 29	Des Moines	Marengo	Davenport, Iowa	220
June 30	Davenport	Rochelle, Illinois	Chicago, Illinois	180[43]

Tour cars assembled first at Cincinnati, where the tour began on June 14. The evening before the big sendoff a banquet was enjoyed by participants and dignitaries, held at the Cincinnati Automobile Club's quarters in the Gibson House. Mr. Glidden, founder of the tour, had planned to be present for the start of the tour, but had wired that he would catch them along the way and would stay with them two or three days.⁴⁴ The next morning, a crowd estimated to be ten thousand strong were lined up to get a glimpse of the khaki-clothed participants and their high powered machines.⁴⁵ Chairman Butler and the referees rode in a Columbia car. The other official cars were one Chalmers, two Cuttings and a Reo for secretary Ferguson.⁴⁶ The first cars left the Queen City about two hours before the contestants. These were the pilot cars, one of which marked the route by spreading confetti while others carried dignitaries and the press. Next were the thirty-four contestants that started at one-minute intervals.⁴⁷ The Automobile Club of Cincinnati had arranged to escort the departing cars across the Ohio River to Covington.⁴⁸ Many of the escorts went a substantial distance into Kentucky wishing the contestants well and anxious to be part of the festivities.

An account of the first leg of the tour was given in the June 15 issue of the *Lexington Herald* with a front-page picture of number 103 ready to begin the tour. The Lexington car number 110 was the eleventh car to start from Cincinnati, leaving at 8:41 a.m., but was the first to arrive in Lexington at 11:42 a.m., 58 minutes ahead of schedule, having passed the other ten cars along the way. The route went south from Cincinnati, through Georgetown entering Lexington via Georgetown Street to Fourth, then to Broadway, on to Main Street to the Phoenix Hotel where they were checked in and a luncheon was served. The cars were then moved to Cheepside for inspection.⁴⁹ There was a forty-five minute delay before each car was checked out and on the road again.

This was obviously an exciting day for the folks of Central Kentucky. The speeding ordinance had been suspended for the day by County Judge Percy Scott and persons with easily frightened horses were cautioned to keep clear of the contestants' route.⁵⁰ "Main Street was thronged with people from Fayette and adjoining counties, with enthusiasm that presented a striking resemblance to the crowd waiting to watch a circus parade." A blue ribbon with a medallion containing a horse's head and the words "She was bred in Old Kentucky," along with a quart of whiskey, were presented to each of the tour participants.⁵¹ It must have been a high old time in town that day! After their break for lunch, the next leg of the tour took the tourists out of town via the viaduct, west on High Street to Versailles, Frankfort and on to Louisville, Kentucky. On the road out of Lexington, drivers who had any hint of superstition may have been tempted to turn back as they encountered three funerals and a one legged chicken, considered to be a bad omen.⁵² Cars in the Chicago Trophy competition that lost points the first day were Lexington number 110 that was penalized four points for having to replace a pin that had dropped out of a brake rod; number 111 Wescott, six points for making two carburetor adjustments, and number 106 Falcar, 60 points for having to replace the magneto. One very minor occurrence happened when the Number 11 Ohio car and a non-contestant's car bumped with a light jolt as Number 11 was hidden by the crowd and pulled in front of it. A quick inspection revealed no damage had been done to either car; the tourists were on their way.⁵³ The most serious accident that damaged a tour car happened when a Cole 30, trying to pass between a Moline car and an approaching horse drawn vehicle, broke a right front wheel when it collided with the buggy. The wheel was replaced with a new one that was procured from Louisville and the work was done so quickly that the car covered lost ground and checked in on time, but was still assessed a penalty of 1042 points. By far the most serious inci-

Top: One of the Glidden Tour entrants for 1910, No. 103, was on display in downtown Connersville before being driven to Cincinnati. *Bottom:* Some of the workers at the Connersville plant with Lexington's Glidden Tour entrant number 103. *Both photographs courtesy Wayne Goetz.*

dent occurred near Frankfort when a Chalmers 30 frightened a horse, causing it to run away, thus throwing a lady from a surrey. The driver of the Chalmers was unaware of the accident, and continued on; however, occupants of a Cino car that was following the Chalmers took the injured lady to the home of a relative. The lady died later that night from her injuries.[54] The Lexington number 103 had a perfect score even though it had been troubled with two tire punctures before

John C. Moore at the wheel of No. 103 with Harry Johnson, mechanic, while on the 1910 Glidden Tour. *National Automotive History Collection, Detroit Public Library.*

reaching Lexington. The distance traveled between Cincinnati and Louisville was 162 miles with travel time of 9 hours and 42 minutes.[55]

From Louisville, the tour turned south, passing through Nashville, Tennessee, and on into Alabama. This part of the tour went very well with no additional penalty points on either Lexington. Driving conditions were still a challenge as they forded 19 creeks and the roads were so rough that observers were thrown out of their seats twice. But when they headed west toward Memphis, various problems arose. An article in the June 18 Connersville *Evening News* headlined "Worst Day in Any Tour, Says Moore" noted that roads were virtually nonexistent.[56] Every car in the Chicago trophy class received penalty points; J. C. Moore lost his perfect score when penalized 159 points for arriving late. Six of the cars were totally disabled, including number 110, which had struck a stone wall of a bridge, demolishing the front end of the car but narrowly missing going over a hundred foot bluff.[57] The June 23 issue of *Automobile* magazine described the situation thus: "Never before in a Glidden Tour has there been so strenuous a trip as today's 162 miles from Sheffield (Alabama) to Memphis." The Lexington no. 110 was withdrawn after breaking a steering arm and not having the necessary replacement parts. Eleven cars were late at Corinth, leaving only four that checked in there on time. The next day was more frustrating as the tourists spent 17 hours on the trip. A good portion of it was crossing the mighty Mississippi River on a ferry. A large lumber barge was secured and all of the cars were loaded onto it at one time, then towed across the river to Helena. The same article describing the trip from Little Rock to Hot Springs, Arkansas, stated, "When the final reckoning was made this afternoon, it was found that several cars had received penalties; one of the most serious being No. 103 Lexington, which struck a very soft spot in the road and broke the right side member of the frame just back of the front axle. Driver Moore at once withdrew from the contest, but later today reconsidered his course."[58] The frame was repaired and Moore continued the tour. The roads of the southwest took a heavy toll on the automobiles. By the time the tour had reached Oklahoma City, there were only 11 cars still in the contest, out of the original 34 that started. However, Moore, in his number 103, continued to perform well and was one hour and thirty minutes ahead of schedule arriving at Kansas City for the weekend layover. Although the run to Omaha was planned for the next Monday, there was a great deal of dissension among Glidden contestants. Some of the unhappiness stemmed from the fact that the Reo carrying the secretary with the contest records didn't arrive until Saturday evening, a full day late. They had been a day behind since the second day of the tour. The committee spent Sunday checking for errors and assessing penalties.[59] So upset were the crew driving the Parry car that the Parry Automobile Company of Indianapolis secured an attorney who worked through the night with the intention of obtaining a court injunction to end the tour in Kansas City, claiming the Technical Committee had been unfair in its decisions.[60] The Glidden Tour did continue to Omaha as scheduled, where the Lexington was first to arrive, then to Des Moines, Davenport and on to Chicago

The Lexington Model C was advertised in *The Evening News*, July 7, 1910.

Fred N. Coats helped bring Lexington to Connersville, but was soon replaced as general manager. The Evening News, *July 27, 1910*.

without court interference. The Lexington No. 103 finished 5th, or last, in the Chicago Trophy Class with 2,042 penalty points. Although it did complete the 2,850 mile course, the broken frame cost them nearly 2,000 penalty points that could not be overcome. The winning entrant in the Chicago Cup contest was a Moline that had only 19 penalty points against it.[61] Lexington did not compete again in the Glidden Tour but would eventually be successful in other types of competition. Moore drove the Lexington back to Connersville after the event had ended, so in all, he had driven the Number 103 nearly 3,200 miles—an impressive trip for any vehicle in that day.

Meanwhile, back at the factory, production was picking up. Cars offered were basically a continuation of those that were made in Kentucky. The Model A, a five or seven passenger touring, was a large car that weighed 3,250 lbs. and rode on 36 × 4½ inch tires and listed for $2,500. Two extra auxiliary seats cost an additional $50. The Model B had a four passenger close-coupled body. The Model C was a two passenger runabout that used the larger engine; and the Model D, a five passenger touring using a smaller engine, but weighing a thousand pounds less and running on 34 × 3½ tires, listed for $1,650. All models used Rutenber four cylinder water-cooled engines; model A, B and C used the 40/50 horsepower model U engine with 4¾ inch bore and 5 inch stroke, whereas model D used a 30/35 horsepower model RA engine with 4½ inch bore and 5 inch stroke.[62] All models continued to use a leather faced cone clutch with cork inserts. The cars that competed in the Glidden Tour were A models, whereas the model D was the record holder in the Kansas City hill climb event.

By July of 1910, the first Lexington known to travel European roads, a 1911 roadster, was sold to C. B. Jenkins, an American, who ordered the car to be delivered at Liverpool, England, in time for him to arrive and begin a tour.[63] Within a few years, a modest export business had developed that took the name of this Indiana made product to many parts of the world. Lexington did not compete in the "low priced field," nor did they intend to. This was noted in their advertising and news release with the statement that Lexington had made no efforts at producing what were termed low priced cars, and that even though some parts of the industry were experiencing a slump, the local plant had booked orders far ahead.[64] Sales for the year were 625. This was a substantial increase over the previous year's 123,[65] even though it was most certainly slowed by the move from Kentucky to Indiana. Connersville area residents showed substantial interest in the new marque with local purchasers being Fred Lightfoot, Alva Bilby, John Hubble, John Doyle, Charles Hull, George Sinks, E. J. Schlichte, Frank Ansted, Wilson Stewart, Dr. B. R. Smith, E. D. Johnston and R. B. Trimball.[66]

Cars for 1911 were the Model A, the "top of the line," offering the touring, a four door touring and a limousine at $2,500. This car was powered by the 50 hp Rutenber engine, rode on 36 × 4½ inch tires with a 122-inch wheelbase and weighed 3150 pounds. The Model D offered a touring and a four-door touring, at $1,650. The touring did not have doors for front seat occupants as standard equipment, producing an openness reminiscent of riding in a buggy. Detachable doors were available for an extra $50. There was also the Model D-F touring at $1,650, the Model E two passenger roadster listing for $1,650 or four passenger torpedo at $1,775, and the Model F touring at $1,860.[67]

Models D, DF, E and F all used the 4½" × 5" bore and stroke Rutenber 40 hp engine that was advertised as the Renault type. Models D, DF and E were classed

When first announced, the 1911 models were essentially a continuation from 1910. Later, the model configurations were redone. The Evening News, *Sept. 17, 1910.*

together because they were built on the same 117 inch wheelbase chassis and rode on 34 × 3½ inch tires, whereas the model F had the 122 inch wheelbase and 34 × 4 inch tires, the same as the model A but using the smaller engine.[68] Lexington continued the unusual use of a sub-frame for the motor and transmission. Since the cylinders were cast separately, the aluminum crankcase supported the entire motor, with the lower part (which could be removed) giving access to the crankshaft.

Double universal joints and a short shaft were used between the clutch and transmission thus placing the gearbox directly beneath the front seats. Shift linkage connected the transmission with the gearshift lever, which was still mounted on the outside of the body on the right hand side of the driver. The clutch was cone type faced with leather and aluminum. Standard equipment included a dual ignition system using two sets of spark plugs, four for the magneto and four for the battery. Also included was a Bosch magneto, Model F Schebler water jacketed carburetor, Goodrich tires, Schwartz wheels, acetylene gas headlights with a Prest-O-Lite tank, kerosene side and tail lights, horn, jack, tools and tire repair kit.[69] There were two sets of brakes on the rear wheels. The foot pedal activated internal expanding and the hand brake lever controlled external contracting binders.

Tops were an extra cost item. A pantasote or mohair top for a roadster was $75, and the touring or torpedo top listed for $90. The Model F was a large car, but used the smaller engine. It was first shown in Connersville in November of 1910, before being shipped to the Lexington Company's representatives Burkhart & Crippen of Los Angeles, California. This car was noted as having been a beautiful golden brown

THE LEXINGTON MOTOR CAR CO
MAKERS OF
FINE AUTOMOBILES.

E.D. JOHNSON, President
A.E. LEITER, Vice President
FRED N. COATS, Secy & Manager
GARRETT D. WILSON, Treasurer
J.C. MOORE, Mechanical Engineer
H.S. JOHNSON, Purchasing Agent
W.F. SEEL, Sales Manager

CONNERSVILLE, INDIANA   Dec. 1, 1910.

S. A. Miles,
    New York City, N. Y.

Dear Sir:-

    We have your favor of the 30th ult. regarding a list of entries which you have for the Show that is to be held at New York, commencing New Year's Eve at the Palace and notice that you have the name of C. S. Baeder as being down for our car, also that this is an <u>Unsanctioned Show.</u>

    Mr. Baeder is a new agent of ours in New York and wrote us several weeks ago, that he wanted to Show our cars at the New York Show, of course we are not Licensed and that probably bars us from the Licensed Show at Madison Square Garden. At the time he took the matter up with us, it was understood that the space he was to have, would cost $800. and that we were to stand half of it, which we have done and the money has already gone to him. Upon receipt of your letter, this morning, we wired to see if the money had been paid to the people running the New York Show.

    As a matter of fact, we gave the matter very little attention when Mr. Baeder first wrote about this matter and <u>it did not occur to us that this was an Unsanctioned Show.</u>

    Since you have brought this to our attention however, we have wired Mr. Baeder and upon receipt of his advice, will then be able to tell you whether or not we shall retain our space at the Chicago Show, by telling him that he must not go into the first New York Show, or else we will go in there and stay out of your Show.

    Mr. Baeder is a new man for us in New York and we have been anxious to give him all the encouragement we could, and it would be rather tough on both of us to forfeit the $800. for space, provided he has paid it, but as soon as we learn whether or not this is the case, will advise you further, so that you will know just what to depend on from us.

                           Yours very truly,

FNC/J
                            THE LEXINGTON MOTOR CAR CO.,
                                    Fred N Coats
                                  Secretary & Manager.

A letter regarding Lexington's entry in the 1911 New York show. The reference to an "unsanctioned show" meant that it was not licensed under the Selden patent. Two separate auto shows were held in New York City, one for licensed and another for unlicensed manufacturers.

color and it was sent, along with two other models, to be displayed at an automobile show to be held in L.A. the next month.[70] Lexingtons were shown at various other auto shows including Chicago, New York, Boston and Philadelphia.

A letter of praise was received from Mr. L. E. Russell, who used his Lexington for touring the New England states during the summer. He wrote, "We received our Auto June 15th at Providence, R. I., and immediately started on our journey, touring out of Providence through Massachusetts, New Hampshire to Newport, Vermont, then back through the White Mountains which is a most beautiful mountainous drive. The car has been attractive and admired by all who have seen it and has given us perfect satisfaction as we drove it through places and over hills that would be almost impossible to go with a team and had no trouble of any kind."[71]

Then there was a story of a Lexington truck. Or was it actually a bus of sorts? This was a vehicle built to take people to and from the Fayette County Free Fair. This fair, which was held the last week of August in 1911, was, and still is, one of very few county fairs in the country that did not charge admission. The fairgrounds was located about two miles north of downtown Connersville in Roberts Park, and several vehicles carried folks back and forth for a small fee. The Lexington that was involved was reported to be a regular touring car except for a larger and heavier body. It was operated sixteen hours a day for four days, during which time it was reported to have hauled 1,870 people, nearly one fourth of the population of Connersville. This same vehicle had been used for passenger service at the previous year's fair and had been used the remainder of the time to transport freight back and forth between the Lexington factory and the railroad freight depot.[72]

The year 1911 brought growth to the company as they increased production by 50 percent over the previous year. A new plant superintendent was hired. "Mr. John A. Edsold came from the 'great Packard factory at Detroit, Michigan,' with which concern he had served five years in different departments." Before that he was at Chalmers for two years and at Ford one year. The company was seeking a man who could take charge and manage thousands of dollars worth of material and labor on a daily basis.[73] Former superintendent Fred Coats retained his position as secretary of the company and remained with Lexington for another year but as a district sales manager.[74] Another sign of growth was evident when it was announced in August that the Lexington factory was going to build a large addition in the rear of the present facility. It was one story in brick, 77 feet wide by 175 feet long, to be used for body finishing. The addition would make the total frontage of the factory facing the east 525 feet long, about the length of one and one half city blocks.[75] Production for 1911 was 939; however, out of total U.S. production of nearly 200,000, Lexington was still a small duck in a large pond.[76]

The 1912 model year brought important changes in Lexington's automobiles and another attempt at a nationally spotlighted competition. Model identifications were shuffled significantly with two entirely new series appearing. The most economical offering was a smaller car that year, the Popular Model K consisting of a touring and a speedster, listing at $1,400 without a top. It used the small 232 cubic inch displacement 30 horsepower Rutenber engine with 3¾ inch bore and 5¼ inch stroke cast *en bloc*. This was a noteworthy change for Lexington as all previous Rutenber engine offerings had cylinders cast separately. The subframe was eliminated on this model, but the unit power plant that included the engine, clutch and transmission continued to use the three-point suspension. A Remy magneto with dual igni-

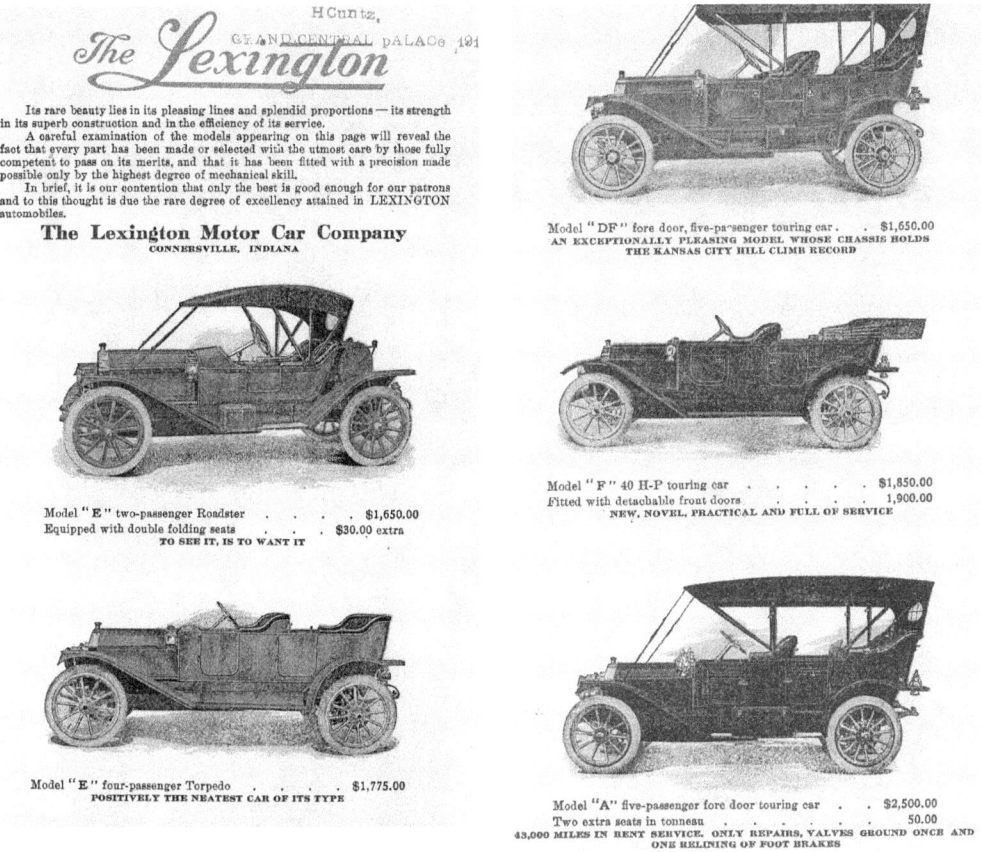

Additional letter series were introduced before the 1911 shows. Lexington would use almost every letter in the alphabet during their nearly twenty years in business.

tion was used instead of Bosch. The car rode on 34 × 4 inch tires with a 116 inch wheelbase. Lexington's most expensive offering was the completely new Perfect Six, available in touring, demi-tonneau or roadster body types that listed for $2,500.[77] Rutenber was again the source of power, providing a six-cylinder with 4⅛ inch bore by 5¼ inch stroke, good for a horsepower rating of 55/60. Cylinders were cast separately making it easy to make repairs or replacement. Two separate ignition systems and two sets of spark plugs were provided, one using the Bosch magneto and the other a battery distributor. The Perfect Six continued the use of the subframe for engine and transmission mountings with double universal joints between the clutch and the transmission intended to relieve all strains. The Perfect Six Model G was a large automobile with 36 × 4 inch tires and a 133 inch wheelbase. This was Lexington's first attempt at marketing a six cylinder vehicle, in a time when most automobile manufacturers competing in the mid to upper price range were offering engines that delivered more smoothness and power than found in four cylinder units.[78] The innovative chief engineer, John C. Moore, had the Perfect Six engine equipped with two exhaust manifolds. He then added two exhaust pipes and two mufflers, creating what was probably the first dual exhaust system on an American production automobile. The idea behind the novel system was to minimize the back pressure caused by a restricted one pipe system while still maintain-

The carburetor of choice for Lexington was the Schebler, from nearby Indianapolis. *Motor Age, Sept. 21, 1916.*

Two exciting modes of transportation in 1912 were combined on the cover of this brochure.

If You Want Full Service

from your automobile or motorcycle—both night and day—you must have a dependable lighting system.

Don't overlook that all-important point when you buy.

Then is the time to

Insist Upon Prest-O-Lite

It is the only safe, sure, efficient and economical lighting system giving satisfaction, night after night, to 350,000 owners.

Its satisfactory service includes 15,000 exchange stations, in every town and village where automobiles go.

Don't take chances by driving at night with a cheap, unsafe, unreliable generator or imitation gas tank.

One accident costs ten times the price of Prest-O-Lite.

Be sure you get Prest-O-Lite. Insist!

MAKERS OF
Prest-O-Lite Gas Tanks
Prest-O-Tire Tubes
Prest-O-Tire Tanks
Prest-O-Carbon Remover
Prest-O-Welder
Prest-O-Starter
Prest-O-Liter
Ask for literature on any or all of them.

THE PREST-O-LITE COMPANY
210 East South Street   Indianapolis, Ind.

BRANCHES
at Atlanta, Baltimore, Boston, Buffalo, Chicago (2), Cincinnati, Cleveland, Dallas, Detroit, Denver, Indianapolis, Jacksonville, Kansas City, Los Angeles, Milwaukee, Minneapolis, New York, Omaha, Philadelphia, Pittsburg, Providence, St. Louis, St. Paul, San Francisco, Seattle.

CHARGING PLANTS
Atlanta, Cleveland, Dallas, E. Cambridge, Hawthorne, Ill., Indianapolis, Long Island City, Los Angeles, Minnesota Transfer, Oakland, Omaha, Seattle, Waverly, N. J.

FOREIGN AGENCIES
Honolulu, H. I.; Manila, P. I.; San Juan, P. R., Toronto, Can.; Vancouver, B. C.; City of Mexico; London, Eng.; Berlin, Germany; Australia.

EXCHANGE AGENCIES EVERYWHERE

By 1912, a car owner could choose either acetylene or electric headlights. Saturday Evening Post, *April 6, 1912.*

ing quiet operation. Three exhaust valves would open into each manifold, so no two valves could send burned gasses into the manifold at the same time. Through this system, one cylinder's exhaust would be completely removed before another cylinder's exhaust valve was opened. For 1912 this system was standard equipment only on the Perfect Six, but it was soon included on all models. Advertised as the Moore Multiple Exhaust, it was eventually patented and became a Lexington trademark as they claimed increased economy along with more power. A carry-over from the previous year was the Standard Model that was available as the E roadster or the DF touring car. This series now rode on a 118 inch wheelbase, an increase of one inch. Either could be had for $1,775 without a top. The Standard Model used the Rutenber Model X 281 cubic inch displacement engine with 4⅛ inch bore by 5¼ inch stroke having cylinders cast separately, giving an output of 40 hp. The three point suspension was used with the front motor support a part of the front crossmember and rear supports being integral arms of the flywheel housing that attached to the transmission and to the frame. The gearshift lever and the hand brake were located to the right of the driver on the outside of the body. The Master Model F offered a touring car and a demi-tonneau for $1,975 or a coupe at $2,500. Interior refinements on the coupe included dull black leather upholstering, an inside electric light and one extra folding seat placed at the left side of the steering column. One could purchase the coupe body separately for $900. This body was interchangeable on the Model F chassis so when colder weather made open car travel uncomfortable, a switch of the bodies would furnish closed car protection. A strong similarity existed between the touring and the demi-tonneau, but the latter body had a longer steering column set at a sharper angle and sported a shroud over the front of the cowl for a snappy effect. Both bodies could accommodate up to five passengers.[79] The Model F replaced the model A of previous years. It continued to use the Rutenber Model RA engine with 4½ inch bore by 5 inch stroke having cylinders cast separately, listed at 45 hp, and rode on a 122 inch wheelbase. This model continued to use the subframe upon which the engine and transmission were mounted. All Lexington models continued using Schebler carburetors and offered standard colors of blue, gray or golden brown, and brass trim added beautiful luster but required frequent polishing.[80] The Lexington company was optimistic and ambitious by offering four different engines and four different powertrain/frame combinations for a small production run.

Shortly after the introduction of the 1912 models on September 1, 1911, significant new innovations became available, as described in literature dated November 20, 1911.[81] Electric lights were offered as an option on all models for an additional $85. Lexington described this system as the "Auto-Lighter," and it consisted of an electric generator, a large Willard battery, a volt meter and a switch on the dash that con-

A novel system for starting the engine was the acetylene powered Prest-O-Start used by Lexington. Saturday Evening Post, *April 6, 1912.*

trolled lighting. The operator could choose either the head lights, side lights or tail lamp, or all of them.[82] The same brochure announcing availability of electric lighting also described the most desirable addition for the year, a self-starter that was included as standard equipment.

Most automobile manufacturers were scrambling to offer devices to make starting the car easier and less dangerous. To be one of the first with this innovation was of utmost importance. A wide variety of self-starters appeared on the market and were advertised in automobile trade publications, including units powered by acetylene, compressed air, electricity, mechanical winding and even gasoline. Lexington chose to use the Prest-O-Start made by the Prest-O-Light Company of Indianapolis. This outfit consisted of a starter pump about eight inches long and five inches in diameter that was mounted through the dash. It was operated by a plunger handle from the driver's seat. One or two strokes of the plunger filled the engine cylinders with acetylene Prest-O-Gas. Then, as soon as the coil box switch was pressed to the battery side, a spark ignited the acetylene gas. The resulting explosion caused the engine to turn over with the expectation that it would start.[83] Some manufacturers preferred the Presto-Start type of starter because it required only minimal alteration to the engine for installation. It did not require a different flywheel with teeth to engage the starter as did the electric type. However, the acetylene starter soon died out because the electric unit, first developed by Charles Kettering for use by Cadillac, was much more reliable and many companies jumped on the electric starter bandwagon and introduced their own versions.

Various promotions encouraged local citizens to purchase Lexington automobiles, and sometimes their names were printed in advertisements. One promotion attracted a great deal of community attention when a new Lexington car was raffled off and tickets were sold far and wide. The Hackelman-Heeb Furniture store in downtown Connersville dedicated a front window where ticket stubs were placed. As the raffle sales continued, the ticket stubs eventually accumulated to about one foot in depth. A large crowd gathered the day of the drawing as excitement reached its peak. Robert F. Williams, about eight years old at the time, was selected out of the crowd to draw the winning ticket. He waded into the mound of ticket stubs in the store window and drew five stubs. The first four received minor prizes, but the last one drawn was the winner of the automobile. Robert's father was in the crowd holding tickets that he had hoped would be winners, but he went home empty handed that day. He did end up purchasing a new Lexington in 1912 and another one a few years later, so the promotion may well have stirred some interest.[84]

One competitive event brought a great deal of excitement and disappointment to the company and to the community. During the spring of 1912, Lexington built a racecar and entered it in the Indianapolis 500 Mile Race. This was Lexington's first attempt at participating in that prestigious event; however, the other automobile manufacturer of Connersville, McFarlan, had raced at the new track the previous two years and was also a competitor that year. With two companies from the community entered in the race, excitement could hardly be contained. It only increased when it was learned that Marmon, the winner in 1911, was not entering the 1912 race. A good showing was almost sure to add lots of sales, and a victory seemed a possibility. The *Evening News* of May 27 had articles telling of the successful qualification runs of the McFarlan and the Lexington. The Lexington, driven by Harry Knight, was the slower of the two, having made the two and one half miles

(A) Model DF. (B) Model E Roadster. (C) The Model K Touring Car. (D) The Model K with Speedster body. (E) Model F Demi-Tonneau. (F) Lexington Coupe.

1912 was Lexington's first year to offer a six-cylinder engine.

This Standard Model Roadster offered a sporty ride. Motor Age, *March 7, 1912.*

Forty Features Which Make the Lexington Your Favorite Car

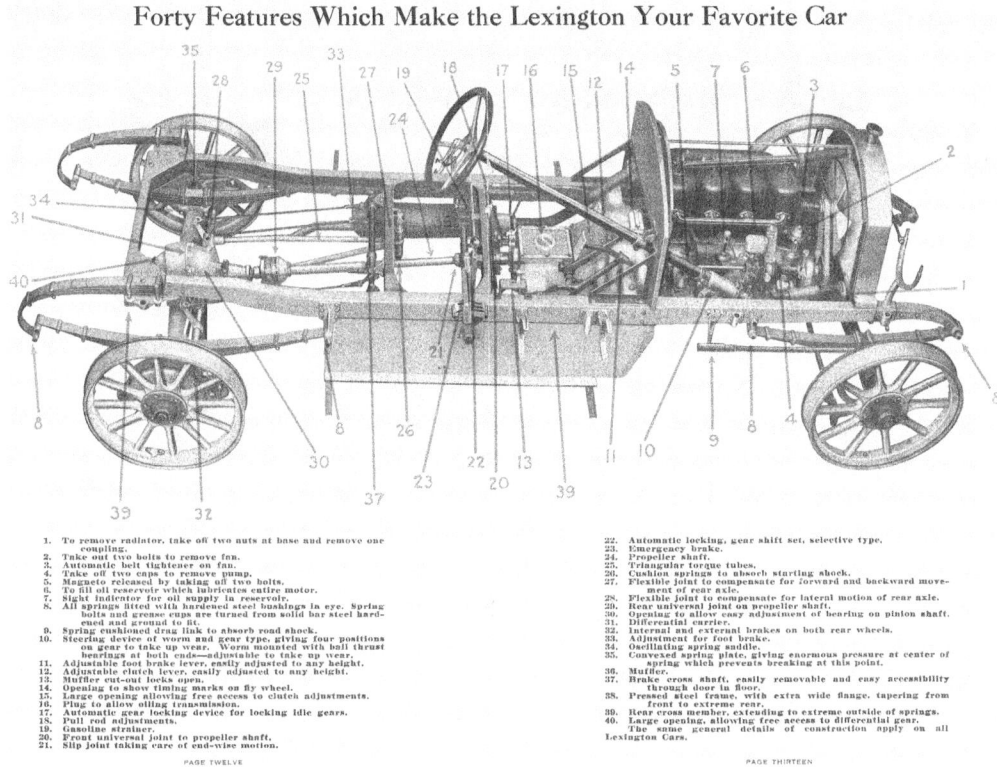

This Lexington chassis offered many quality features.

in one minute and 58.54 seconds for 75.92 m.p.h., compared with the McFarlan's time of one minute and 53.26 seconds for 78.08 m.p.h. Twenty-four cars qualified for the 500-mile race.[85] A special train was commissioned to take race fans to Indianapolis for this great event. But disappointment came early when, in the sixth lap, the golden brown Lexington being driven at a rate of 76 m.p.h. broke a pin in one of the cylinders, locking the engine and forcing it out of the race. The McFarlan, running in tenth place at the 100 mile mark, made it for 63 laps before a tire blowout sent the car atop the retaining wall where it slid for nearly 100 feet before hitting a telephone pole, splitting the pole in two and badly damaging the car.[86] The drivers and mechanics of both vehicles escaped without injury, but the end of the 500 mile race career had come for both of these Connersville companies.

Lexington production showed a slight gain for 1912, with 1,013 cars leaving the factory.[87] Nonetheless company finances were in disarray, and a committee of creditors was brought it. In an attempt to continue production locally, a new company, the Connersville Securities Corporation, was formed, composed of local businessmen. They proposed to the creditors, rather than foreclosure, the payment of 25 percent of their claims within 30 days. The value of assets was placed at $134,000 and liabilities at $140,000. The proposal of the securities company was the best one that was received.[88]

One member of the creditors committee, Frederick I. Barrows, became the secretary-treasurer of Lexington and stayed with the company for more then ten

Purchasing and keeping track of the multiplicity of parts used in assembling automobiles was a major task. This inquiry must have been one of many.

years. Frederick was born in Portage County, Ohio, in 1873, and was about seven years old when his parents moved to Connersville where he completed high school in 1890. He taught in Fayette County schools for three years beginning in 1891, before earning a Ph.B. degree at DePauw University and later a law degree from Georgetown University Law School. Barrows served as mayor of Connersville from 1905 until 1910 and had become connected with the Central State Bank where he was elected vice-president in 1913.[89] Mr. Barrows, along with other local businessmen, tried to save this financially embarrassed company that had been spirited away from its city of origin just three years earlier.

3

A New Name Is Born

By mid–1912, when the 1913 line was introduced, the Lexington Motor Car Company was experiencing serious financial difficulties. The new car line was scaled back, offering only two selections at the time of introduction. The Standard Model G that had been labeled the model DF the previous year was for those who wanted a mid-sized automobile with many of the features of more expensive cars. It had the four-cylinder 40 hp Rutenber engine with 4 × 5 inch bore and stroke, on a 118 inch wheelbase. Standard equipment included the top, top boot, Electric Auto-Light lighting system, Prest-O-Starter, Stewart Warner speedometer and steering wheel and driver controls remaining on the right hand side. The Moore Multiple Exhaust was also standard feature on the four cylinder cars beginning with this model. This medium priced car with proven dependability listed at $1,775. For those with deeper pockets, the six-cylinder model D was rated at 55/60 hp, had a 129 inch wheelbase, rode on 36 × 4 inch tires and sold for $2,500. The top of the line six cylinder Lexington had plenty of competition in the mid–$2,000 price bracket. As a comparison, the Cole Six with 132 inch wheelbase sold for $2,485, the Chalmers 18 with 130 inch wheelbase listed for $2,400, the McFarlan M with 128 inch wheelbase at $2,750, the Oakland 6–6 with 130 inch wheelbase at $2,400, the Stutz 6 with 130 inch wheelbase at $2,300 and the Wescott 50 with 127 inch wheelbase at $2,525, to name just a few.[1] The Lexington six was offered only a short time before being replaced by a similar car with a new nameplate.

A natural disaster made production more difficult that year. In March a major flood; recounted in the March 23, 1913, *Evening News* under the headline "Fayette County Swept by Terrible Flood," swept away all of the railroad and trolley lines, telephone and telegraph lines in the area and made nearly every country road impassable.[2] This disaster became known as the terrible 1913 flood, an event so catastrophic that it became the standard with which to compare other floods. Many communities suffered worse than Connersville as major cities such as Cincinnati and Dayton were cut off from the outside world and suffered loss of life. Local factories were required to cut back on electric use because of a shortage of fuel to run the generating plant. The Lexington factory was undamaged but lost production due to the damage done to railroads. Raw materials could not be shipped in and finished products could not be shipped out. It took about thirty days before the plant was running at a normal rate again.[3]

This was a year of forced reorganization. A committee of creditors had been called in mid-way through 1912 to deal with financial difficulties and seek possible reorganization. The first announcement on impending change was made in mid-October of 1912, noting that Lexington was to manufacture 1,000 six-cylinder cars the coming year, and a new selling company would market them.[4] On January 16,

Even after the company reorganization, Lexington automobiles continued to be manufactured by the Lexington Motor Car Company. Motor, *June 1913*.

1913, the Central Car Company was founded "to manufacture and build motor driven and other vehicles."[5]

Articles of Association were signed on that date establishing the company that was funded at $100,000. The agreement named a Board of Directors with seven members: E. W. Ansted, the recognized organizer, Joseph E. Huston, Robert T. Huston, Frederic I. Barrows, James M. Heron, Thomas C. Bryson, all from Connersville, plus John W. Burk, of Springfield, Ohio.[6] Burk was the only out-of-towner in the group, but he was a brother-in-law of E. W. Ansted. The Central Car Company was to produce the Howard six cylinder automobile that would to sell for $2,375 "fully complete."[7] The Lexington Motor Car Company was still in operation producing the Lexington Standard Model G four cylinder automobile. Both companies were using the same facility.

The formation of the Howard Motor Car Company represented an effort for the manufacturer to make profits without the cares of sales and advertising. The new company had the sole purpose of advertising and marketing a new line of automobiles, to be designated as the Series C Howard. "Articles of Association" for the Howard Motor Car Co. were signed by the Board of Directors, Raymond S. Springer, Allen Wiles and Frederic I. Barrows, and were filed Jan. 21, 1913. Objectives of this organization were listed as "to manufacture and build automobiles; to buy and sell such material and articles as may be necessary or convenient to manufacture and build automobiles; to buy and sell automobiles and automobile parts."[8] In spite of the broad listing of objectives, in reality, this organization was just for sales and promotion. The corporation was funded at only $10,000 with officers being Howard Babcock, Guilford C. Babcock, Harry Tuttle and Clarence L. Millard.[9]

Even the company noted that the sale of the Series C Howard was conducted under a peculiar condition. Apparently established Lexington dealers were not

Preparing for a trial run in a pre-production six-cylinder Howard test car. The company had several test drivers who sometimes angered the public by speeding on city streets and country roads. *Courtesy Wayne Goetz.*

automatically franchised to sell the Howard. One of the company ads noted that sales manager Ansted and advertising manager Huston were choosing a select list of dealers in all parts of the country. The company did not intend to deal with "fly-by-nighters" or "one-season dealers." They wanted the car to be well represented wherever it was represented at all.[10] This marketing strategy of having one company produce the car and another company advertise and sell it probably was the elder Ansted's idea as his other businesses were not directly involved in the retail sales but, instead, sold to other manufacturers. The end result was there were major parts of the country that had no dealer representative for Howard automobiles, and sales suffered accordingly.

There is no explanation why the name was selected for the car, but it seems probable that Howard Babcock used his connections as a distributor and provided finances enough to be honored by having his name on the front of the radiator. Another of the officers, Harry Tuttle, had been with Stoddard Dayton for the past five years and was an acquaintance of district sales manager Fred Coats, who himself had been employed at Stoddard before joining Lexington a few years earlier. The Stoddard Dayton Company had been hit especially hard by the 1913 flood and was soon to go out of business.

The Howard Motor Car Company didn't last long in its original form because of its ineffectiveness with marketing. By late September, the owners of the Central Car Company had secured a majority of stock for the Howard Motor Car Company and had taken it over. The capital stock was increased from $10,000 to $100,000 with the new officers being Edward W. Ansted, president, Emery Huston, vice-president, and Frank B. Ansted, general sales manager.[11] The McDuffee Automobile Company of Chicago continued to be the major distributor for the Howard automobile, focusing their efforts in the Chicago area and on the West Coast. For a few months, the Central Car Company and the Howard Motor Car Company co-existed producing and marketing the Howard, while, in the same facility, the Lexington Motor Car Company quietly continued producing and selling the four cylinder Lexington.

This automobile manufacturing concern was soon to be under the control of one family with Edward Willard Ansted at the helm. In a booklet, *A Little Journey to Connersville*, written by Elbert Hubbard and published in 1914, Mr. Hubbard describes E. W. Ansted as the one man who "constituted Connersville," because he owned or had a financial interest in so many businesses. Edward was born in Clayton, New York and was raised in a modest home. His father was a blacksmith, no doubt an inspiration to him as he started manufacturing wagon springs when just eighteen years of age. His father was of Mohawk Dutch and his mother of Irish descent. They taught the virtues of hard work, thrift and a love of craftsmanship. The book learning that he acquired was through the efforts of his mother who taught at the little school E. W. attended. His first job away from home was making wagon springs across the border in Ganaoque, Canada, and he was one of the first to make wagon springs of steel, placing one leaf on top of the other with each leaf getting shorter toward the top. Seeking adventure, Edward moved to Racine, Wisconsin, where he worked for the Racine Springs Works. He eventually bought their equipment and opened his own factory along with a partner, Michael Higgins. In 1889 the partners were induced to move their factory to Indianapolis to make springs for the Perry Manufacturing Company. Three years later, this factory was moved to Connersville as the Ansted Spring and Axle Company.[12] Other industries started by

Ansted were the Central Manufacturing Company, Indiana Lamp Company, Hoosier Castings Company, and many other business interests.[13] The Central Manufacturing Company was already supplying bodies and Indiana Lamp Company was the source of lamps for Lexington while Ansted Spring and Axle Company supplied springs and axles. It was a logical move for E. W. to own the car company as well. From humble beginnings, Edward W. Ansted had become a very wealthy person. Before moving to Wisconsin, he married Catherine Burk. They had five children, George W., Arthur A., Frank B., Nellie and Edward W. Jr.[14]

Emery Huston, vice-president of the new company, had just graduated from Wabash College in the spring of 1913 when he became advertising and assistant sales manager for Lexington. Emery was a local boy whose family was also involved with Connersville industry. Emery became E. W.'s son-in-law in November of 1914 when he married Nellie Ansted.

Edward W. Ansted became the president of the Lexington-Howard Company in 1913. He was recognized as Connersville's leading citizen.

This opulent residence at 1205 Central Ave. was built in 1902 as the home of Edward W. Ansted. It is the present home of Connersville's mayor, Max Ellison, and his wife. *Photograph by author.*

Then there was the general sales manager, Frank Ansted, E. W.'s third son, who was becoming very involved in his father's manufacturing interests. Frank was born in Racine, Wisconsin, in December 1884, but moved with his family to Connersville when he was about six years old. He attended local schools and later graduated from the University of Michigan Law School and opened a practice upon returning to Connersville. He married Isabel Heron, whose father, James M. Heron, was secretary-treasurer of the Rex Manufacturing Company, treasurer of Hoosier Castings Company, and secretary of Central Manufacturing Company. All of these firms were closely affiliated with Lexington-Howard. Frank and Isabel had one son, Dale.[15] Frank became interested in automobiles and journeyed to Kentucky to purchase a large Lexington touring car during the Spring of 1910, at the time that the factory was being relocated, but before a locally made vehicle was available. Soon after, he took on the Lexington dealership under the name of Ye Motor Shop, later known as Inland Motors. His position with the Howard Motor Car Company and Lexington-Howard, as general sales manager, ended after a couple of years when he resigned over differences of opinion on marketing. At the urging of his father, in September of 1915, he returned as vice-president and general manager. At the passing of E. W., Frank became company president, and he was very much involved in the company's successes and failure.[16]

The Howard Six made its debut at the Chicago Motor Show in early February of 1913. It had been advertised in Chicago newspapers and was on display at the McDuffee Automobile Company, the Howard distributor for the Great Lakes states.[17] Designers were Harry Tuttle and John Moore. In overall appearance, the Howard was almost a twin of the Lexington Six Model D it had replaced, but there were some major differences.

The new Howard Model C used a Continental model Six-C engine instead of Lexington's Rutenber. This was a large power plant, having a 421 cubic inch displacement with 4⅛ × 5¼ inch bore and stroke, and was rated at 60 horsepower. The cylinders were cast in threes with valves enclosed by cover plates. The engine, clutch and transmission were one unit with three point suspension. The subframe system was not used. Fuel was supplied to the engine through a model G Stromberg carburetor. The Howard came equipped with an electric starter instead of the Prest-O acetylene unit, and the steering wheel was moved to the left hand side of the car.[18]

The proper location of the steering wheel was one of the controversial issues of the time in automobile circles. Henry Ford's Model T popularized the left-hand location of the steering wheel and gradually all other manufacturers in the U.S. followed, with Pierce Arrow holding out until the 1921 models were introduced to make the switch. The time had arrived when it was more important to watch the car coming toward you than to watch out for the side ditch.

The Howard was a large car with a 130-inch wheelbase, riding on 36 × 4½ inch tires, and was offered only in a five-passenger touring the first year. Equipment included a gasoline gauge, electric lights and horn, high-grade mohair top and top boot, one-inch-thick Turkish upholstery, speedometer and grade indicator. The wiring for the electric lights was concealed inside the lamp brackets, thus giving protection to the wires while keeping an uncluttered look. Cowl lights were mounted nearly flush in the cowl and could provide additional lighting along with the headlights.

CONNERSVILLE EVENING NEWS. SATURDAY, MAY 16, 1914.   PAGE THREE

Value Received-- And More!

The HOWARD Six is worth all we ask for it, and then some.

"Value Received—and More!"

In the first place it is a real Six. Not because we say so; not because of salesmanic fireworks; but because of scientific engineering.

The Moore Multiple Exhaust System (patents pending) enables our six-cylinder motors to develop 22.8 per cent. more horse power than is otherwise possible. And the Lexington-Howard Co. is the only motor car manufacturer in the world which has a right to use it at the present time!

So, no matter how much more than $2375.00 you may be willing to pay for an automobile, you cannot elsewhere secure this epoch-making device which is included without extra charge in the price of the HOWARD Six.

This is worthy of your investigation.

THE LEXINGTON-HOWARD CO.

THE SIX *Howard* THAT HITS SIX

Howard "D"—$2375.

The Howard received the bulk of the advertising for 1914. The Evening News, *May 16, 1914.*

The spark lever on the steering column operated in the ordinary way to vary the timing of the spark; however, pressing it down would blow the electric horn which was mounted at the left side of the motor inside the engine compartment with the bell projecting through the hood for maximum sound effect. The Howard also had two ignition systems, a Bosch high-tension magneto and an Atwater Kent battery system. The battery box was located on the driver's side running board.

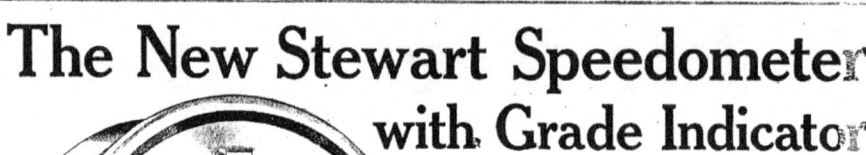

The Stewart Speedometer with Grade Indicator was standard on the Howard. The grade indicator could give the driver bragging rights on how steep the hill was that he had climbed. The Saturday Evening Post, *July 20, 1912.*

Some unusual features included the accelerator pedal being globular in form, so that it could be operated from any angle. It was also made in such a way that it fit under the instep of the ordinary shoe, so that the driver could actuate it or release it by just moving his foot slightly backward or forward. The gasoline tank was of 18-gallon capacity. The tank was located under the front seat with pressure being maintained by a fuel pump driven by the camshaft. A novel feature of the tank was its shape with an inclined bottom to assure fuel pressure at the carburetor when the car was tilted or was on an uneven surface. The fuel gauge was located on the front floorboard where it could easily be monitored. In the rear passenger compartment, hassocks were used instead of a foot rest and were fastened to straps so that they could be pulled backward or forward according to the desire of the passengers.[19] Both lines of cars seemed to be more subdued since the brass plating on the radiator and headlights had been eliminated in favor of painting them to match the fenders, usually black. In spite of the year's problems, Lexington and Howard production increased significantly to 1,915.[20]

The year 1914 dawned with yet another name change for this company with the announcement that the Lexington-Howard Motor Car Company had filed papers of incorporation and was capitalized at $150,000. The Howard Motor Car Company and the Lexington Motor Car Company were combined to form this organization. The Central Motor Car Company was dissolved. Officers for the new corporation were E. W. Ansted as president, Frederic I. Barrows, secretary and Frank B. Ansted, sales manager. The Board of Directors was also comprised of just three men, E. W. Ansted, Joseph E. Huston and Frederic Barrows; however, additional members to the board were added January 6 and September 14, 1915, and again on June 28, 1916, at which time there were a total of ten directors.[21]

Two lines of cars were marketed for 1914, the Lexington Four, labeled the Series H, and the Howard Six Series D.[22] The larger Howard received the most promotion and was expected to bring in the biggest revenue. It was essentially the same car as the previous year's model C. Power was provided by the Continental Big Six engine that developed 60 hp at 1500 rpm. The cylinder blocks, made of gray iron, were cast in two blocks of three cylinders each. The aluminum alloy crankcase was made in two pieces. The upper part carried the crankshaft bearings and the lower part formed the oil reservoir which could be removed when it was necessary to adjust connecting-rod bearings. The valves were operated by a single camshaft with the inlet and exhaust valves being interchangeable. Valve stems were made of carbon steel and the heads of nickel steel. The pistons were the three-ring type with an oil groove to prevent excess oil from getting into the combustion chamber.

The engine, clutch and transmission formed a unit power plant that was suspended at three points to eliminate vibrations. The single point of suspension was located at the front of the engine and was lubricated by a grease cup mounted on the bronze-lined bearing supporting the motor.[23] The Stromberg carburetor received fuel from the tank that had been relocated to the rear of the chassis. A 14-inch leather surface cone clutch included a brake to reduce gear clashing and make shifting easier without the need of double-clutching. A Warner-Toledo gearbox with three speeds forward plus reverse was used with the gearshift lever mounted directly above the transmission. The rear axle was full floating with the differential having a 3.44 to 1 gear ratio.[24] The ignition was Bosch high-tension magneto with an Atwater-Kent battery system also. A Howard-Jesco starter made by the Jones Electric Starter Company was used, and a newly designed Howard integral spare tire holder was standard equipment. This holder was noted for extreme strength, being attached directly to the frame, and either one or two tires could be carried without straps as the spares clamped into place securely using the same type of bolts that attached the demountable rims. Brakes were located on the rear wheels with

FACTORY NO. 1.

Buying at Home

no matter what you buy, has so many undisputed advantages that there is little need to argue the question further.

This is especially true of automobiles because, among other things, it means:

1st. Prompt Service.
2nd. Superior Service.
3rd. Cheaper Service.

It means prompt service because you can drive your car to the factory in a few minutes.

It means superior service because the men who built your car are the best men to keep it tuned up.

It means cheaper service because you have no expense of getting repair parts by C. O. D. express.

WE BELIEVE THAT PRETTY NEARLY EVERY CAR BUILT NOW-A-DAYS IS A GOOD CAR AND THAT LEXINGTONS AND AND HOWARDS ARE AS GOOD AS THE BEST.

That is why we feel perfectly free in discussing service with you. For you know as well as we do that EVERY car, sooner or later, needs adjustments and replacements. LEXINGTONS and HOWARDS are in the "later" class, it is true, but when that time does finally come at which it is necessary to give them expert attention, it is gratifying to know that the factory is not far away; the factory with its well equipped service department where you may receive prompt, courteous, and thorough attention.

Think these points over when considering the LEXINGTON or the HOWARD among ALL the rest.

The HOWARD six IS truly wonderful value at $2,375.00 and we court an opportunity to prove it.

The LEXINGTON four is as sturdy, powerful, and classy as any car you can buy anywhere for $1,335.00.

Phone 80 or 81 for a demonstration of either, or both.

Visitors at the factory always welcome.

THE LEXINGTON-HOWARD CO.

This factory building was the home of three car companies in 1913: Central Car Company that built the Howard car, the Howard Car Company that marketed the Howard car, and Lexington Motor Car Co. that continued production of the Lexington car. The Evening News, *May 4, 1914.*

6-Cylinder $2375 Fully Equipped

130 inch Wheelbase

YOU find in the Lexington-Howard cars these three essential selling requisites.

1. Those elements of service and comfort demanded by the motor car buyer.
2. Specifications that we as manufacturers know to be of sterling value.
3. Exclusive features that make it easy for the dealer to sell cars.

Upon these points, cars are made, bought and sold.

Every Lexington-Howard specification has been tested and proven to be of superior worth.

Every essential of service has been selected because of its successful performance in the most rigid tests.

As manufacturers the Lexington-Howard Company admits of no superiors.

Conservative and careful attention to details has marked every change or advancement.

Motor car manufacturing finds its highest expression in the Lexington-Howard plant at Connersville.

Both the Lexington "Four" and the Howard "Six" present exclusive features that make either car the choice of careful buyers who want full value for their money—

The Howard "Six" stands out strongly and in an individual position because of the Moore Multiple Exhaust System—

Through this remarkable System the Howard "Six" presents 22.8% more horsepower at less fuel consumption than any other car of similar size made.

The Howard "Six" sells for $2375, and this price alone is indicative of what you may expect in quality.

$2375 is the result of careful manufacturing; elimination of waste; sane promotion; and a solid financial foundation.

You should not pay more than $2375 for any car that does not at least show equal value—

Lexington-Howard cars sell easily and quickly and at a fair margin of profit for the dealer.

Lexington-Howard dealers receive every cooperation and help that can be conscientiously given a dealer.

And your Lexington-Howard dealers pay only for the actual value represented in Lexington-Howard cars.

Territories are being closed every day—because they know that such an organization as the Lexington-Howard Company is an asset in their business and because Lexington-Howard cars deserve the acceptance they are sure to receive.

Write today for the Lexington-Howard selling proposition for your city.

4 Cylinder $1335 Fully Equipped

114 inch Wheelbase

Lexington-Howard Co.
126 Main Street
CONNERSVILLE, INDIANA

Even though the Howard received top billing, it was never a good seller. Motor World, *April 9, 1914.*

the foot brake activating contracting shoes on the outside of each drum and the emergency hand brake lever causing shoes to expand inside each drum.

Body styles offered included a five passenger touring that listed at $2,375, or by special order, a seven passenger touring, a limousine or a three passenger coupe could be had for $2,500.[25] Features of the body included large doors with concealed hinges and ebonized cap or garnish moldings that matched the ebony finish used on the instrument board. Instruments included the speedometer, air gauge, ammeter, light and ignition switches, priming button and an instrument panel light.[26] On December 12, 1913, two rail cars loaded with Howards left the factory bound for California. Of the six cars, four were five-passenger tourings, one was a seven-passenger touring and the other was a coupe.[27]

Each Howard was road tested before being loaded for delivery. Superintendent E. B. Brown saw to it that no Howard left the factory until he had taken a ride in it. One favorite test route was to go west on what is now 21st Street out over Widener Hill on what was known as the Elephant Hill road. Several years before, when Van Amberg's circus menagerie wintered on the Frost farm, Tip-Po, the largest elephant then in captivity, died and was buried on the hill, resulting in the name Elephant Hill. The bones were later removed and placed on display in a museum at nearby Earlham College at Richmond, Indiana.[28] The hill was a good challenge for checking performance, but there was public outcry over the speed and carelessness of some test drivers. There were threats of prosecution for test drivers who might injure or kill an innocent person.[29] In spite of all of its quality features, the Howard was not a good seller and was phased out at the end of the model run.

Both the Howard and Lexington lines shared the benefits of the Moore Multiple Exhaust system. In a test of this system conducted at the Wheeler and Schebler laboratory in Indianapolis, it was found that the Continental six cylinder engine equipped with Moore's dual exhaust system developed 50 hp at 1,400 rpm, whereas with the standard type manifold with single exhaust and muffler the engine developed a maximum of 42.5 hp at 1,400 rpm for a 22.8 percent gain in horsepower with the dual exhaust.[30] A difference in the operation of the carburetor was also noted with the two different systems. Before fitting the double exhaust the 1.25 inch carburetor required a number 6 needle, number 21 air spring and .5 inch venturi to obtain the best results. With the Moore system a finer number 8 needle, a lighter number 17 air spring and a wider .625 venturi were required indicating probable greater fuel economy with the double exhaust. The same tests were also made on a Lexington four cylinder engine with comparable results.[31]

The Lexington Four Model H was restyled for 1914. A roadster finished in pink with white striping was an unusual attraction at the Lexington-Howard booth in the Chicago auto show.[32] The Model H rode on a shorter 114 inch wheelbase and had been restyled offering smoother lines with the cowl sloping upward from the rear of the hood to the windshield, eliminating the use of cowl lights. It was offered in a five passenger touring or roadster. One of the appealing features on this four cylinder roadster was adjustable seats. A hand wheel under each seat controlled the height and also the angle of the seat.[33] Other body features included large doors with concealed hinges and ebonized cap moldings to match the ebony finished dash. Tool pockets were fitted on each side under the cowl to be readily accessible.

Power was supplied by a Rutenber engine whose dimensions were unchanged from the previous year with 4 × 5 inch bore and stroke and *en bloc* casting. All valves

Left: Right side of the Howard six cylinder engine, showing high mounting of carburetor, neat method of carrying wires over the top of the motor and exhaust manifold. *Right:* Left side of the Howard six, showing mounting of Electro lighting and ignition system on the pump shaft, manner of wiring and placing of petcocks on sides of cylinders. *Both photographs:* The Automobile, May 29, 1913.

were interchangeable and the valve mechanism was enclosed and worked in a spray of oil. Other standard features were an Atwater-Kent ignition with automatic spark advance and a Schebler carburetor. The system for starting and lighting was changed significantly. The troublesome gas ignited starter was replaced with a more reliable electric unit. A combination starter-generator that was driven by a silent chain that ran off of the crankshaft at the front of the motor provided a charge for the storage battery or, at the press of a button, cranked the engine for starting. The transmission was the selective sliding gear type with three speeds forward and one reverse; a specially designed H slot prevented accidentally shifting into reverse when shifting from low into second gear. The transmission was built by the Warner Manufacturing Company of Toledo, Ohio, the case being made of aluminum alloy and gears of chrome vanadium steel.[34] Gone was the subframe system for supporting the engine and transmission. Also gone was the short shaft between the clutch and transmission in favor of the more conventional engine, clutch, transmission unit and conventional drivetrain. A triangular torque rod swiveled at the rear axle and was fastened in heavy cushion springs at the front intended to minimize torsion strains.[35]

The Model "H" also came equipped with an illuminated instrument board, a Stewart speedometer, windshield, electric horn, electric lights with dimmer, the Howard patented spare tire holder and the steering wheel now on the left hand side. Springs were by the Ansted Spring and Axle Company with the front ones being 35 inch semi-elliptic and the rear, 50 inch long three-quarter elliptic. Both front and rear axles were made by Hess, the front I beam and the rear three-quarter floating. Body colors for the Series H were blue-black with black enamel fenders and hood. Brightwork trim items such as hub caps and headlight rims were nickel plated instead of brass. The roadster listed at $1,295 and the touring at $1,335.[36] The Lexington Series H had the bulk of the sales for the year.

There were distributors throughout the country for the Lexington-Howard Company, many of whom had been with Lexington before the corporate changes occurred. Notable among them were Owen Schoeneck Co., Chicago; Edrus Motor Car Co., St. Louis; J. H. Ward, Minneapolis; Phoenix Motor Car Co., Lexington, Kentucky; and Thomas Motor Car Co., Los Angeles.[37] There were several local sales

CRITERION OF ITS CLASS

THIS staunch four is well worthy to bear the name which, since 1908, has stood consistently for high quality and sincere worth.

The same engineer who has designed every LEXINGTON ever built is responsible for this latest thoroughbred. To the great host of LEXINGTON owners scattered over the United States this will be more than sufficient guarantee that this new car is absolutely right.

For confirmation of this broad statement your attention is invited to the specifications recited. Here you will find set out a list of sterling parts which goes far toward insuring the correctness of the completed whole.

To the numerous people who find the four best suited to their needs, the new LEXINGTON will come as a welcome surprise, combining, as it does, plenty of power, perfect comfort, and unusual economy at a remarkably reasonable figure.

SPECIFICATIONS

MOTOR—Especially designed motor, incorporating Moore Multiple Exhaust; four cylinders, cast in Block, 4x5", L head; enclosed valve mechanism; three point suspension, and unit power plant.
COOLING SYSTEM—Cellular type radiator and centrifugal pump geared to motor.
CARBURETOR—Schebler.
TRANSMISSION—Selective sliding gear type.
CLUTCH—Cone type.
IGNITION—Atwater-Kent automatic spark advance, Willard battery.
STARTING—Efficient electric starter driven by silent chain to motor.
LIGHTING—Electric generator; large headlights, with dimmer, and tail light.
FRAME—Unusually heavy pressed steel.
TORQUE TUBE—Triangular, cushioned on heavy springs.
SPRINGS—Lexington-Ansted; front, semi-elliptic, 33 inches long; rear, three-quarter elliptic, 50 inches long.
AXLES—Front, Hess, I-beam; rear, Hess, three-quarter floating.
BRAKES—Four internal brakes, foot and hand, 1¾" x 14" each.
STEERING GEAR—Worm and gear; eighteen-inch notched wood wheel.
DRIVE—Left side drive, center control.
WHEELBASE—115 inches.
BODY—Five passenger touring; blue-black finish, with black enameled hood and fenders; nickel-plated bright-work; high quality, real leather upholstery.
EQUIPMENT—Illuminated instrument board; Stewart speedometer; Howard patented tire holder, all metal; mohair top; demountable-detachable rims, one extra; 34 x 4 inch tires; windshield; electric horn; foot rail; robe rail; and complete set of tools, jack, pump, etc.
PRICE—$1385.00 f. o. b. factory.

The 4-cylinder Lexington, restyled for 1914, accounted for most of the sales. Motor, *January 1914*.

that fall including a touring to Mrs. Louisa Snider, a roadster to Dr. J. M. Mountain, a roadster to T. C. Bryson, a touring to W. H. Sherry and also one to George Brown of Lyons Station. Lexington and Howard sales for the year were down 16 percent at 1,612.[38] Reasons for the decline may have been that sales emphasis was placed on the ill-fated Howard, an unknown make that the public did not embrace. The con-

The Howard was a large car with luxurious appointments, though ads like this one offered no specifics.

tinued name changes and personnel changes undermined the company's credibility. Prospective customers may also have been reluctant to make major purchases with the deteriorating world situation caused by the beginning of the Great War in Europe.

Whatever the problem was in 1914, it seemed to have been solved in 1915 as sales increased dramatically when 2,814 Lexingtons rolled out of the factory.[39] There was significant restyling this year with more streamlining. All models now had the cowl tapering smoothly from the windshield to the hood, the front fenders dropped sharply down to meet the running boards and curved over the front wheels more in front, to slightly resemble fenders on cyclecars that were enjoying a brief period of popularity. Models offered were the Model K Minute Man Four, the Model L Thoroughbred Six, and the Model M Six Supreme, all of which carried the name Lexington. The Minute Man and the Thoroughbred designations would be used extensively in advertising and were retained through most of the remainder of the company's existence. At the 1915 New York Automobile Show held in January, Lexington had space C-19 on the third floor of Grand Central Palace while at the Chicago show they had spaces E-5 and E-6 in the Armory.[40] The reception of the crowds at the shows was expected to set the tone of sales for the season, so a great deal of effort went into each display.

Tests conducted at the Wheeler & Schebler laboratories showed a 22.8 percent gain in horsepower using the Moore Multiple Exhaust System. From left: C. P. Grimes, research engineer; J. C. Moore, chief engineer of Lexington-Howard; William Schebler, general superintendent; Forest Hughes, production manager; and Aaron Handy, experimental laboratory engineer. Motor Age, *April 9, 1914.*

The Minute Man Four was offered in a five passenger touring, two passenger roadster or coupe. Instead of the Rutenber engine used since Lexington started production, the four cylinder engine was made by Teetor-Hartley of nearby Hagerstown, Indiana. Known as the Teetor T-head, it had 3⅞ × 5⅜ inch bore and stroke and developed 40 hp. The engine came equipped with Westinghouse starting, lighting and ignition systems. The fuel system involved a Schebler carburetor and the Stewart vacuum system with a 22-gallon pressed steel Janney-Steinmetz gas tank moved from under the front seat to the rear of the chassis.[41] The springs were Ansted semi-elliptic in front and cantilever in the rear and both axles were supplied by Hess. Cantilever springs were unusual in that they were turned upside down so that the spring curved downward and the rear axle fastened to the rear of the spring. Additional equipment included a rain vision ventilating windshield, Neverleek one-man top with Collins curtains, engine driven tire pump, jack and tools. One item listed as an option was five Houk wire wheels for $85 extra. This car had a 115-inch wheelbase, an increase of one inch over the past year's. It weighed 2,900 pounds and listed for $1,375.[42]

The Thoroughbred Six Model L was introduced at the beginning of the season as the Light Six, but dealers complained that the name was misleading because

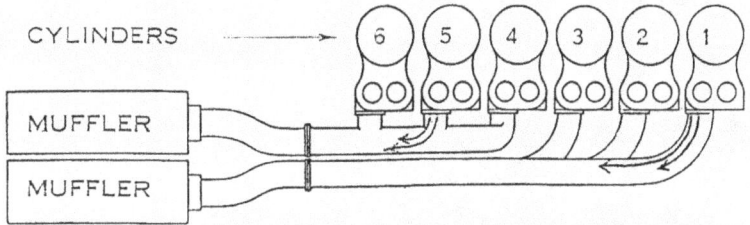

A Clean Path for Every Exhaust—Above cut illustrates the operation of the Moore Multiple Exhaust System: Cylinder No. 1 has just fired and its exhaust is passing out one of the *two* exhaust manifolds. No. 5 is next, in order, and its exhaust is shown passing out the other manifold—the exhaust lines are thus used alternately.

The Moore Multiple Exhaust was the first dual exhaust system that was standard equipment on an American automobile.

this 3300-pound car was not a "light duty" automobile.[43] Body styles offered were four, five, or six passenger tourings or a roadster listing at $1,875.[44] Front seats were individual buckets, each of which could be adjusted separately for angle of seating or distance forward or back. This was a Lexington exclusive. The rear compartment contained two auxiliary seats to accommodate extra passengers when needed. The Thoroughbred Six rode on a 128 inch wheelbase and was powered by the 50 hp Continental engine that was cast *en bloc* with 3½ × 5 inch bore and stroke. As in the Minute Man Four, the ignition was from Westinghouse and a Schebler carburetor was used in connection with the Stewart vacuum fuel system. A multiple dry disk clutch and internal expanding brakes plus axles by Hess were also part of the running gear.[45] Standard equipment was the same as on the four cylinder models.

The Model M Six Supreme also received a name change, after starting the season labeled the "Big Six." It was offered in a five-passenger or a seven-passenger touring or a roadster, carrying a weight of 4100 pounds and riding on a 130 inch wheelbase. The Supreme was powered by the larger Continental engine with 4⅛ × 5¼ inch bore and stroke with the block cast in threes and using a Stromberg carburetor along with the Stewart vacuum fuel system. A dual ignition consisted of a Bosch magneto plus an Atwater Kent distributor. Springs were by Ansted and axles came from Timken. Selling at $2,575, it was a luxury car that provided deep upholstery with adjustable front seats to assure driving comfort. Standard equipment included elegant foot and robe rails, silk mohair top with Collins curtains, Kellogg tire pump and Non-skid tires in the rear, if desired, without extra cost.[46]

All models used a drive-line consisting of a triangular torque tube with the front cushioned by a spring mounted on the frame cross member and a single universal at the rear axle. Also used across the line was the exceptionally strong spare tire carrier that would carry two tires without using straps. The open cars did not have outside door handles. This had been a practice with Lexington in the past few years and it gave a clean unobstructed look. Even with side curtains in place, it was easy to reach inside the car to unlatch the doors. Each model had an illuminated instrument board, Stewart hand type speedometer, motor-driven Spartan horn and the highly advertised Moore Multiple Exhaust system, and all models emphasized the use of long springs for a smooth ride.

Increased sales had put a strain on the factory, pushing space use to the limit,

The Minute Man was a model designation first used by Lexington in 1915. It became their best-known trademark.

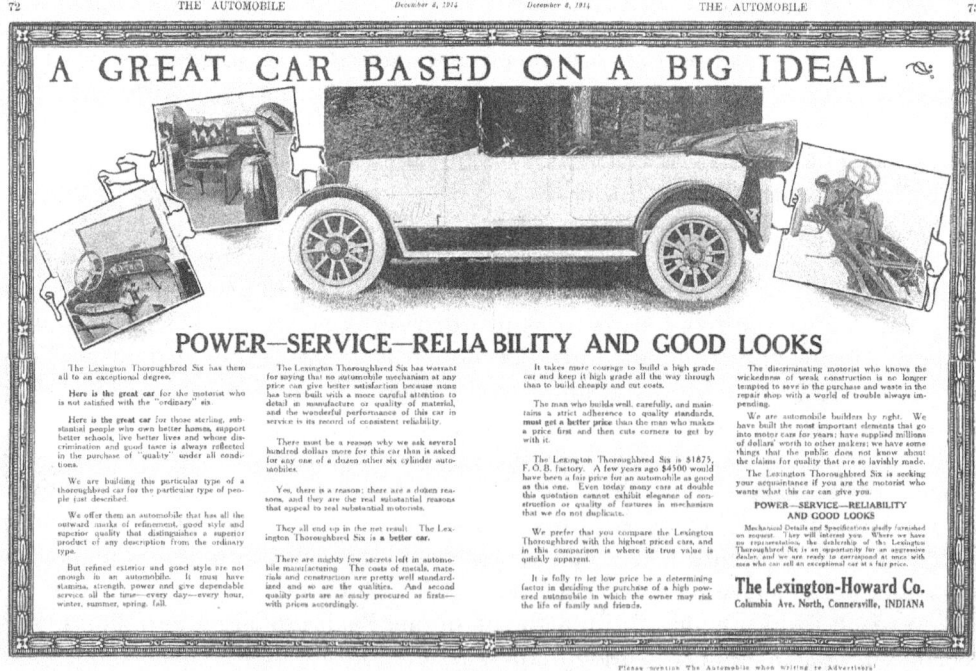

The 1915 model year was a prosperous time for the Lexington-Howard Compay. *The Automobile, Dec. 3, 1914.*

LIGHT SIX, $1875.00
Announcement of the 1915 Series

The same remarkable value, utmost refinement in design and finish, advanced engineering practice that have characterized Lexington cars in the past are features that guarantee service to you in the Lexington 1915 series.

Choose Your Car in a Straight Business Way

Too much attention and thought cannot be put into the purchase of your car. You should consider the master minds designing it, the materials from which it is made, the reliability and financial standing of the company manufacturing it, and their past manufacturing records, etc. All of these are vital factors in the choice of a car. In the Lexington we gladly invite your most careful consideration of them.

The Lexington Has Proven Its Value

You find your ideal car embodied in the new, beautiful Lexington Light Six. Each essential in motor car building has been included.

The Lexingtons for 1915 are worthy successors to the long line of motor cars that have, in every way, stood the strain and tests of daily use in owners' hands for six seasons past.

Included in the series are a superb Big Six at $2575.00, and a beautiful Four at $1375.00, in addition to the extra-value Light Six.

Write for complete descriptive matter of any or all models.

The wise dealer, who wishes to build his business on the firm foundation of owner satisfaction, will do well to investigate the Lexington proposition. Wherever procurable, Lexington Territory means dealer profit, because Lexington cars assure owner satisfaction.

The Lexington-Howard Co.
Park Place, Connersville, Ind., U. S. A.

Specifications

Motor—50 H. P., Continental.
Carburetor—Warmed by connection with exhaust, insuring a volatile mixture.
Starting, Lighting, Ignition—Westinghouse.
Cooling—Honeycomb type radiator and centrifugal pump.
Clutch—Multiple dry disc.
Springs—Front, semi-elliptic; rear, Cantilever type, 52" long, special suspension.
Brakes—Four internal expanding, completely protected against mud, dust and water, large diameters and broad faces.
Steering Gear—Worm and gear type, with 18" notched, ebonized wheel.
Drive—Left side, with *right*-hand control.
Wheelbase—128".
Bodies—Four, five or six-passenger touring, and two-passenger roadster.
Black enamel hood, fenders and splash plates, and blue black body. Nickel-plated bright work, high quality, straight grain, semi-bright leather.
Equipment—Illuminated instrument board with all instruments bunched in an aluminum plate. Stewart hand-type speedometer. Unique tire carrier. Never-leak one-man top, curtains quickly attached from interior of car. Demountable-detachable rims. Rain-vision, ventilating windshield. Sparton motor-driven horn under hood. Foot rest. Robe strap. Motor-driven tire pump. Complete set of tools, jack, etc.
Prices—Touring car, completely equipped as above, $1875.00 f.o.b. Connersville. Roadster, completely equipped as above, $1875.00 f.o.b. Connersville.

An exclusive feature, found on no other make of motor car, is the Moore Multiple Exhaust System—a simple device that adds 25% more power to the engine with a decided decrease in gasoline consumption.

The name of the Light Six was changed to Thoroughbred soon after introduction. Motor, *Oct. 1914.*

so a huge tent was erected in order to provide adequate facilities for testing. The tent, which extended across Columbia Avenue and was parallel to the main building, was in addition to the frame building built the previous year for a testing facility. In order to provide more space for automobile assembly, the second floor of the North building was used entirely for trim and paint shops, and the lower floor for offices, machine shops and final assembly. The company was experiencing a rush of orders, requiring an increased output of up to six cars per day.[47] Even the export trade was experiencing growth as this Hoosier product boasted of a franchised dealer overseas in the United Kingdom at Peters and Sons in St. James.[48]

Things seemed to be about as good as they could be at Lexington in 1915. When a new sales showroom was established in Indianapolis at 425 North Meridian, district manager F. T. Day predicted substantial sales in Central Indiana with this new location.[49] In mid–September Frank Ansted returned to Lexington as vice-president and general manager after resigning several months earlier as sales manager over a disagreement concerning marketing techniques. Also, L. A. Hanson was brought in from Chicago's Fulton-McCutcheon Company to assume the position of assistant secretary-treasurer.[50]

A large celebration and promotion for dealers was held over Memorial Day weekend attracting nearly forty out-of-town guests from as far away as New York City, Baltimore, Pittsburgh, Chicago, Kansas City and Des Moines. The gathering got under way on Thursday with a tour of the city and entertainment provided for all at the Auditorium theater by Joseph Santley and his cohorts in "All Over Town." Sumptuous meals were provided at the McFarlan Hotel and at Glenbush.[51] Business sessions and promotions were held at the Commercial Club. After being entertained, fed and inspired, the guests were to travel to Indianapolis to view the 500 Mile Race. The race was scheduled to be run on Saturday, May 29, but was postponed until Monday the 31st, so the party went on through the weekend. To occupy the guests, a Saturday trip to nearby Hagerstown permitted inspection of the Teetor-Hartley plant that produced Lexington's Teetor four cylinder engines.[52] This big fling was at the expense of a young company that was beginning to prosper.

The war raging in Europe seemed far away and not affecting Hoosiers. That changed when E. A. Woodruff, a company official, was thought to be aboard the British liner *Lusitania* that was sunk by a German submarine torpedo on May 7 with a loss of 1,198 lives. A sigh of relief came when a cable arrived from London more than two weeks later notifying friends that he had arrived safely after changing ships at the last minute.[53] Elbert Hubbard, who had written the booklet *A Little Journey to Connersville*, wasn't so fortunate, as he perished along with 197 other U.S. citizens. As the end of the year was nearing, sadness was brought to the Ansted family on December 12 with the death of Edward W. Jr., the youngest Ansted son. He had experienced health problems all of his life and died as a young man.[54] Also in mid–December, rumors were going rampant of a merger of some Indiana companies that included Lexington-Howard. Other prominent companies said to be involved were the Interstate Motor Company of Muncie and the Cole Motor Company of Indianapolis, whose president, J. J. Cole, was born and raised near Connersville in Fayette County. The reason given for the proposed merger was to place small automobile companies in a more favorable position for purchasing parts.[55] Frank Ansted answered the rumor with an assurance that Lexington would not enter such a merger. He cited the advantage that Lexington already had with sev-

Top: The Inland Motors building opened in 1916 with a gala celebration. It is now the home of Commercial Printing Company in Connersville. *Bottom:* Inland Motor Sales and service in Indianapolis was located at 846 N. Meridian Street. *Both photographs: Distributorships H. W. Dubiske & Company 1920.*

Top: The Thoroughbred received a dramatic restyling for 1916, sporting a V-shaped radiator shell. *Bottom:* Body panels of the 1916 Thoroughbred were higher and wrapped over the back of the front seat. There was an aisle way between the front seats.

eral local factories supplying parts. Local sales were good with purchasers including J. H. Duncan, Fred W. Lightfoot, M. K. Jemison, H. M. Williams, Charles C. Cassell, Dr. I. E. Booher, Carl Sherry, Dr. N. G. Wills, H. R. Gray and other proud Lexington owners supporting local industry.[56]

In 1916 the state of Indiana celebrated its centennial. In Connersville, preparations were made well ahead of time including a pageant, a large parade and pyrotechnics. War clouds were still hanging heavy, but Germany was being less aggressive in submarine warfare and United States industry was keeping busy supplying arms for the Allies. Woodrow Wilson was re-elected to a second term as President, running on the platform "He kept us out of war."

At home in Connersville, a new building for the Lexington dealership, Inland Motor Sales Corp., was built just north of the post office on Central Avenue. The grand opening for this new building was held Friday and Saturday, May 26 and 27.

The Literary Digest for December 25, 1915

Tobogganing Up Hill

NOT by the slightest jerk or tremor do you realize the acceleration of this new Minute Man Six. For it is virtually a symphony in mechanism—a machine of Herculean power, but docile to the touch of your finger tips, and clothed in a design of surpassing grace and beauty.

The master touch that completes this car's perfection is the Moore Multiple Exhaust System which gives to motoring a new criterion of comfort and zest in the

Lexington "Minute Man" SIX $1075

This Exclusive Lexington feature creates 22.8 per cent more power; it adds to the engine's flexibility, saves gasoline, and is largely responsible in making the Lexington the only car that can "toboggan uphill." Without adding appreciable weight, this system eliminates high back pressure in the exhaust by not letting any two cylinders exhaust into the same tube at the same time. Thus the Lexington alone removes the handicap to multi-cylinder construction, gives you the benefit of *all* the engine's power and resultant economy.

Here, and here exclusively, is an advantage that warrants your becoming acquainted with this remarkable low-priced car with its high-priced looks, and *performance*.

**New 50 H. P. Thoroughbred Six Touring Car,
Canti-Lex Spring Suspension Front and Rear**

In stylish appearance this large Lexington creates a genuine sensation. Write us for a photo reproduction of this beautiful car with its V-shaped radiator, back from which flow sweeping lines that form the symmetrical body—with triple cowls—a unit of grace and *ensemble* beauty. Left drive, center control, and divided front seats with wide aisle between—exquisitely finished in every detail. Six-passenger $1875—132″ wheelbase—six cylinders en bloc—50 h. p.—over-size tires. Also adjustable head lamps that are integral part of radiator.

This 50 h. p. Thoroughbred Six is also furnished in a three-passenger Clubster of latest type with aisleway between individual front chairs, making easy access to third or rear seat, and regularly fitted with five wire wheels, at same price—$1875.

**THE LEXINGTON-HOWARD CO., Offices and Works: Columbia Square
CONNERSVILLE, IND., U. S. A.**

Six Cylinders en bloc
40 Horse Power
Moore Multiple Exhaust System
Five Passenger
Aisleway between divided front seats
Left Drive
Center Control
Genuine leather upholstering
116″ Wheelbase
Convex Mud Guards
Over-Size Tires

Price includes one man leatherette top and boot, full ventilating windshield, speedometer, ammeter, and demountable rim.

Write for all the facts about this marvelous car.

The Minute Man Six was the price leader and major seller. The Literary Digest, *Dec. 25, 1915.*

Entertainment for the first evening was music by "Sugar Smith" and his corps of 14 musicians.[57] Loads of flowers adorned the showroom and gave off a pleasing aroma. W. H. Thome and Emery Huston provided the formalities of an opening ceremony. Saturday evening the Commercial Club Boys Band played eight numbers, closing with a medley of patriotic songs. One of the dealer representatives from Indianapolis commented that the new facility was big league stuff and was certainly a credit to Connersville.[58] The building was built by E. W. Tatman, who owned one of the Connersville newspapers and originally intended to move the printing operation into it. Instead it became Inland Motors. Various businesses have used the building for periods of time, but ownership has never left the Tatman family. It is presently the home of Commercial Printing with George Tatman as owner.[59]

The parent company, Lexington-Howard, increased their advertising during the year using popular magazines such as the *Saturday Evening Post* and *Leslie's*. The Thoroughbred model designation provided a connection with the company's place of origin. Lexington also continued to use the "Minute Man" logo, which had a patriotic ring at a time when much of the world was at war and most Americans recognized that it was just a matter of time until the United States would be more directly involved in it. Several years later, Lexington added to their patriotic theme with the Series Seventy-Six and the Concord models.

The need for expansion had become very clear when huge tents were used the previous year to increase plant space. In preparation for

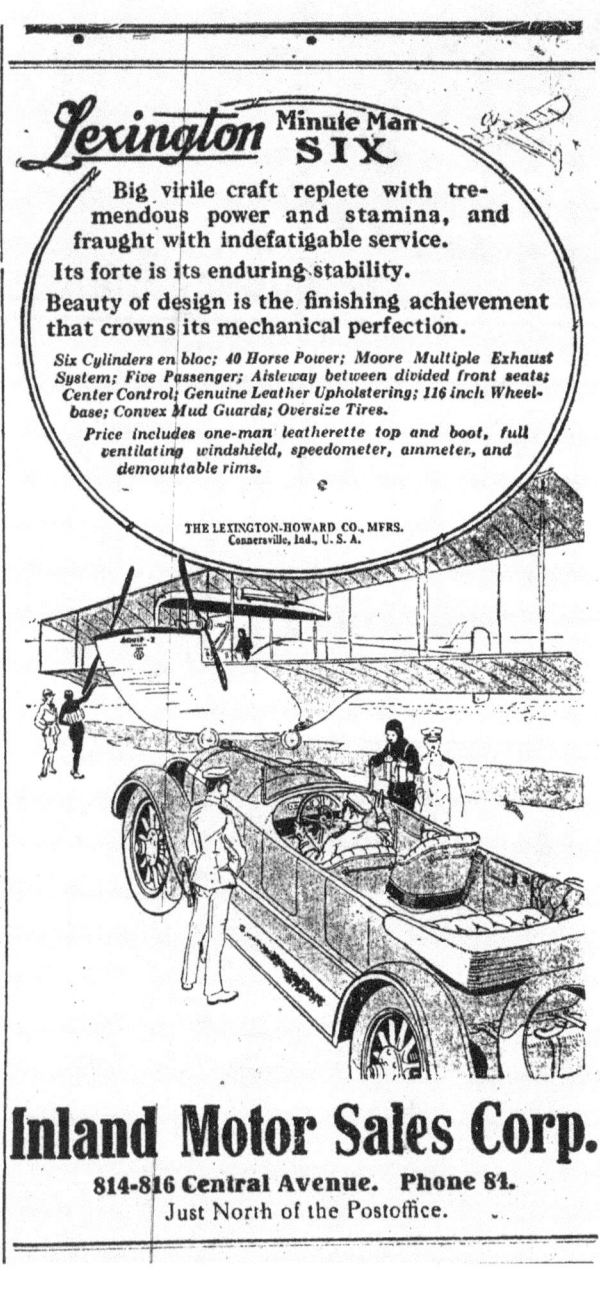

The Minute Man Six also had divided front seats with an aisle between. The Evening News, *May 2, 1916.*

3—A New Name Is Born

Lexington
MINUTE MAN FOUR

This small illustration shows the unusually long, thick Canti Lex springs which are largely responsible for the soft riding qualities of the Minute Man Four—the springs that make the Minute Man ride like a car of twice its cost.

The spring rides the axle with a peculiar saddle construction, exclusive in Lexington cars. This construction adds to the flexibility, and at the same time, to the long life of the springs.

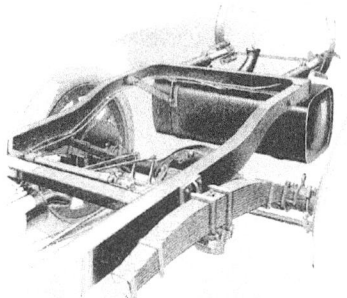

The above view of the new Minute Man Four conveys a further impression of sturdiness. There is nothing flimsy looking about the rear of the Minute Man so characteristic of moderate priced cars.

The gasoline tank is a seamless, pressed steel affair—the kind found on cars costing many times the price of the Minute Man.

One is impressed with the apearance of the tire rack which is just as efficient as it looks. One or two tires may be carried with equal ease. The wrench which loosens the lugs on the wheels loosens the lugs on the tire rack also, thus simplifying matters.

The cross brace of the tire rack forms a very neat license bracket and tail light support, all of which contribute to the owner's satisfaction.

The increased height of the rear seat back is here apparent.

The Lexington-Howard Co.
Connersville, Indiana, U.S.A.

The Minute Man Four Series 4-KA was carried into the 1916 model year but was soon dropped because the six was much more popular.

The state of Indiana celebrated its centennial in 1916 with numerous parades. *National Automotive History Collection, Detroit Public Library.*

expansion, on April 26, a special meeting of the stockholders of the Lexington-Howard Company was called for the purpose of increasing the capital stock from $150,000 to $300,000. The stockholders who were present at the meeting were E. W. Ansted, Joseph Huston, George Ansted, Frederic Barrows, Frank Ansted, L. A. Hanson, Emery Huston and Ezra Brown. These men were listed as being "all of the stockholders and the persons who own all of the stock in the Lexington-Howard Company."[60]

Corresponding with the increase in financial leverage were some major improvements in the plant that included installation of overhead tracks and carriages to facilitate movement of heavy objects.[61] Then, on August 17, construction began on a major addition that was to be completed by November. This new building was one story, 60 feet wide by 500 feet long, nearly doubling the floor space of the previous buildings. Construction was done by the Hoosier Construction Company using mainly brick and concrete. Building costs for this new addition were reported to have been $50,000 plus an additional $3,500 invested in new equipment.[62] The C.I. & W. Railroad extended a switch along the entire east side of the new building to aid delivery of construction materials and, later on, loading and shipping the finished automobiles.[63] Construction was completed by the end of the year, thus increasing production capacity substantially.

Frank Ansted and Frederick Barrows spent the 1916 New Year in New York City

MOTOR AGE

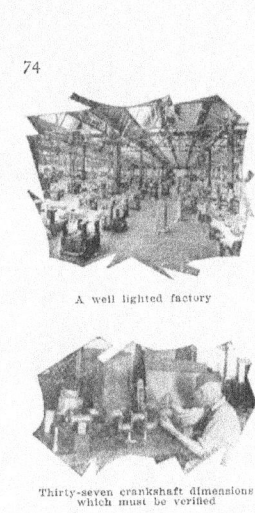
A well lighted factory

Testing with Scleroscope for proper hardness

The tool room of the Detroit plant

Thirty-seven crankshaft dimensions which must be verified

Special Boring Mill which operates ten cutters

Drilling ninety-five holes in seven minutes

Balancing a crankshaft on final test

The Room of Silence in testing department

"*For Heaven's sake, give me cars,*" hundreds of dealers will wire frantically.

"*We cannot get motors,*" many manufacturers will be forced to reply.

Continental Motors

The early months of next year will see a time of rush and turmoil in the automobile industry. Makers and dealers are holding back to an unusual degree this fall; and when demands come crowding— say next March — every manufacturer will press with might and main for delivery of parts, as his dealers begin to pour in their specifications.

There will be a shortage in some quarters. There must be.

But not of motors (the most important unit) for any car Continental equipped. Every firm that uses Continental co-operation in the building of its motors, knows to a certainty that its specifications will be carried through on the dot.

Every dealer who handles a car or truck Continental equipped, knows to a certainty that he will not be hampered in his sales campaign because the factory cannot get motors.

Two immense factories, ample resources and an organization intact year after year—these are the safeguards that insure Continental deliveries.

A reputation for service, universal good will, and a motor that is America's Standard—these are the safeguards that insure your sales.

Continental Motor Mfg. Co.
Detroit, Mich.
Factories: Detroit and Muskegon

When Writing to Advertisers, Please Mention Motor Age.

By 1916, Lexington was using Continental six cylinder motors exclusively. There were still concerns about being able to get motors when needed, not because of production problems, but because of rail strikes holding up delivery. Motor Age, *Dec. 11, 1913.*

as two Lexington 6-N Thoroughbreds were on display at the National Automobile Show on the second floor of the Grand Central Palace. The show ran from December 31, 1915, until January 8, 1916, under the auspices of the National Automobile Chamber of Commerce. The two cars in the show were a six passenger touring finished in olive green with black fenders and crème wheels and a three passenger Clubster, crème color with black wire wheels. There was substantial model reshuffling as the Supreme Six was dropped and the Thoroughbred became the top of the line model. The Thoroughbred Series 6–N had dramatic restyling with a V-shaped radiator and the headlamps mounted on the shell. The touring had disappearing auxiliary seats and tonneau lamps for interior lighting. The body side panel curved over the back of the front seat making a clean appearance. An aisle between the front seats gave easy passage from front to back, making it possible for passengers to change places without leaving the car. The Clubster's third seat was behind the front seats with an aisle allowing for entry or exit. These cars had a 132-inch wheelbase and a 50 hp Continental engine and listed at $1,875.[64] The sales leader was still the Minute Man, but now it had a six cylinder 40 hp engine. Lexington would not market a four-cylinder car after this model year. The Minute Man Six rode on a 116-inch wheelbase and also sported the aisle between the divided front seats. Upholstering was genuine leather and the car came equipped with a one-man top. All of this was in the five passenger touring that offered tremendous value for $1,075.[65] The hood line was raised on the Minute Man and the Thoroughbred making it nearly even with the bottom of the windshield. The Minute Man also sported restyled front fenders that now curved into the running boards and were advertised as being convex or lightly crowned.

Mass drive-aways were used at times when rail transportation wasn't available. This group of Minute-Man Sixes was readying to make the trip to the N. C. Bowen Motor Sales Co., the Lexington agent in Columbus, Ohio. *Courtesy* Connersville News-Examiner.

In April, when it is often rainy in the Midwest, Frederick Barrows drove a Minute Man Six to Muncie. Between New Castle and Luray the road led through a cut where heavy rains exposed fresh clay without any gravel. Ahead of Mr. Barrows was a partially loaded farm wagon that, upon entering the cut, sank to the hubs on one side. The teamster loosened his team from the wagon, and turning back, giving a word of warning to Barrows who had been watching from a distance. Frederick decided that the cut was not bottomless, but just extremely muddy, and having complete confidence in the Minute Man Six, he set the machine in second gear and pulled right through what he described as about five rods of the stickiest clay in Henry County.[66] The previous month, however, a Lexington being driven to Richmond, Indiana, for display at the Richmond Auto Show showed up a day late because it got stuck in the mud along the way.[67] The company neglected to make mention of this incident.

Production for 1916 had been slowed because of materials shortages, especially steel, and difficulties obtaining rail transportation due to the war in Europe. One Chicago agent was so anxious for delivery of cars he had already sold that he brought a crew of men and drove eight new Lexingtons to the Windy City rather than wait until rail shipping could be arranged.[68] The foreign trade was showing promise as a rail car load of Lexingtons was shipped to Chile and another load to Cuba in mid–November.[69] In spite of hindrances with materials availability and some transportation problems, it was a good year. Minute Man prices were substantially lower and production increased to 3,115 units.[70]

4

The War Years

The year 1917 was one of challenges and many changes, but, overall, one that would be considered a success. Prices were increased when the new Model O was introduced in late August of 1916. The model 6-O-17 Minute Man Six listed at $1,185 for the five-passenger touring, the four-passenger Clubster, or the open roadster. The 6-OO-17 at $1,350 was offered in the convertible roadster, the four-passenger convertible Clubster or the five-passenger convertible touring. The Model O rode on a 116 inch wheelbase. Touring and sedan models were finished in dark green with black fenders and cream wheels. Roadsters were a deep wine color for the bodies.[1] Power was provided by a 40 hp Continental engine with 3¼ × 4½ inch bore and stroke using the model M Rayfield carburetor and Connecticut igniter or distributor.[2] The driveline included a three speed gearbox and a multiple dry disk clutch, universal joints at each end of the propeller shaft and three-quarter elliptic rear springs made from vanadium steel.[3] The Thoroughbred Six Series 6-P continued the dramatic V shaped radiator and body panels that curved over the back of the front seats. It offered a seven-passenger touring on a mammoth 144 inch wheelbase at $2,875 or a four-passenger Clubster on a 130 inch wheelbase at $2,675. The Clubster was unusual in that the two doors opened into the rear compartment. The driver and front seat passenger reached their seats by stepping forward through the center aisle. Power was by a 50 hp Continental engine with a 4⅛ × 5¼ inch bore and stroke.[4] The larger engine continued having cylinders cast in blocks of three with the crankcase divided horizontally with both upper and lower halves made from aluminum. Lubrication was by a combination of force feed by pump to the main bearings and splash for the connecting rods.[5] Two separate ignition systems using 12 spark plugs were fitted to this six cylinder engine. Since the Thoroughbred was considerably larger, a heavier transmission with wider gears with bigger pitch and a leather faced cone clutch transferred power to the rear wheels.[6] Both lines shared improvements such as double universal joints, full-floating rear axle with spiral bevel gears, a cut steel starter gear on the fly wheel, double-bulb adjustable headlamps, Motometer temperature gauge, a large oil pressure gauge fitted in the cowl board, a motor driven tire pump, and a trouble lamp.[7] The Moore Multiple Exhaust system continued to be touted in every advertisement and article about Lexingtons. By this time, the company also made it known that on August 29, 1916, J. C. Moore had been granted a patent on his novel exhaust.[8] It is remarkable that this exhaust system or a similar unit wasn't copied by other American automobile manufacturers and was used on only one or two foreign cars. Styling changes for the year included front fenders that curved so as to flow into the running boards, providing smoother lines, and outside door handles that were nearly flush with the doors.

(A) Series 6-O-17, Open Touring Car, $1185. (B) Series 6-O-17, Open Roadster, $1185. (C) Series 6-OO-17, Convertible Touring Car, $1350. (D) Series 6-OO-17, Convertible Roadster, $1350.

Body styles labeled as "Convertible" were new for the model year, having been developed by the Rex Manufacturing Company, also of Connersville, to provide a fixed-top enclosed vehicle for colder weather. By removing the plate glass side windows and center doorposts, one could have completely open sides providing a plentiful supply of fresh air during warmer weather. Jiffy curtains, carried in a concealed compartment above the driver's head, could be quickly installed in case of sudden showers.[9] This type of body style became popular with the motoring public again in the 1950s and were called "hardtop convertibles." The closed car was just beginning to gain acceptance as the automobile was becoming a four season vehicle rather than being used just for summer fun. Headlights that could be dimmed when in town had become a necessity. As traffic increased, cities were passing ordinances trying to control the blinding brightness of headlights. The dual bulb lights were introduced to comply with the new laws that were becoming common throughout the nation.

One of the major challenges of the year was posed by railroad strikes that held up shipping. This made it difficult at times to keep a supply of Continental engines that came from out of state. Obtaining other parts to assemble wasn't so much of a problem with many supplying factories being located within a few blocks of Lexington-Howard in the industrial park. Some ads read, "Ten big affiliated plants, each independent, take part in production of the Lexington."[10] Getting the finished automobiles to dealers presented a challenge that was partially solved by mass driveaways. On March 1, 103 Lexingtons left Connersville and were driven to Chicago. Before they left, they were lined up, parked on 12th Street from Central over to Grand, then north on Grand past the City Cemetery. Fifty men came from Chicago to drive cars and the rest of the drivers were from the local area. The procession began at 10:30 a. m., leaving in groups of ten. The overnight stay was in LaFayette with Chicago reached the next evening. A later report stated that the trip was made "without anything deserving to be called an accident" occurring during the long

Foresight

THE favor of car buyers for the convertible type of car which is now so evident, was forecast by LEXINGTON designers many months ago.

As a result the LEXINGTON Minute Man Six Convertible Coupe and Convertible Sedan are carefully designed cars whose perfect lines would be impossible in convertible types hastily built to ride with the current of popular interest.

This element of foresight, which has always marked LEXINGTON design, produces a car which is fully abreast of the latest developments of motor car construction yet includes *not one* untried, doubtful, or experimental feature.

A car of manifest class at a price which is not prohibitive, a car that looks good to the buyer who decides quickly, and looks better to the buyer who is both critical and cautious.

Lexington Salient Superiorities

Lexington-Continental Engine
Moore Multiple Exhaust System
Cut Steel Starting Gear on Flywheel
Independent Ignition, Lighting, and Starting Circuits
Double Universal Joints
Full-Floating Rear Axle with Spiral Bevel Gears
Wick-Feed Oil Cups

Engine-Driven Tire Pump
Double Bulb Adjustable Headlamps Rigidly Mounted on Radiator
Largest Size Motometer
Bolted-on Tire Rack and Spare Demountable Rim
Oil Pressure Gauge
Convex Mud Guards
Genuine Leather Upholstery

In addition, the regular equipment includes full ventilating weather-stripped windshield, speedometer, electric horn, ammeter, and portable electric lamp.

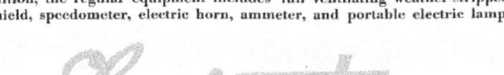

MINUTE MAN SIX

5-Passenger Touring Car - - - $1185
4-Passenger Clubster - - - - -

5-Passenger Convertible Sedan $1350
4-Passenger Convertible Coupe

If you are a dealer looking for a connection that is worth something, write, wire — or visit the factory

THE LEXINGTON-HOWARD CO.

1950 Columbia Avenue   Export Managers—Messrs. Chipman, Ltd. 8-10 Bridge Street, New York City   CONNERSVILLE, IND., U. S. A.

The Convertible Coupe also had a fixed top with removable windows.

parade. Noted observers recording this event leaving Connersville were two "moving picture men" and a "Mr. Miller of the *Cosmopolitan Magazine.*" The girls and faculty of Elmhurst School watched the parade as did A. L. Cline, formerly of Connersville, at that time service manager for the Chicago company where the cars were delivered. Charles Keller, traffic manager at Lexington-Howard, helped organ-

 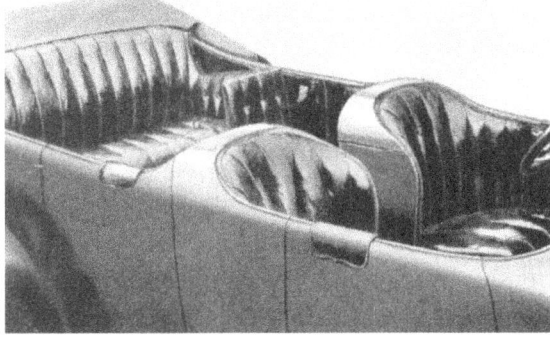

Top: The 1917 Thoroughbred Touring had distinctive styling from the V-shaped radiator to the metal covering that curved over the back of the front seats. It rode on a mammoth 144 inch wheelbase. *Bottom, left:* The single leg of the folding seat would seem to limit occupants to smaller children. *Bottom right:* Note the unique styling with metal curving over the top of the front seat and the aisle between the seats.

ize the trip. E. W. Ansted, in failing health at the time, watched the parade pass by his home at 12th and Central.[11] The first drive-away was so successful that, by the middle of March, a second one was planned, this time with the destination of Milwaukee.[12] Whether the publicity of the mass drive-aways helped draw attention to the need, or the railroad strike eased, is not clear. But on March 29, 15 rail cars were loaded with Lexingtons, all bound for New York City.[13]

Another concern was the worsening world situation. Germany resumed unrestricted submarine warfare early in the year, bringing about more loss of American lives and causing the United States to enter the war on April 6. As material shortages multiplied, prices increased, and by May, the price of the Minute Man Six had been raised an additional $100. Restrictions were placed on production and various programs were implemented to conserve goods, including gasoline. In spite of these hindrances, production went well and the additional space gained by the previous year's expansion was put to good use. By mid–December, Lexington had landed a government war contract to make a type of hemp rope called Picket Rope, a stout string bound at the ends with metal. Each rope was 33 feet long.[14]

One benefit of the Great War to American manufacturers, including Lexington, was an increase in their export trade. In New South Wales, Australia, on September 1917, six Lexingtons were registered. By February 1919, the number had increased to 25. New South Wales accounted for about one-fourth to one-third of the vehicle population in Australia. The total exports, just to Australia, would have been a significant number. There was a high import duty on automobile bodies, so most manufacturers sent just the chassis, with the bodies being built in Australia. The three Williams brothers, who had been cycle dealers in a rural area, bought into a dealership in Sydney and by 1919, had become Williams Bros. Ltd. They handled Lexington along with other makes. One of the brothers, G. H. Williams, visited Connersville late in 1922. The dealer continued offering the Lexington line at least through 1923.[15] A number of Lexingtons were also sold in New Zealand where the remains of five cars await restoration.

Another death occurred in the Ansted family on June 20, 1917. This time it was Edward W., Sr. He had been in failing health for two years, but his passing was still a loss, not only to the Ansted family, but to the entire community.[16] He had lived the American dream during the industrial revolution. Being born into a modest home, he had become very wealthy through hard work and wise investments. Mr. Ansted had been the founder or president of six manufacturing companies: Ansted Spring and Axle, Central Manufacturing Company, Indiana Lamp Company, Hoosier Castings, Ansted Engine Works and Lexington-Howard. He was also financially involved in a number of banks and other businesses and was well known for being a philanthropist, especially in his later years. He donated his former residence at 1939 Virginia Avenue to be the Fayette County Sanitarium. On July 5, 1916, bonds valued at $12,000 were given in his name to the medical facility.[17] This institution has continued to prosper and grow into what is now the Fayette Memorial Hospital, encompassing nearly a full city block of modern construction. Edward was buried in the family crypt in Dale Cemetery.

Within a few days of E. W. Ansted's death, his son, Frank, who was a second vice-president, but was already the general manager, skipped a step on the promotion ladder by being elected to the presidency of Lexington-Howard. He had formerly been vice-president and manager of the Indiana Lamp Company and was the owner of Inland Motor Company, the Lexington distributor for central Indiana. Even as the company was struggling to survive, Frank was accepting praise for his leadership and business savvy.

Just 32 years old when he assumed the presidency, Frank received numerous accolades for heading an automobile manufacturing company at such a young age. As sometimes happens when youth replaces the older generation, things started changing rapidly. In July, a new 100 by 200 foot annex west of the main building was under construction.[18] Earlier in the year improvements had been made by enclosing the offices, installing a sprinkler system in part of the factory and adding a complete telephone system that connected offices, factory and even the yard.[19] On August 29, Articles of Association were filed for a new corporation, changing the company name again; dropping Howard, it became the Lexington Motor Company. It was capitalized at $1.8 million, a substantial increase that helped finance additional expansion. The charter included, in addition to automobiles, the building of aeroplanes, hydroplanes, motorboats or any mechanism that was power driven.[20] This could have been quite useful for war production, if needed. The arti-

Many Connersville and nearby factories supplied parts for the Lexington. The Saturday Evening Post, *July 12, 1916.*

cles of incorporation listed five men, all from Connersville, as directors: Andrew H. Rieman, Benjamin F. Thiebaud, Charles Cassel, E. Ralph Himelick and Allen Wiles.[21] Frank Ansted, the new company president, was looking for ways to increase production and there was a modest increase for 1917 with 3,917 automobiles leaving the factory, an increase of 802 cars.[22]

Increased power and increased economy were claims made for Lexingtons equipped with the Moore Multiple Exhaust System. The Literary Digest, *Dec. 30, 1916.*

The 1918 Lexingtons were introduced on September 15, 1917. The unveiling at Inland Motor Company in Connersville attracted a sizeable crowd with Louis Heeb and Herbert Baganz dressed as Minute Men and the Commercial Club Boys Band providing entertainment.[23] All of the excitement was over the new Model R which had a completely new "Brush type frame design" using a rigid bridge box and incorporating the running boards as part of the frame unit, instead of the pressed steel frame of the past. The steel running boards, with both ends curved upward to meet the fenders, became an identifying trademark with Lexington. Marmon had pioneered this design for running boards on some of their 1916 models and they used it for several years also. The purpose of redesigning the frame was an attempt to solve the problem of jammed doors whenever the car was parked on an uneven surface. This frame, the work of chief engineer John C. Moore, was advertised as eliminating 126 separate parts. Instead of bolting or riveting the separate parts together, they were welded into an integral unit.[24] Another notable improvement was moving the emergency brake to a location behind the transmission on the propeller shaft. The claim was that it could be operated with the slightest pressure of the little finger.[25] The new Model R rode on a 122 inch wheelbase offering a five-passenger touring that included two auxiliary seats that folded into the rear floor when not in use. Also available were the four-passenger Sport-tour that listed for $1,585 and the five-passenger Convertible Sedan for $1,785. The Model O with 116-inch wheelbase was continued from the previous year in two body styles, a four-passenger Convertible Coupe listing at $1,510 and a four-passenger Clubster at $1,345. The carryover model did not share the improvements of the new Model R. They still boasted that the frame was made from special analysis steel that was 30 percent better than SAE specifications. Running boards were also the old type, which were thoroughly creosoted to prevent warping. Both models were powered by Continental with the Model R using the 7W 50 horsepower engine.[26] The Model O used a 224 cubic inch displacement engine that developed 40 horsepower.

Lexington increased their advertising this year, concentrating on nationally circulated weekly magazines such as *Leslies*, *Life*, the *Literary Digest* and the *Saturday Evening Post*, in which they ran a full two-page spread to announce the new Series R. This company was also one of the first automobile companies to use color ads that helped promote the numerous color selections they had available.[27] Many of their ads were highlighted with color, but some were full color scenes, which were unusual for that time and quite expensive for a small company to sponsor.

Frank B. Ansted was just 32 years old when he assumed the position of company president. He received many accolades for his leadership, even as the company was failing.

The United States' involvement in the Great War brought certain hardships at home, although of no comparison to the suffering in the war zone. Maintaining a strong working force was a problem both locally and nationwide, as well over 1,000 of Fayette County's young, able-bodied males were serving the war effort. In order to fill the void, girls and women were welcomed into factories to do certain jobs that had previously been done by men.[28] War contracts were sought after by most companies including Lexington, both for reasons of profit and to be patriotic in support of the war effort. In mid–July, an additional order to make thirty thousand picket ropes for the Navy was announced. This project was aided by a device invented by Ezra Brown that twisted the ends of the rope into the eye of the steel clout, making the end secure while speeding production.[29] Another product that was being made under government contract was exhaust manifolds to be used on engines for military tanks. In early August, Lexington announced plans to build 500 three-quarter to one-ton Class AA GMC truck chassis that would be used by the U. S. Army as ambulances or rapid transit commissary wagons. The cost to the government was $1,225 for each chassis.[30] In early October, a $2.25 million contract was awarded to build heavy-duty trailers that could be used to haul smaller tanks or light duty tractors.[31] Another order for 1,000 additional truck chassis was awarded to Lexington just a few days before the November 11 Armistice that ended the Great War.[32] This second order was later cancelled and attention eventually turned again to strictly automobile production.[33] As a security measure, 3,731 feet of 10-foot-high fence topped with barbed wire was installed around the plant. Employees were issued badges that were to be shown to gain admittance.[34]

The Quartermaster Department was attempting to standardize all Army cargo-

The emergency brake drum was moved to a location immediately behind the transmission of the drive shaft, and was supposed to require less effort to operate as claimed by this *Saturday Evening Post* ad from March 16, 1918.

A major advertising commitment was this two-page ad introducing the 1918 Model R in *The Saturday Evening Post*, Sept. 15, 1917.

carrying vehicles. Nash Quads and F.W.D. trucks were ordered for ammunition and other ordnance work. The Engineer Corps had adopted the Mack 5½ ton and the Medical Corps had gone in for the GMC model 16 type AA truck for ambulances. A number of Ford ambulances were also purchased for light duty service.[35]

This Eastern Indiana community gave outstanding support to the war effort. Fayette County was the first community in the nation to "go over the top" in the Thrift Stamp Sales Drive. One event that brought some recognition to the local community was the naming of a wartime supply ship *Connersville*. The steel ship of 3,500 tons was 300 feet long with a beam of approximately 50 feet, drew 14 feet of water forward and 16 aft and had a speed of 15 knots. A motorcade of four Lexingtons left Connersville on September 12, 1918, for the shipyards at Ashtabula, Ohio on Lake Erie. Ray Fowler, a well-known test driver for the Lexington Motor Car Company, drove one of the cars. Local persons who were prominent with the Red Cross made the trip and witnessed the launching, including Mr. and Mrs. Thomas Bryson, Mr. and Mrs. Minor Lelfingwell, Mr. and Mrs. Fred Neal, plus Miss Ethelyn Sample, who had been selected to break the bottle of champagne, christening the ship.[36]

Restrictions during the wartime that limited the number of cars that could be produced were tightened as the war continued to the point that automobile production eventually ceased altogether. Even so, the previous year's expansion benefited Lexington as they were able to fulfill their defense contracts and still show a slight increase in the number of cars built for the year, at 4,123.[37] Shortages of railroad cars for shipping continued to be a problem. In early April, 25 Lexingtons were driven to Cincinnati where rail cars were available to ship the new Minute

The Clubster

The Convertible Coupe

Top: The Clubster. Bottom: The Convertible Coupe. The Model O was continued into 1918 in Clubster and Convertible Coupe body styles.

Man Sixes to points south.[38] For the first quarter of 1918, Lexington outproduced every other automobile manufacturer in the state.[39] Production was good enough for the entire year that Lexington led all Indiana automobile manufacturers with the exception of Studebaker.[40] This means Lexington outproduced such well known makes as Apperson, Auburn, Cole, Haynes, Marmon, Premier and Stutz.

The U.S. involvement in the Great War focused attention on the exciting airplane. Lexington dared to suggest that the Series "R" was comparable by calling it "The 'Ace' of the Road." The Saturday Evening Post, *May 4, 1918.*

Lexington
MINUTE MAN SIX

Like A Machine Gun That Does Not Choke

ONE advantage of the new Browning machine gun for United States soldiers is its *continuity* of shots without choking.

The engine under the hood of every Lexington can be compared aptly to this marvelous machine gun's efficiency, because—

The Lexington engine can not be choked by dead gas.

In a sense every automobile engine is a *gun*—it must load, explode, shoot piston-projectiles, and discharge used-gas.

With the Lexington, due to its exclusive Moore Multiple Exhaust System, no two cylinders discharge their dead gas into the same exhaust line at the same time. This avoids choking, and gives every discharge a quick and clear exit.

Official tests prove this one of many Lexington advantages increases power and makes a substantial saving in fuel, adding much to its ease and range.

More than 100 parts are integral with our improved non-rattle frame. The emergency brake can be operated by the pressure of one finger.

Its beauty of design and color scheme is self-evident but its excellence of performance, driving ease, and riding comfort are appreciated only after *demonstrations*.

Consider its moderate price for a quality car, possible only because ten large factories, devoted to automobile parts, are affiliated with and contribute to Lexington.

See your Lexington Dealer or write to us.

Orders filled in rotation.

Lexington Motor Company, Mfrs., Connersville, Ind., U. S. A.

The reliability of military equipment was used as a comparison for Lexington automobiles. The Saturday Evening Post, *July 6, 1918.*

Two actions occurred that indicated the Ansteds' intention to continue expansion. In early April 1918, Frank Ansted and his brother George purchased a controlling interest in the Teetor-Hartley engine factory of nearby Hagerstown. Charles Teetor and Ralph Teetor retained a large block of stock and were expected to continue their involvement with this plant. The Teetors retained control of another automobile parts business known as the Indiana Piston Ring Company. That concern remained in Hagerstown and eventually became Perfect Circle.

The Teetor-Hartley Company was founded in 1896 by the Teetor family of Hagerstown. At first they built railroad inspection cars, but eventually the company evolved into automobile engine and parts production. The engine producing part of the organization provided power plants and various engine parts for several makes of automobiles, including the other Connersville manufacturer, McFarlan, and for some models of Lexington. One reason for Lexington's purchase was to assure a steady supply of engines if Continental could not meet their needs; another reason may have been to acquire a source of engines that did not depend totally on rail shipments, as work stoppages in the past had caused serious problems for receiving materials and for shipping finished vehicles. Yet another reason was to develop their own engine design. With this purchase, a group of Connersville directors were chosen with F. I. Barrows named as president, George and Frank Ansted serving as vice-presidents, Charles Teetor being retained as general superintendent and Ralph Teetor as the engineer, John C. Moore serving as a consulting engineer, Ray Teetor as assistant treasurer and A. E. Smith as assistant secretary.[41]

Within two days of the first announcement, another new annex to the Lexington plant was announced. The new building was 100 feet wide and 979 feet long, a single story of brick construction, built by the Hoosier Construction Company with John Doyle in charge.[42] This building was west of the original main building and extended all the way to 18th Street. Work started in April but was not completed until the next February. As the building passed from one construction stage to another, trucks that were being manufactured for the government were stored there until nearly all of the floor space was occupied. After the trucks were shipped out, machinery was moved in to enable increased production of the Minute Man Six.

The labor situation had eased somewhat toward the end of 1918, as servicemen began returning from the war. However, the Spanish Influenza was now taking its toll. By early December, it was estimated that there were probably 250 cases in the county that were seriously affecting people.[43]

The deadly flu continued to affect Connersville, and the nation as a whole, well into 1919. In early March, the local newspaper stated that more Americans died in the past four months from the Spanish Influenza than had been killed fighting during 19 months of the Great War. Schools were closed for several weeks and even churches were not permitted to hold services. Any gathering of people was apt to spread the disease, so industries found it challenging to keep operating at a normal rate.

The Lexington factory had been totally devoted to war production for a time, but on February 10, 1919, they reported having produced 12 pleasure cars that day.[44] Government contracts were still being completed and on March 13, Lexington received authorization to ship 260 army motor trucks to Jeffersonville. This was reported to be the largest shipment of vehicles ever made from this part of the state.[45] After the armistice was signed, Jeffersonville, Indiana, was designated as the

The Expert Six—
A Leader for 1918!

EARLY returns from all over the country indicate an overwhelming success for this new Lexington Minute Man.

Because it strikes a fresh note—meets the higher efficiency standards and coincides with the economy demands of the times!

It is both *comfortable* and *competent!*

No type has ever had more thorough testing and perfecting than the Six. And *this* car represents the very acme of six cylinder achievement. It is the *only* engine dead gas cannot choke, due to our exclusive Moore Multiple Exhaust System.

To benefit by the latest improvements you should see this beautiful car at once.

Our sales have broken records by their increase of 1000% in three years.

Intrinsic superiority did it—the kind of performance you should get with *your* money.

On top of this achievement now comes this bigger value than ever with the same unalloyed character of its successful predecessors—

Combined with wonderful improvements and refinements, possible at its moderate price only because of—

Our modernized manufacturing system of a whole chain of affiliated factories *specializing* in automobile parts.

One big improvement is the new Lexington frame, eliminating 100 separate parts, which are now made integral with the frame instead of being bolted on. This prevents rattles and squeaks.

There is a new easy-to-handle emergency brake. You can operate it with one finger!

The motor develops 40 horsepower. The wheelbase is 122 inches.

Get acquainted thoroughly with the bigger value of this new car—Call upon your Lexington Dealer or write us.

Series "R," five-passenger Touring Car, with two auxiliary seats, $1585; four-passenger Sport-tour, $1585; and five-passenger Convertible Sedan, with two auxiliary seats, $1785.
Series "O," four-passenger Clubster, $1585, and four-passenger Convertible Coupé, $1545.

All prices f. o. b. factory and subject to change without notice

Lexington Motor Company, Mfrs., Connersville, Ind., U. S. A.

Lexington
MINUTE MAN SIX

Auxiliary seats that folded out of the floor were a novel way to add seating capacity. The Saturday Evening Post, *Jan. 26, 1918*.

depot to store much of the surplus equipment. Additional storage sheds were hastily erected in order to accommodate up to 80 train car-loads of incoming materials per day. Among the items stored there for a period of time were the GMC type AA ambulance chassis that were shipped from Connersville. These chassis along with surplus Nash Quads, four-wheel-drive trucks, were stored on end, resting on the front bumpers, until eventually disposed of.[46]

Top left: **The Four-Passenger Sedanette.** *Top right:* **The Five-Passenger Salon Sedan.** *Bottom left:* **The Five-Passenger Limousine-Brougham.** *Bottom right:* **The Three-Passener Coupelet.**

With the war behind them, motorists began thinking of using their automobiles for pleasure including cross-country travel. The only coast-to-coast route that was supposedly well marked was the 3,389 mile long Lincoln Highway. This route generally coincided with the present US 30.[47] Some utility poles were marked with red, white and blue signs and the "L" to help keep tourists on track. The June 1919 *American Automobile Digest* boasted, "Those traveling on the Lincoln Highway this year will encounter the best touring conditions ever provided in the history of the great road." The same article noted, however, that of the 400 miles of highway passing through the state of Iowa, 276 miles were dirt and 95 miles were gravel.[48] This left approximately 29 miles of paved road. After a rain, the dirt roads turned to gumbo mud, making travel next to impossible, and in dry weather clouds of dust enveloped the travelers as well as nearby residents.

One effort at improving travel conditions that had been ongoing for several years was the Good Roads movement. Various organizations and, especially, companies involved in the motor vehicle industry were encouraged to adopt a specific road and help with improvements. The Lexington Company helped sponsor the Minute Man Route that was to be a trans-state highway running from the Indiana-Ohio border to the Indiana-Illinois border. Frank Ansted was secretary of the Minute Man Route and took an active interest in the development of this and other efforts to improve roads.[49]

Another movement that gained prominence after the war was women's suffrage, a long-standing cause that was gaining national attention. Congress passed the Eighteenth Amendment in June 1919, giving women the right to vote, and it was ratified the next year. Lexington sponsored advertising that recognized the influence of women in the selection of the family automobile, and even featured a woman behind the wheel when a gentleman was also present.[50] This was taking a rather bold stand at the time.

This 1918 Lexington Series RT was purchased in the United States by Gastav Larsson, an immigrant from Sweden. He took his car with him when he returned home in 1920. *Courtesy Mats Heder.*

The Memorial Day weekend brought an excited group of Lexington distributors to Connersville for entertainment, a pep talk and, especially, a trip to the Indianapolis 500 Mile race. Lexington had sponsored a similar event in 1915 but dropped it during the war years. Guests began arriving on Thursday, and by Friday noon at least 50 distributors and their associates assembled for a luncheon at the McFarlan

After the Armistice, GMC truck chassis that had been made by Lexington were stored at the general supply depot at Jeffersonville, Indiana, standing on end, resting on their bumpers, until eventually disposed of by the government. *Benedict Crowell,* Report on America's Munitions, *1919.*

Hotel that was hosted by the Rotary. Formal entertainment was provided by Pryor's Orchestra of Eaton, Ohio, and the Indianapolis Vaudeville Company. On Saturday morning the group went en masse to the Speedway by a special train consisting of a diner, two Pullmans and a coach.[51]

A huge celebration was held in Connersville on July 4. Known as Peace Independence Day, it celebrated the return to peacetime, observed Independence Day and let the community know that the Lexington Motor Company was having a profitable season. The celebration was billed as Community Play Day with all costs being picked up by Lexington and other local companies that were suppliers of parts, namely the Central Manufacturing, George R. Carter Leather Company, Indiana Lamp Company, Standard Parts Company and Rex Manufacturing Company. The Play Day was billed as the banner Independence Day of Fayette County's history with an estimated 10,000 people taking part in the festivities.[52] The celebration was held at Roberts Park at the north end of the city where the Fayette County Free Fair was also held. Workmen had placed a floor in the pavilion and had smoothed it with holystone to make it suitable for dancing.[53] Pryor's orchestra provided music throughout the afternoon and evening while vaudeville shows and athletic contests were held in other parts of the park. One of the main attractions of the day was the landing and eventual takeoff of an army aeroplane, the first army plane ever to have landed at the local fairgrounds. The army birdmen soared above the city, made a perfect landing on the race track infield, allowed inspection of the craft and then

114 The Lexington Automobile

Women's suffrage became a major issue after World War I. Lexington took the bold position of featuring women drivers in their ads, even with a gentleman present. The Saturday Evening Post, Jan. 4, 1919.

took off and performed numerous stunts before heading for Indianapolis. Another highlight of the day was a flag salute as flags of the Allied nations floated across the sky in parachutes as the crowd cheered, followed by the "greatest pyrotechnic display in the county's history." The Jessup brothers handed out thousands of packages of cracker-jacks and seven whole hogs were roasted. Orangeade, lemonade

Lexington recognized the influence of the woman of the house in selecting the family automobile. The Saturday Evening Post, *Aug. 2, 1919*.

and soft drinks were given out to help quench the crowd's thirst on the hot summer day.[54]

Frank Ansted received some positive recognition by the *Chicago Evening American* newspaper noting that he was possibly the youngest "captain" of industry. He had now been at the helm at the Lexington Motor Company for about 18 months.[55]

Top: 1919 Lexington Convertible Sedan. *Middle:* 1919 Lexington Tourabout. *Bottom:* 1919 Lexington Touring. *Lexington Minute Man Six Motor Cars, 1919.*

In what had become a yearly ritual, Mr. Ansted announced two construction projects for the year. First was building a test track. This was to be a driving circuit, just west of the plant, to be used as a testing loop for Lexington's cars.[56] This announcement surely made many townsfolk happy, as there had been numerous articles in the newspaper complaining of the reckless speeding of the test car drivers. In July, it was announced that a new building was being erected in Connersville for the Teetor-Hartley Company northwest of the Indiana Lamp Company.[57] This building became the home of the Ansted Engineering Company with William H. Freed as plant manager.[58] Lexington also built a new stock and receiving depot that would be 100 feet square. In the process, they relocated their boiler house and heating system and constructed a large smokestack. The plant had grown substantially over the years, and as the space increased, so did the need for more steam for heat and to power machines. This smokestack stood more than 100 feet tall and had the name lexington spelled in vertical letters made of lighter colored bricks inlaid in the structure. The extreme height created a strong draft for fires under the boilers, but it also created a landmark that stood for approximately 50 years before more recent tenants H. H. Robertson and D & M had the structure razed. It was no longer used and there were concerns of it possibly falling, causing injury or property damage.[59] Eldon Brown was Superintendent of Maintenance at D & M when the stack came down. He had acquired the services of Jess McFarlan, a local demolition contractor, who climbed to the top of the structure and knocked bricks down, inside the chimney, working his way around and then down as layer upon layer of bricks were safely brought down.[60]

Frank Ansted's plan was to be able to complete 30 cars a day and to continue production year-round and not just in the "motor season."[61] The actual assembly process took place in the original two story building that had a sloping floor to make it easier to move cars from department to department, taking on added equipment until they were driven out of the south end of the building.[62] On July 18, a sizeable fire at the Lexington plant caused a great deal of excitement but little damage. The fire, described as a gigantic bonfire, was discovered about 10:30 p.m. It destroyed a frame structure just northwest of the main buildings that contained a quantity of oil, paper and wooden shipping crates. The sky lit up as it burned quickly; however, there were no injuries and the cause of the fire was not determined.[63]

Some of the year's production ended up overseas in places such as Australia, South Africa, England, Finland, France and Sweden. Lexington export sales in central Sweden were handled by August Huzell and his son Eski. They owned a hardware store in Karlstad, the provincial capital of Varmland, located on the North shore of Lake Vanern, approximately halfway between Stockholm, Sweden and Oslo, Norway. Eskil came to the United States in 1919 or 1920 and probably visited Connersville. Mr. Huzell acquired the right to sell Lexingtons in Sweden, ordering the first batch of five Minute Man Sixes and also a McFarlan Town Car, an expensive prestige vehicle also made in Connersville by the McFarlan Motor Car Company. The first batch of Lexingtons arrived in Sweden in the spring of 1920. Oskar Karlstrom, sales manager at the Huzell Company, acquired one of the cars, a Series S with chassis number S 20492 that was registered May 21, 1920. The remaining four cars were sold and registered within the next few days. In less than a month, the car registered to Mr. Karlstrom was sold to Mr. Per Person of Langav in the northern part of Varmland. This car is still in the same family and is preserved in excellent running condition.

The first five Lexingtons that were imported into Sweden had been assembled in Connersville; however, later arrivals were shipped disassembled because import duties were lower on automobile parts than on a completely assembled car. A rather small company in Karlstad called Mekanisk Industri assembled the cars at a rate of two per day. It is believed that Lexingtons were the first American car to be assembled in Sweden. Both Ford and General Motors started building cars in Stockholm at a later date. Lexingtons were imported into Sweden for several years with the last known registration being in 1925. The cars were sold all over central Sweden with at least one registered in Sundsvall, an industrial town approximately 500 kilometers north of Karlstad. Yet another was on the island of Gotland in the Baltic Sea. It is not known just how many Lexingtons were imported and or assembled in Sweden, but 30 of them were registered as new cars in the province of Varmland and another 16 were registered in other provinces. The Huzell Company apparently sold between 50 and 100 Lexingtons over a period of several years. Five Lexingtons were sold new as taxicabs in Karlstad, although most were sold to land owners and businessmen. The Minute Man Six even had some success competing in speed trials in Sweden in the early twenties.[64]

Another Lexington that was imported into Sweden was owned by Gastav Lars-

Top: Lexington's export trade flourished during this period with overseas customers in Australia, New Zealand, Europe and Africa. Motor Australia, *June 2, 1919. Bottom:* One of the few Minute Man Sixes fitted with a custom body was this car built for Kinzea Stone of Georgetown, Kentucky. Stone had been a major investor in the company when it was organized. Newt Thomas was the family chauffeur. *Courtesy the Stone Collection.*

son, who had immigrated into the United States in the late 1800s from Stanga, a small community located on the southern part of the island of Gotland in the Baltic Sea. While living in Brooklyn, New York, Mr. Larsson purchased a 1918 Series RT. Because of restricted traffic over the Atlantic Ocean during the Great War, he did not get back to Sweden until 1920, but he took this car with him when he made a trip back home. The car was left behind when Mr. Larsson returned to the states. He had given it to his brother, Gcorg Larsson, who used the Minute Man Six for his wedding in 1920 and for about a year after. Next it belonged to the Slitbergs who ran a car shop. It was registered there until about 1924 when the registration number I115 was taken over by another car.[65]

Lexington's offering for the year 1919 was the Series R Minute Man that included the five-passenger Touring, five-passenger Tourabout, and the Convertible Sedan. The touring listed at $1,785, and had two auxiliary seats so it could actually seat seven. The seats could be partially unfolded and used as a footrest. It had a shipping weight of 2,875 pounds. The front seats were indi-

LEXINGTON MOTOR COMPANY
Connersville Indiana U·S·A
Cable Address ·Lexho·

FIB-EC

Saturday
May
17-1919

Mr. Robt. A. Brannigan,
Manager, Patent Department,
National Automobile Chamber of Commerce,
7 East 42nd Street,
New York City,
New York.

Dear Brannigan:

Will you please wire us immediately on receipt of this letter the number of the patent granted to M. T. Wildau on a "No-Door" car?

It is a body patent giving an isle with side guards and a peculiar type of wind shield front and back, without running boards.

Very truly yours,
LEXINGTON MOTOR COMPANY
F. J. Barrows,
Vice-President.

Most companies were careful not to infringe on patents that were owned by another person or company. Lexington would have their own problems with this later on.

vidual bucket seats with an aisle between them. The Tourabout body was somewhat narrower than the touring, giving it a sporty look. It had a full front seat that could seat three, eliminating the center aisle, and a back seat more suited for two passengers. The shipping weight was 2,800 pounds. The Convertible Sedan had a shipping weight of 3,050 pounds. The removable windows and center posts reduced its weight by 65 pounds when they were removed, in addition to providing the open-air feel. Other features of the Convertible Sedan included a dome light, a silk roller curtain for the rear window, massive coach handles on the doors with Yale locks and two auxiliary seats that folded out of the rear floor. The standard wheelbase was 122 inches.[66] Lexington advertised costly molded fenders which were softly crowned.[67] Some ads also promoted Lexington as the "white footed Thoroughbreds" as they were equipped with white enamel wheels. Production for the year dropped significantly to 3,124 cars,[68] as a result of commitments for war production plus numerous national strikes that affected the motor car industry. Strikes included the railroad shop men in August, bituminous coal miners beginning October 31, and the steelworkers, beginning September 22, lasting for the remainder of the year. As the year 1919 came to a close, there were major changes brewing in the Ansted industries.

5

Lexington Goes to the Races

Lexington's first few years were marked by notable successes and failures in competitive events such as races, endurance runs and hill climbing events. The company's first effort at competing in a speed contest came within weeks after production started. A fifty-mile race was held at the Kentucky Trotting Horse Breeders' track with $100 in gold having been deposited in the Phoenix Bank as prize money. The local Lexington distributor, along with the factory, sponsored the event that was open to any stock car as long as it did not have a special motor or a professional driver. The Lexington Motor Car Company said that anyone who entered the race would be "up against a car that can run long and fast." Cars could be stripped to have less weight, so the hood of the Lexington was removed along with the fenders. Hopes went sour when dirt got into the carburetor forcing a stop, and the home-town car was defeated by a Packard from Cincinnati.[1]

Another early experience in racing was on August 26, 1910, when a Lexington was entered in a speed contest at Elgin, Illinois. Along with the prestige of winning, the Elgin trophy was much sought after by participants and the Lexington Number 8 driven by Bob Drach, though outclassed, turned in a good performance making a full run of 200 miles without stopping for oil, water or repairs.[2] In this contest, Lexington claimed fourth place coming in behind the winning National, Marmon and Benz.[3] The company's most ambitious venture during those early years was probably entering the 1912 Indianapolis 500 Mile Race. Lexington had secured the services of a talented young driver, Harry Knight, who was one of the youngest in the game and was considered to be a fearless but cautious driver.

Knight was a true Hoosier race driver, born near the small town of Jonesboro in Grant County, Indiana. Before he was fourteen years old, he was employed at an automobile sales company in Indianapolis and attracted the attention of Russell Harrison, son of former President Benjamin Harrison. Russell hired Harry as a chauffeur. While in Harrison's employ, Knight made a thirty-day trip through the East and South driving the car the entire way. He later drove a Cole in the 1910 Glidden Tour, and competed in several meets at the Indianapolis Motor Speedway.[4] On September 3, 1910, he finished second while driving a Wescott in a 100 mile free-for-all.[5] In the first 500 mile race he drove a Wescott that was made at Richmond, Indiana.[6] In the second 500 mile race he drove a Lexington that had come from Connersville, Indiana; both the Wescott and Lexington used the Rutenber engine that was made at Marion. After the 1912 race, Knight went to Atlanta, Georgia, and took on the Cole agency. Cole automobiles were an Indianapolis product.

In the 1911 500 mile race, Knight had been recognized as something of a hero.[7] He was driving the Wescott at 86 miles per hour when he came upon and swerved to miss C. L. Anderson, a mechanic who had been thrown out of Joe Jagersberger's

Top: **This Lexington was being prepared for the 1912 Indianapolis 500 Mile Race. Driver Harry Knight is sitting behind the wheel while mechanic Edgar is relaxing in the passenger seat.** *Bottom:* **Harry Knight (left) and Edgar with the 1912 Indy car.** *Both photographs courtesy Wayne Goetz.*

Case when it broke a steering knuckle and suddenly swerved. Although Knight missed the dazed mechanic, in doing so, he crashed into the pits. The Wescott first hit Herb Lytle's Apperson that was getting a tire change, then turned end over end in the air and dropped upon Caleb Bragg's Fiat, which was being repaired. The impact was so great that it moved the structure of the pits. Both Knight and his mechanic, John Glover, were thrown from the car and received injuries. Knight suffered a possible skull fracture and lacerations; Glover had fractured ribs and internal injuries.[8]

Excitement ran high in Connersville during the spring of 1912 as the Lexington race car was being prepared for the Memorial Day event. A surprise decision by Marmon, which had won the 1911 race, was to not enter the 1912 event since their driver, Ray Harroun, had retired after his win the year before.[9] Wescott was not having an entry in this year's race after last year's car was destroyed in the pileup, so driver Harry Knight was available to pilot the Lexington. The Lexington and last year's Wescott had some similarities, especially with their power source, as both used the Rutenber six cylinder 421 cubic inch displacement engine. This was not a regular production Rutenber power plant, but was the largest engine the Western Motor Company had built up to this time using a bore of 4⅛ inches and stroke of 5¼ inches.[10] It is possible that the Wescott engine was rescued and reused in the Lexington. The car was assembled in the Lexington factory under the personal supervision of the driver and was displayed in downtown Connersville prior to being transported to Indianapolis for the race. The race car was painted a pleasing brown with a big white number 10 for identification. The crew wore outfits somewhat similar to the golden brown[11] color available on production Lexington automobiles.

Qualifiers for the 1912 500 Mile Race were required to show an average speed of at least 75 miles per hour for a two and a half mile lap. Knight piloted the Lexington around the track in one minute and 58.54 seconds for an average speed of 75.92 m.p.h., fast enough to start in the second row. By the time race day came, 24 cars had qualified under the direction of starter Fred J. Wagner.[12] In addition to the Lexington, there were three Stutz cars, three Nationals, two Mercedes, two Cases, two Loziers, and one each of Fiat, Simplex, White, Cutting, Firestone-Columbia, Marquette-Buick, Schacht, Knox, Mercer, McFarlan and Opel.[13] Engine sizes varied dramatically with the Mercer having just a 301 cubic inch displacement, whereas both the Knox and the Simplex machines had a whopping 597 cubic inches of displacement.[14] The Lexington engine was considerably smaller at 421 c.i.d.

The Indianapolis 500 Mile Race was known for the thrills and spills that contributed to its success, and the 1912 race was no exception. Ralph De Palma, in a Mercedes, set the pace and led almost the entire race. After 450 miles, he was five laps ahead of his nearest competitor. Many in the crowd began to leave as De Palma looked to be unbeatable. But with just five miles to go, De Palma's Mercedes suddenly lost power and began slowing down, leaving a trail of oil behind as a broken connecting rod had punched a hole in the crankcase.[15] The Mercedes finally quit altogether, stopping on the fourth turn of the 199th lap. A dejected De Palma and his riding mechanic attempted to push his car over the finish line in a desperate effort to salvage the victory.[16] But Joe Dawson, running in second place driving an Indianapolis made National, increased his speed passing the ailing Mercedes on the main straightaway to win the race.[17]

Harry Knight also had a disappointing day as he was the first one to drop out of the race on the eighth lap because of engine trouble. Initial reports indicated that a pin had broken in one of the cylinders locking the engine. The engine had been rebuilt a few days before the race by Rutenber mechanics and speculation was that they were in too big a hurry and didn't reassemble the engine properly.[18] After the race fiasco, the engine was again rebuilt at the Rutenber factory in Marion. At that time, Harry Knight faulted the riding mechanic, Edgar, saying that he had not

Above: **Ready to take on the "Brickyard."** *Courtesy Wayne Goetz. Left:* **A Rutenber motor powered the Lexington in the 1912 Indianapolis 500 Mile Race. Motor Age,** *Sept. 5, 1912.*

given the engine enough oil and that caused it to lock up. Harry Knight purchased the Lexington racecar and, after it had been repaired, had it shipped to Atlanta.[19]

Knight died during a July 4, 1913, race at Columbus, Ohio, during an incident not unlike the one that had brought him commendation two years earlier. Knight was driving a Rovan front-wheel-drive racecar on a half-mile track, rounding into the quarter stretch on his 125th lap. He blew the right rear tire, causing the car to turn over twice, ejecting both Knight and his 19-year-old mechanic, Milton McCullis.[20] Knight was then run over by Johnny Jenkins, driving a Schacht, killing Knight almost instantly. McCullis died about an hour later because a rib had punctured a lung.[21] Knight's mother and fiancée were in the stands and witnessed the accident. The two of them accompanied his body as it was returned to Indianapolis that evening.[22]

Lexington made little corporate effort at organized competition for several years after the ill-fated run at Indianapolis. Occasionally individuals drove Lexingtons in local contests, but they did so without factory sponsorship. Although the Lexington was never known to be one of the fastest cars for flat-out speed, it did capture a couple of racing events in other countries. Two such events involving Lex-

The Lexington No. 10 recorded a disappointing performance in the 1912 Indianapolis 500. Because of engine trouble, it was the first car to drop out of the race. *Indianapolis Motor Speedway Museum.*

ingtons caught the attention of the home office and were touted in news accounts locally and in some advertising.

In Sydney, Australia, in early June 1919, a Minute Man Six driven by Albert V. Turner captured the stock chassis race event at Victoria Park Course, beating several other competitors with an estimated 20,000 spectators cheering the winner.[23] In the first heat of 20 laps, the Lexington won easily by 60 yards with the time of 28 minutes and 32 seconds and the fastest lap time of 1 minute, one and 1⅖ seconds. In the second heat of 20 laps, Lexington was again the winner, this time by half a mile. The time of this heat was 25 minutes 52⅖ seconds with the fastest lap at one minute 11⅖ seconds.[24] Other makes that were also competing included Buick, Studebaker, Crossley, Chevrolet, Australian Six and Daimler. A Buick won the free-for-all with an Australian Daimler coming in second.[25]

Albert Valentine Turner was the Lexington distributor for the Sydney area. He had gone into the motor business forming the firm Stanton, Turner and Company in about 1911. Turner wanted an agency for cars and in an American magazine, ads for two makes caught his eye. He cabled both companies and within weeks had the Lexington and the American Underslung franchises. In addition to the American makes, he eventually sold Bugatti and Itala automobiles. Public acceptance was not enthusiastic as their prices were high and the marques were untried in the wild rough country where there were few roads. In order to convince potential customers that his merchandise could survive the Australian frontier, he plunged into the whirligig of reliability trials and interstate records. Turner became so successful he was sometimes called "the record master," best known for inter-capital records—Melbourne to Sydney in an Underslung in March 1913, 19 hours 2 minutes, Sidney to Melbourne in a Delage, February 1923, 13 hours 47 minutes, and

Lexington wins at Sydney, Australia's, Victoria Park in June 1919. *Courtesy State Reference Library, State Library of New South Wales.*

February 1924 in an Itala, 12 hours and 34 minutes.[26] He competed in Australian motor sport from 1912 through 1914 and after the First World War from 1919 until 1926. He entered every reliability contest he could and in every case either won outright or won his class. Turner was born in 1887 into a substantial family and received the normal schooling until he was apprenticed at the age of 14 to an engineering firm. In an era when cars were beginning to go really fast, A. V. Turner was considered to be the best driver the country had produced, but he died tragically in an accident at a minor Sydney hill climb in 1926.[27]

Back in the Northern hemisphere, Lexingtons were involved in another speed contest. On February 27, 1921, in Karlstad, Sweden, two Lexingtons—one a touring, the other a stripped chassis—took prizes while racing on a frozen lake. The race was held under the auspices of the Royal Swedish Automobile Club on Lake Vanern over a distance of five and a half kilometers. The ice had started to thaw and had a coating of water on the surface. Carl Johnson drove the stripped chassis and was said to have "thrown up slushy water like a sea plane." His most formidable competitor was a Scania Vabis, a Swedish make driven by Hans Osterman. The touring car was driven by O. J. Carlstrom, sales manager for Eskil Huzell, the Lexington dealer for Scandinavia. His nearest challenger was a Buick.[28] In November of 1921, two Lexingtons competed in a Johannesburg to Durban Reliability Trial in South Africa. The contest went over a hard course covering 418 miles with 21 cars competing. A Buick six cylinder was the winner with one of the Lexingtons, driven by H. Ackerman, placing ninth and the other, driven by C. C. Haine, coming in last. Lexington didn't advertise the results of that contest.

The competition picture began to favor Lexington as the new, more powerful overhead valve Ansted engine was introduced in July of 1920. The company again chose to sponsor racecars in a nationally known event, the Pikes Peak National Hill Climb. A carriage road had been built to the summit of Pikes Peak in 1880 and, of course, as automobile racing progressed, the challenge developed to be quickest to the top on what was considered to be the world's highest highway.[29] The Pikes Peak National Hill Climb was first run in 1916, but was discontinued during the war years, so the next hill climb was in 1920. Sanctioned by the American Automobile Association, the race was run over a course with an average grade of 7 percent and a maximum grade of 10.5 percent with 156 turns and no guard rails. The distance covered was 12.42 miles with an elevation gain of nearly 5,000 feet beginning at 9,402 feet

Ready to tackle Pike's Peak. The race was run on Labor Day, Sept. 6, 1920. Left to right: Garner Lewis, mechanic; Al Cline, drover; Henry Paul Goetz, mechanic; and Otto Loesche, driver. *Courtesy Wayne Goetz.*

and ending at 14,110 feet above sea level. Each event started at Cascade, a small settlement about eight miles up the mountain from Colorado Springs. The race was a timed contest where each participant raced against the clock. Spectators would arrive early to select their vantage point along the graveled race route, often choosing to watch from one of the turns. Cars slid and threw gravel as they rounded the curves, headed for the summit at full throttle.

In addition to prize money, the winner would be awarded the Spencer Penrose trophy. This exquisite cup was named for its donor, a wealthy Colorado automobile enthusiast, sportsman and part owner of a silver mine. The trophy stood 43 inches high sitting on an onyx base, was silver and gold plated with a reported value of $1,000.[30] It was first awarded in 1920 and was expected to be a "traveling trophy," meaning that it would be transferred to the winner each year until the next year's race. There was a provision that anyone who won the race twice would get to keep the trophy.

A party of four men left Connersville in a Lexington touring car on August 11, headed for Colorado Springs to prepare for the upcoming Pikes Peak Hill Climb to be held on Labor Day, September 6, 1920. They were Otto Loesche and Albert L. Cline, contest drivers, Garner Lewis, relief driver, and Henry Goetz, mechanic. A few days later, two other men, John Moore, chief engineer, and Fred R. Leeds, assistant director of sales, also headed for Colorado.[31] As Labor Day approached, they were joined by Clinton Patrick, engineer, Clarence Lawton, superintendent at Ansted Engineering, and Emery Huston, a company vice-president and head of advertising.[32] It was apparently Huston's idea that they should compete in this event. He had even released advertising copy ahead of time proclaiming victory, to be run the day after the race in major newspapers.[33] A roomy cabin had been leased by the company near Cascade, about twelve miles above Colorado Springs, along the route the race would be run.

These Connersville cars and drivers were going up against some of the world's best-known hill climbers. There were three events scheduled. The first was for cars with an engine displacement of 183 cubic inches or less, the second for cars of 300 cubic inch displacement or less, and the third, a free-for-all that anyone could enter. Both Lexington Specials had been entered in the last two events.[34]

The Lexington Specials had been shipped to Colorado earlier in order to be there when the race crew arrived. The cars were on the shorter Thorobred chassis with the Ansted overhead valve engine. Fenders, running boards and bodies had been removed and were replaced with seats for the driver and the mechanic. The steering wheel had been moved back and cowling had been extended to provide limited protection for the occupants, who sat just in front of the rear axle. It was normal to have a mechanic, who could make adjustments as needed, riding in the extra seat. Loesche saved on weight by not having the extra person ride with him during the hill climb, but Cline took along a riding mechanic.

On race day, a large number of fans showed up, the most popular vantage point being at mile fourteen of the course. From there, nearly the entire eight miles of the lower course could be seen and also stretches of the upper four miles.[35] Spectators dressed warmly and brought blankets, knowing that the weather on the upper part of the mountain was unpredictable. But it was a cold day and even those who were well prepared shivered through the afternoon of uphill racing. A large fire had been built at the summit to warm observers and participants after they reached the top.

The small displacement event was won by William Bentrip driving a Chevrolet with a time of 24 minutes and 5 seconds. The second place winner in that event was Dave Lewis in an Essex with a time of 25 minutes and 56 seconds. The next event was for larger engine cars, and then the free-for-all for any who would brave the mountain switchbacks and the cold temperatures. Although the sun was shining brightly at the start, the course became more of a challenge as a heavy snow storm had set in over the upper part of the mountain.[36] A Packard driven by Roy Duncan was the first car to leave the starting line, but it had carburetion problems and was delayed ten minutes with adjustments and had a poor showing. Ralph Mulford, driving a Page, was picked by many to win this year's event because he had won the 1916 race setting a record that still stood. However, Mulford was forced to abandon the race at mile sixteen because of the blinding snow. The Oldsmobile also went out of the race when a tire exploded. The other entrants in the large engine class and the free-for-all completed the course, so when the last car had reached the summit, officials declared the races over.

The order of starting was determined by lot. Cline was the fifth to start and Loesche ninth. When it was Ot Loesche's turn, he thundered up to the starting line in his Thorobred. A forest ranger rode up to his car, leaned down and hung a bear's claw strung on a string around his neck, saying, "Take this son, and you will come through a winner." This was a claw taken from the third toe of the left hind foot of a black mountain bear. Ot jammed the bear's claw into a pocket, forgetting about it until he reached the top.[37] A week earlier, Loesche had shot a jack rabbit so that he might have the left hind foot to carry with him as a good luck charm.

Otto faced the same slippery curves, sleet and low clouds that caused problems

Important Announcement!

Mr. Otto Loesche Assumes Management of Ye Motor Shop Repair Department.

Mr. Otto Loesche of Cincinnati, O. has consummated an arrangement whereby he will assume active management of the repair department of Ye Motor Shop, 125 West Seventh Street, Connersville, Indiana. Mr. Loesche has been for years Instructor in the Y. M. C. A. Automobile School at Cincinnati and most recently acting in the capacity of Repair Manager for the Schacht Motor Car Co, Cincinnati, O.

We are here to serve the public and only ask a trial.

Your patronage solicited on the basis of high class workmanship and a thorough knowledge of the business.

NOTE. Don't delay having your motor car overhauled. NO TIME LIKE NOW.

Otto Loesche came to Connersville in 1913 to manage the local Lexington repair shop. He became better known as a champion driver in hill climbing events. The Evening News, *Feb. 26, 1913*.

for others, but the snow had let up somewhat. He ended up winning by turning in the best time of the day at 22 minutes and 25 seconds.[38] For his efforts, he received $500 in prize money for each event, a gold cup and the coveted Penrose trophy. Loesche's time was several minutes slower then Mulford's record time in 1916 due to the horrible weather. Ot's recipe for winning the Pikes Peak race was "a Lexington car, a bear's claw, a true eye, a steady hand, and the nerve to give'er the gun."[39]

Al Cline was the next closest competitor to Loesche, running the second best time for the day, just five seconds behind the leader. Cline fought more severe elements, and at one point, his goggles got so obscured with snow and sleet that he yanked them off and threw them away. He drove the rest of that event steering with one hand as he shielded his face with the other hand. His mechanic was so cold when they reached the summit he had to be lifted from the car.[40] Second place winnings were $200 for each event and a silver cup.

Otto Loesche was originally from Cincinnati, Ohio. He was born April 26, 1889, and had only the normal education common in that day, but he had a real knack for anything to do with automobiles. Early in his career, Otto was an instructor for the Y.M.C.A. Automobile School in Cincinnati. In this position he was employed to teach Cincinnati police and fire personnel how to drive motorized vehicles.[41] He was also repair manager for the Schacht Motor Car Company, a Cincinnati concern.[42] In February of 1913, Loesche came to Connersville to manage the repair department of Ye Motor Shop, the local Lexington dealership. This company was owned by local businessman Frank Ansted. As Ansted became more and more involved with the Lexington factory operations, he recognized Ot's talents and moved him to become laboratory foreman of the engineering department.[43] Although he had had no previous experience with racing, Loesche became recognized nationally for his hill climbing skill. It is possible he learned from driving the hills of Cincinnati the techniques that made him so successful in this field. Ot was

The Pikes Peak Hill Climb was recognized by newspapers and automobile trade magazines as a major racing event. Motor Age, *Sept. 23, 1920.*

not known as a "lead foot," but he clearly knew how to give it the gas when it counted. Loesche stayed with the Lexington company until it folded, then returned to the Queen City where he became a partner in Loesche and Yost, operating a garage and service station on Spring Grove Avenue for nearly thirty years before retiring in 1954. Often, after working on a car, the champion hill climber would test his repair job by climbing the Straight Street hill in the Queen City.[44] Loesche married Carrie Lepple in 1909 and had two children, Ruth and Chester. Otto passed away January 8, 1975, and was buried in Spring Grove Cemetery.[45]

Albert L. Cline had worked for the Lexington company for a number of years working in various positions. He had left the Connersville area for a period of time, taking on the position of service manager for the Chicago Lexington distributor.[46] But, by 1920, he had returned to the home plant with the title of sales engineer.[47]

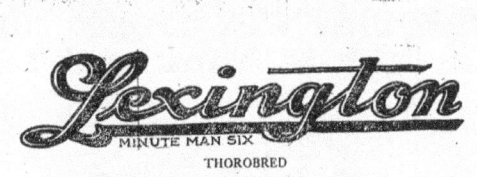

In Connersville, winning this contest was a major event. The News Examiner, *Sept. 7, 1920.*

News of the victorious afternoon of racing reached Connersville quickly as Emery Huston telephoned Frank Ansted. Frank was attending a banquet being held at the Connersville Country Club in honor of Josephus Daniels, Secretary of the Navy. When he returned to the banquet hall after being summoned to receive the news, his announcement had an electric effect on the audience and word spread throughout the community in less time than it took the drivers to win the Penrose trophy. Daniels joined in giving accolades as he also owned a Lexington.[48]

The Lexington contingent was to arrive back home at 6:00 p.m. on Tuesday, September 14, on the C.I. & W, but a small wreck of boxcars west of Rushville delayed them for 45 minutes. A community celebration began as soon as the train arrived. The Dan Patch Company whistle blew a long welcome home blast. Police cleared the right-of-way using ropes to keep enthusiastic onlookers off of the tracks. A bright light was attached to a utility pole and shined upon the returning celebrities so a

Otto Loesche became a celebrity overnight as a champion hill climb driver. Lexington Motor Company, *Sept. 1920.*

motion picture crew from Cincinnati could film the scene in its entirety. As soon as they were off the train and into automobiles, a parade was formed which went from Tenth and Eastern Avenue, near the C.I. & W. depot, south to Third Street, over to Central and north to Ninth Street. Col. J. H. Fearis was the parade marshal and was in charge of the extravaganza. Cheers thundered from every quarter as the procession made its way, with great throngs of people showing enthusiastic appreciation.[49]

The Davis Brothers had erected their large tent on the vacant lot at the corner of Ninth and Central where 3,000 chairs had been set up, brought in from Roberts Park.[50] There, each of the drivers, mechanics, and company officials was introduced and encouraged to make a speech. E. P. Hawkins, as the master of ceremonies, using a megaphone in order to make himself heard, introduced the approximately thirty Lexington dealers who were in attendance and was able to coerce several notables to give speeches.

After the program under the tent was done, the Rotary Club hosted a banquet for about 250 distinguished visitors and representatives of the press. This was held at the McFarlan Hotel with entertainment by cabaret singers from Chicago who were reportedly pleasing to look at and listen to. The audience also enjoyed a performance by a Spanish dancer, and E. P. Hawkins kept the party going until midnight.[51] This tribute to Lexington's victory was sponsored and planned by the manufacturers and merchants of Connersville, and factories had agreed to stop work at 4:00 p.m. in order for their employees to have time to prepare for the celebration.

The two racing Thorobreds, Number 7 and Number 6, that had brought so much excitement to the community finally arrived home on September 20. They had been driven from Pikes Peak to Denver and shipped the rest of the way by rail. The cars were on display that evening and the next day at Inland Motors, the Lexington dealership, where a large turnout of visitors viewed them.[52] The coveted trophy arrived in Connersville in late October and was also placed in the dealership front window for all to admire.[53] On October 6 and 7, the Auditorium Theatre showed a motion picture of the Pikes Peak race, described as "the most thrilling automobile race ever observed in this country." The Auditorium management announced that this program would be given without any advance in price, but children were urged to attend the Saturday afternoon matinee.[54]

Top: **Frank Ansted, president of Lexington, congratulates Otto Loesche after his 1920 victory.** *Courtesy Jim Robinson.* *Bottom:* **Emery Huston and Frank Ansted with the prized Penrose trophy.** *Courtesy Fayette County Historical Museum.*

Lexington made the most of their success at Pikes Peak with considerable adver-

Winning the Pikes Peak Hill Climb provided fodder for this *Saturday Evening Post* **ad from Nov. 27, 1920.**

tising. Ot Loesche even took the winning Number 7 car on tour, going all the way to Massachusetts, where he and the winning Lexington were photographed in front of the original Minute Man statue. The photographs were used for publicity. Of course, he stopped at dealers along the way to promote the victory in the hopes of increasing sales.

Though both victorious drivers returned to their regular jobs with the company, they also occasionally competed in hill climb contests. In early May of 1921, Ot Loesche made the news in Kansas City by twice climbing a hill said to be a 17 percent grade. With a flying start, carrying four passengers, he reached the summit at a speed of 29½ miles per hour. Next, starting from a standstill in high gear, he reached the top, running 29 miles per hour. At almost the same time, Al Cline raced a Thorobred in New York, where he impressed onlookers with the car's hill climbing before running an impressive 77 miles per hour on a straightaway.[55]

Actually, as early as April, Al and Ot were looking toward another run at Pikes Peak, intending to make the Penrose cup a permanent fixture at the Lexington plant. Otto had an ideal position in the company lab to work with chief engineer John Moore, fine tuning the Specials. The cars for 1921 were basically the same as those that were so successful last

Otto Loesche's daughter, Ruth Bauer, and grandson, Jerry Corbett, with the gold cup that Loesche was awarded for winning his class in the 1920 Pikes Peak Hill Climb. *Photograph by author.*

year, continuing to use the shorter Thorobred chassis with the 70 horsepower Ansted engine. There was slight alteration to the cockpit area as a panel on each side partially enclosed the occupants to provide more security.

The crew left for Colorado in late July 1921, planning to get six weeks of practice before the big day. Al Cline, Ot Loesche and two mechanics drove out to meet their cars that had been shipped by rail. J. C. Moore, chief engineer, and Emery Huston, a company vice president, joined the others and set up camp at Cascade.[56] Expectations were high as preparations continued for the race. The drivers' wives, Carrie Loesche and Rose Cline, also arrived in time to watch the race.

The Pikes Peak Hill Climb was to be held on Labor Day, September 5, over the same course as the previous year with $4,100 in prize money plus the Penrose cup up for grabs. A preliminary speed trial was held on September 1 to determine the order in which the racers would start. This contest consisted of a five and a half mile run from the regular starting line to Goken Cove Inn. The order of finishers was Loesche in Number 7, 1st, Cline in Number 6, 2nd, Rhiley in a Hudson, 3rd, Chapin in a Dodge, 4th, Shultz in a Ford, 5th, Williamson in an Allen, 6th, and Nemesh in a Page, 7th. The results of this trial run gave added excitement to the Connersville crew.[57] Both Thorobreds were entered in Event 2, non-stock class C.

Loesche was the first one away from the starting line in Lexington Number 7

Pike's Peak Race Pictures
SPECIAL ATTRACTION FOR
FRIDAY AND SATURDAY

See Otto Loesche and the Lexington in Action

First view of official pictures showing Lexington, No. 7 and Lexington, No. 6, driven by Otto Loesche and Al Cline, respectively, as they dashed across the tape at the top of Pike's Peak in the most thrilling automobile race ever observed in this country. The pictures show Mr. Loesche and Mr. Cline making the hairpin turns and the cars are seen shooting up the steep mountain road through snow and sleet. It is believed that every Connersville person will be interested in these pictures.

Pike's Peak pictures, while the most interesting part of the bill for Friday and Saturday, are by no means all the program, as splendid photo-plays and vaudeville will be given at each performance.

VAUDEVILLE AND Other Photo Plays

OTTO LOESCHE.

The Auditorium management announces that this unusually interesting program is to be given without any advance in price. On Saturday afternoon the usual matinee will be observed and it is urged that children attend the afternoon show.

VAUDEVILLE AND Other Photo Plays

AUDITORIUM THEATRE

The new exciting entertainment of the day was moving pictures, especially when local talent was featured. The community was invited to see the race in moving pictures at no increase in admission. Children were urged to attend the afternoon show so adults could enjoy evening entertainment without the noisy kids. The News-Examiner, *Oct. 6, 1920.*

at 10:30 a.m. when the starter's flag dropped. He carried with him the same rabbit's foot that he had the year before. The weather was kinder that day and he was able to keep good speed, cutting about three minutes off of the previous year's time at 19 minutes, 47⅗ seconds. Cline was next away from the starting line, and for the first few miles was making possible record time. Something caused him to throttle down on one of the curves and he dropped out before he had driven three miles. Initial reports were that Al had gone over the edge. Mrs. Cline, who was waiting at the summit, had several uneasy moments until she learned otherwise.

The fastest time of the day and the winner of the Penrose trophy went to King Rhiley of Kansas, driving a privately modified Hudson. Rhiley was known as the king of dirt track racing. He ran in Event 3, non-stock class C. Loesche had the best time in his class and received the first place award for that event.[58] The Lexington Number 7's showing for the day was excellent, but not good enough to keep the Penrose cup. The lack of an overall victory was a disappointment to the Lexington team after such a successful time in their first attempt plus being the fastest qualifier. Mr. and Mrs. Loesche, Mr. and Mrs. Cline, J. C. Moore and the rest of the expedition

The sendoff for the 1921 Pikes Peak race. Left to right: Ot Loesche, Frank Ansted, Emery Huston, J. C. Moore and Al Cline. *Courtesy Fayette County Historical Museum.*

arrived back in Connersville on September 11. Ot's only request was that he be given one more chance to fight the battle of the curves and bends with King Rhiley.[59]

The 1922 race did not provide that opportunity as the cash-strapped United States Automotive Corporation, of which Lexington was the prime company, did not compete at Pikes Peak. Initially, 1923 didn't look any more promising with cash flow even tighter at the beginning of the year. But after the company went into receivership, limited funds again became available to sponsor a racing entry.

As the 1923 Pikes Peak event drew near, the Lexington Motor Company decided to enter one car, and Ot Loesche was ready to drive it. The Connersville crew, consisting of Loesche, G. C. Patrick, the new chief engineer, and Gus McClanahan, service expert, left for Colorado on August 16. This gave them a much shorter practice time than in previous years, but would afford Ot the opportunity to, once again, race against King Rhiley. The Number 7 racecar had been shipped ahead of time by rail.[60]

Again, there were three classes of competition. The small class was for cars with engines no larger than 183 cubic inches and weighing at least 1,600 pounds. The mid-size class was for cars between 183 c.i.d. and 300 c.i.d. weighing 1,800 pounds or more, and the large engine class for engines over 300 c.i.d. weighing no less than 2,000 pounds. There was prize money for the winners of each class, and the driver

Otto Loesche navigated the sharp curves and switchbacks with all of the skill of a professional driver to win first in his class in 1921. *Courtesy Ken Lane.*

with the fastest time of the day would get the traveling Penrose cup. The Labor Day event was under the auspices of the *Denver Post* and the AAA.

The Lexington Special was in the mid-size engine group, as was a second Lexington entered independently by Jack Knight of Denver. Ot drove the same car that he had driven in the 1921 Pikes Peak event, a Thorobred chassis with an updated 272 c.i.d. Ansted engine. Knight's car was of similar construction.[61] Overall, there were 23 cars entered in the uphill battle. In addition to the two Lexingtons, other makes represented included Mercer, Wills St. Claire, Essex, Dodge, Hudson, Chevrolet, Studebaker, Oldsmobile, Duesenberg, Page, Allen, Ford, and Stephens.[62]

Labor Day 1923 fell on September 3. By the time action had ended, Otto Loesche had won another first place in his class and Knight, in the other Lexington, had won second place. The other cars in the mid-size class that placed were Hudson, third, Stephens, fourth, Oldsmobile, fifth, and Wills St. Claire, sixth. Of the twenty-three cars entered, seventeen started the climb and only eleven finished. The real shocker was the best time of the day, won by Glen Schultz driving an Essex that had been entered in the small engine class. The Essex Company accepted the cash prizes, but declined accepting the Penrose trophy because of insurance requirements imposed by the race organizers.

Opposite, top: **Ot Loesche at the summit of Pikes Peak before the 1921 race.** *Bottom:* **Al Cline at the summit of Pikes Peak before the 1921 race.** *Both photographs courtesy Fayette County Historical Museum.*

Once again, the Penrose trophy had eluded Loesche. However, by the rules governing the Penrose trophy, the Penrose cup went to the driver having the highest number of points at the end of six years. If Loesche were able to win first, second, or third in the next year's event, the cup would go to him because he had accumulated more driver points than anyone else with his winnings in 1920, 1921 and 1923.[63] The recognition of his victory that year was a special program held on September 13, at the McFarlan Hotel. At the regular Kiwanis meeting, E.P. Hawkins introduced Otto Loesche, Clinton Patrick, chief engineer, Gus McClanahan, service department superintendent, and William Herod, head of the Lexington plant. Each man was encouraged to speak. Loesche responded by expressing appreciation for the interest shown by the Kiwanis Club.[64] He was a man of few words, but others gave more detailed accounts of his accomplishments.

During the spring and summer of 1924, automobile production was not setting any records. But there was excitement within the ranks as four short wheelbase Lexington Specials were being readied for the upcoming Pikes Peak Hill Climb. Each car was built to conform to the rules established by the American Automobile Association, promoter of the classic. The engines were Ansted 272 c.i.d. plants developing 75 horsepower, the same as were used in the Minute Man Six. Frames were shortened dramatically so that each of the Specials had a 90-inch wheelbase, except Bob Rudd's, which was 98 inches. This aided maneuverability for the serpentine road up the mountain, and also lessened the overall weight. There was only one seat as the riding mechanic was no longer needed. The cars weighed in at 1,799 pounds, but surpassed the required 1,800 pound minimum when fuel and water were added. It was quite a financial commitment for this small company, still in receivership, to sponsor four entries in this prestigious event.[65]

Labor Day 1924 would fall on Monday, September 1. The four Lexington Special racecars were shipped out of Connersville by rail on August 2. The entourage that journeyed West included four drivers; Otto Loesche, who won his class in 1921, and 1923 as well as the free-for-all in 1920; Albert Cline, who placed second in 1920 and raced but did not finish in 1921; Clarence Lawton, superintendent of Ansted Engineering; and Robert Rudd. Accompanying them were G. C. Patrick, chief engineer, Clarence "Cuz" Bullard, mechanic, and "Bud" Stewart of the service department.[66] As race day approached, these were joined by Herbert Clay, sales manager, Ray Barbin and Joe Rudd.

The youngest of the Connersville drivers was Bobby Rudd at just 21 years of age. Bobby was well known in his hometown as a happy-go-lucky kid who always had a smile. Young Rudd was from a family of six boys and two girls, and he was enthralled with racing. He had participated in races at the Winchester, Indiana, track and at other events where opportunity presented itself. Robert's brother, Joe, had built his Pikes Peak car while Joe was superintendent of production at Lexington.[67] After Bobby's Pikes Peak run, he continued to be active in Eastern Indiana racing events until he died of injuries sustained in an automobile accident August 18, 1933. Bobby was not in a race and was not even driving at the time of the accident.[68]

Labor Day started out with beautiful weather, but as the day wore on and the

Opposite, top: Clarence Lawton behind the wheel of his Pikes Peak race car in 1924. *Bottom:* Bobby Rudd behind the wheel of his Pikes Peak race car. This car was eventually sold during the Depression for $25. *Both photographs courtesy Jim Robinson.*

racers continued their attempts to reach the peak in record time, conditions deteriorated with the later participants encountering snow and sleet which slowed them somewhat.

The Lexington Specials made a clean sweep, taking the first three places in their engine size class plus the free-for-all. Otto Loesche, driving Number 7, did it again! He not only shattered his own record, but also broke the record set by Ralph Mulford during the first Pikes Peak race in 1916. Ot's time was 18 minutes and 15 seconds, a remarkable feat, but one that is even more amazing because he encountered two incidents, either of which could have put him out of the race. Just three miles into the race Ot didn't negotiate a turn properly and drove off the road but was able get back and continue without stopping. In a more serious incident, with three miles to go, he hit a large rock, bending the front axle. For the last part of the race, Ot could make left turns only. Fortunately all of the turns on that part of the course were left hand turns.[69] Second place in the mid size engine class went to Lawton at 19 minutes, 5⅖ seconds, and third place to Cline with a time of 19 minutes and 38⅖ seconds. Bob Rudd dropped out after blowing two tires while rounding a hairpin curve. Rudd controlled his car and there was no damage or injury.[70]

Ot Loesche not only came away with the class prize, but he won the free-for-all, thus claiming the coveted Penrose trophy for permanent ownership by Lexington. Second place in the free-for-all was C. H. Myers driving a Van Dyke Special, his time just two-fifths of a second slower than Loesche's. C. H. Brinker, in a Peerless, was third with 18 minutes, 55⅖ seconds.[71] Competition was outstanding for this event.

The race was over and the celebrating began. First, a gala banquet was held in a Colorado Springs hotel where the cars were displayed in the lobby. When the victorious crew arrived back home, festivities were planned to involve the entire com-

The Lexington team at base camp before the 1924 race. Left to right: Ot Loesche, Herbert Clay, Bob Stewart, Al Cline, Ray Barbin, Joe Rudd, Bob Rudd, C. E. Bullard, Clarence Lawton and Clint Patrick. *Courtesy Fayette County Historical Museum.*

> **Join With Us on Pikes Peak**
> # VICTORY DAY!
> ## Connersville, Indiana
> ## TUESDAY, SEPTEMBER 16
> ### Afternoon and Evening
>
> Come out and welcome home Connersville's winning boys and cars! See Ot Loesche, winner of the magnificent Penrose Trophy, and Al Cline, Clarence Lawton, and Bob Rudd, in action on Fifth Street Hill! Climbing demonstrations at four-thirty o'clock. Big street parade at eight o'clock. Fireworks! Bands! Industrial Floats! And Sixty Lexington Automobiles, showing all models since 1912. You are invited to take part.
>
> Race Cars and the Trophy will be displayed at corner of Ninth and Central after the parade.
>
> SPONSORED BY
> ## KIWANIS - ROTARY - LIONS

A mammoth Victory Day celebration was held in Connersville after the 1924 Pikes Peak win. The News-Examiner, *Sept. 11, 1924.*

munity. Tuesday, September 16, was declared Pikes Peak Victory Day. Daylight fireworks, known as aerial bombs, were set off at intervals throughout the afternoon to remind everyone that this was the day of celebration. Festivities began at 4:30 p.m. with hill climbing demonstrations on the serpentine Fifth Street hill by all four Lexington drivers and their cars. This hill, with its gravel surface, was every bit as challenging as any stretch of the mountain highway except it lasted for only a couple of blocks. Sizeable crowds watched as the racecars made haste sliding around the curves and throwing gravel, much to the delight of spectators. Interviewed in 2002, eighty-eight year old Wayne Goetz, whose father was one of the mechanics who traveled to Pikes Peak, remembered the 5th Street Hill demonstration and said some nearby houses had windows broken from flying gravel as the race cars barreled up the hill.[72]

Next on the evening's agenda was a giant parade. Efforts were made to encourage as many people as possible to be a part of it. Local businessman George Beeson was the grand marshal and he was assisted by Sam Balsam, manager of the local Lexington dealership. The parade route was south on Eastern to Third Street, west to Central, than north to Ninth Street. This was called a "red fire parade" because parade participants were given sparklers and red torches, the kind commonly seen in parades of that period. Central Avenue was lined with torches that gave off a glow of red or green. At intersections, pyrotechnic fountains of fire lighted the surrounding area. The first units were the local police and fire departments. Music was provided by the Connersville Boys' Band and the Connersville Military Band. School children were encouraged to be a part of this huge parade and those who marched

GREETINGS, LEXINGTON!

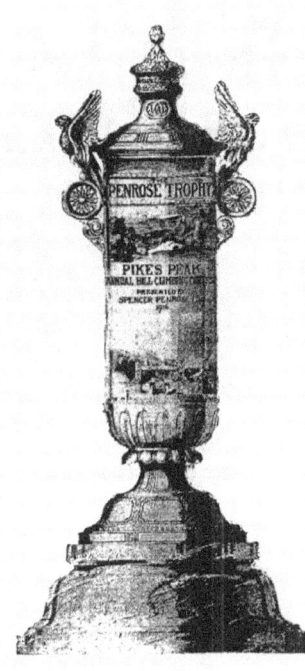

In Colorado September 1, 1924 The Lexington Motor Company Won the $10,000 Penrose Trophy In the Premier Hill-Climbing Contest With the World's Record on Pikes Peak —18 Minutes and 15 Seconds.

The Lexington Drivers were

OTT LOESCHE
(Winner)

AL. CLINE

CLARENCE LAWTON

AND

BOB RUDD

All Residents of Connersville

John Shelpman
The Letter Shop
The Levinson Company
The McFarlan Hotel
Fayette Bank and Trust Company
Smith's Dry Cleaning
Harry Blieden
Seele Furniture Company
The Boda Press, Inc.
Lincoln Manufacturing Company
Neal & Stoll
C. B. MacDaniel, Optometrist
Fayette Restaurant
Fayette Hotel

The A. E. Leiter Company
Guttman's Underselling Store
Silvey-Luking Company
Walker Restaurant Company
First National Bank
Buehler Bros. Meat Market
Castle Sales Company
Roth's Gift Store
Kehl Jewelry Store
V. J. Barker, Hardware and Stoves
Central State Bank
R. W. Smith Music Company
W. H. Sherry & Son
Lewis Sweet Shoppe
Cut Rate Shoe Store

Central Restaurant
Western Union Telegraph Company
H. W. Jones Grocery
Connersville Lumber Company
Fayette Music Shop
The City Shoe Repair Shop
Edward Israel
Interstate Public Service Company
Bell Tire Service
Moritz Friedmann
Palace Hotel
Pratt's Shoe Store
Remedial Loan Company
Chas. Myers

The community was thrilled when the Penrose trophy came home to Connersville for good. The News-Examiner, *Sept. 16, 1924.*

were given a balloon. In addition to the hundreds of people watching and cheering the parade, there were several hundred people marching, each with a red torch held high for all to see. There were about 60 Lexington automobiles that represented nearly every model ever manufactured, including one of 1910 vintage, the year that Lexington came to Connersville. The four race drivers paraded in their cars also. All of the car dealers were invited to have their products in the parade.

Participants included Balsam Automotive with Dodges; Fechtman and Cooley (Ford and Lincoln), George R. Beeson (Chevrolet), Baker and Thomas (Hudson, Essex and Jewett), Dragoo Motors (Oakland), Greene and Halliday (Overland, Willys-Knight and Buick), Stewart Sales Company (Chrysler, Maxwell and Oldsmobile), and De Camp Sales Company (Reo and Studebaker). Another colorful part of the parade was floats that had been prepared by various manufacturers and businesses. To record all of the excitement, Clarence Rooney, of the Pathe Motion Picture Company of Cincinnati, brought his equipment and helped shine the limelight on Lexington.

The end of the parade was at Ninth and Central where there was a mass meeting with Rev. J. S. E. McMichael, pastor of the First Presbyterian Church, as chairman. Speeches honoring the drivers and crew were given by Raymond Springer, Harry Wainwright, Herbert Clay and William Herod. This was followed by an aerial fireworks program. The elaborate display, put on by the A. O. Due Company of Cincinnati, included artillery flares that gave a brilliant light over the whole city, and American flag shells with various designs that lit up the sky. Three service clubs, the Kiwanis, Lions, and Rotary, sponsored the day's activities. Expenses for this gigantic celebration were covered by donations from local citizens.[73] Made in Connersville products were displayed in downtown business houses all during the week. The plan was to give local citizens as well as the many expected visitors an opportunity to see the variety of products manufactured in this East-Central Indiana city.[74] This was a celebration many would remember for a number of years to come. But just two years later, the Lexington Company would have gone belly-up, its factory closed and soon to be auctioned off.

There would be no more factory involvement with Pikes Peak, but individual Lexington racecar owners continued to place in three more Labor Day events. J. V. Plenderlith drove a Lexington Special to a third place finish in 1925.[75] Joe Unser, also in a Lexington Special, placed second in 1926 and again in 1928, but by that time, the name of the car had been changed to Ansted Special.[76] Lexingtons truly dominated Pikes Peak during the 1920s.

It is remarkable that Otto Loesche, Albert Cline, Clarence Lawton and Bobby Rudd, all from the Midwest, without previous experience, could have the success that they had at Pikes Peak. Bobby had dirt track racing experience before his Pikes Peak attempt, but had not driven hill climb events. Although the men deserve the bulk of the credit, the Specials they piloted were also outstanding. The Ansted engines performed flawlessly for their talented drivers, maintaining exceptional power and flexibility in the thin mountain air. Joe Rudd, who put together the car his younger brother drove, was offered $2,500 for his car while it was on display in Colorado Springs. But pride of ownership was too strong, and the car was brought back home where, after the Victory Day celebration, it ended up in his back yard for years. During the Depression, a friend of his paid $25 and took it away.[77] The Number 7 Special, driven by Ot Loesche, was more fortunate. It was saved by Harry Diamond, the New York Lexington dealer. He purchased two of the Pikes Peak cars from the factory, all other dealers having declined. The Number 7 was kept in the basement of his showroom until the 1940s when it was purchased by the du Pont family and later was acquired by the Pikes Peak International Hill Climb Museum in Colorado Springs.[78] After this museum lost their display space, Number 7 was loaned to the Fayette County Historical Museum in Connersville in September of

The winning No. 7 Pikes Peak car, in original unrestored condition, was on display at the Fayette County Historical Museum for several months during 2001 and 2002. *Photograph by author.*

2001 and was on display there until it was returned to Colorado Springs in June of 2002. It is presently owned by the El Pomar Foundation of Colorado Springs, and is on display at a museum in that area.

The Ansted engine that was so successful in conquering Pikes Peak during the 1920s continued as a force to be reckoned with in racing circles. One such application was in the Ansted Special, driven by William Walthall. William was an African-American racecar driver from Chicago who participated in dirt track racing using a car of his own design that was powered by a 1922 Ansted engine.[79] This car competed on the Gold and Glory racing circuit, a series of races that was started in 1924 for Negro drivers. Walthall's car was raced up until about 1950.[80]

The gold cup awarded to Otto Loesche for winning the 1920 Pikes Peak race is still a prized possession of his family.[81] The Penrose trophy or cup has also been preserved and is on display at the Fayette County Historical Museum. This beautiful trophy, a metal cup plated with gold and silver, stands 34 inches high without the onyx base it originally had. In 1920, the trophy was valued at $1,000.[82] The next year, the value was listed at $2,000, a doubling in value, while on display at the Lexington plant in Connersville. In 1923, when the Penrose cup was won by Essex, they declined to accept it because they would have been required to insure it for $6,000 and provide a $5,000 bond to assure its safe return.[83] In 1924, when the trophy again returned to Connersville, this time for permanent display, it was valued at $10,000[87]—quite an amazing increase in value over a rather brief period of time.

When one considers the proclaimed value of this beautiful trophy, it is no small wonder that it is still available for people to admire and enjoy, especially considering the fate of the Minute Man statue. It was made of plaster of Paris with a gilded coating that resembled copper. That piece of art was brazenly taken in broad daylight. Actually, the Penrose cup also disappeared from the Connersville Reynolds Museum in the 1940s or early 1950s, in unknown circumstances, and its whereabouts were not known for several years. Beginning in 1953, the museum curator was Harry M. Smith. He had never seen the trophy until it was returned nearly 20 years after he had started working in that position.[85]

This author had a hand in recovering the prized gem in the 1970s. While I was administrator in charge of Connersville's Junior High South, a student ran up to me one beautiful fall afternoon and excitedly told me of a gunny sack lying on the front step of the school with something in it. I immediately went outdoors, wondering all the while if it were wise to open it. Could it possibly be a Halloween prank? But I did look inside, and to my amazement, there was this beautiful trophy that turned out to be the Penrose cup, somewhat dirty but undamaged. To this day, it is still a mystery where this treasure had been. Who took it or who returned it is not known for certain, though there are several theories. It is nice to have it home!

The following parody poems by an unknown author were written about 1920, to celebrate the Lexington Pikes Peak victory[86]:

Pikes Peak Homecoming Celebration

Long, Long Trail

There's a long, long trail a winding
Into the land of my dreams
Where the nightingales are singing
And a fair moon beams
There's a long, long night of waiting
Until my dreams all come true
Till the day when I'll be going down
That long, long trail with you

Parody

There's a long, long trail a-twisting
Unto the top of Pikes Peak,
Where the touring cars a steaming
And about to spring a leak—
There were anxious, watchful moments
Until the boys come round the curve,
Till the Lex-es crossed the finish line
Without a single swerve!

Till We Meet Again

Smile the while you kiss me sad adieu
When the clouds roll by I'll come to you
Then the skies will seem more blue
Down in lovers' lane my dearie,
Wedding bells will sing so merrily,
Every year will be a memory,
So wait and pray each night for me
Till we meet again

Parody

Smile the while you hail the victors here
When they pass give both of them a cheer.
Then the skies are sure to clear
Over old Pikes Peak my dearie
Vict'ry bells will chime so merrily,
Everything will look more cheerily
So come to join to praise with me
Oh the Minute Men.

Maryland, My Maryland

Thou wilt not cower in the dust
Maryland my Maryland
Thy beaming sword shall never rust,
Mary-land! my Maryland!
Remember Carroll's sacred trust
Remember Howard's war-like thrust,
And all thy slumb'rers with the just,
Mary-land, my Maryland

Parody

Your Ot and Al are Minute Men,
Lexington, oh Lexington!
They acclaim with tongue and pen,
Lexington, oh Lexington!
Who was is said,
Pikes Peak or Bust?
They had the faith, and hope, and trust
And climbed that peak— they felt they must!
Lexington, oh Lexington!

6

A New Corporation and Continued Expansion

Lexington began 1920 with a major announcement. On January 12, at the National Automobile Show in New York City, Frank Ansted announced that a new organization had been formed: The United States Automotive Corporation, to be headed by the Lexington Motor Company. Other companies included in the new corporation were the Ansted Engineering Company, Connersville Foundry Corporation, and Teetor-Hartley Motor Corporation of Hagerstown. Actually, these companies had been owned or controlled by the Ansted family for some time. Now they were pulled together into a corporate structure with Frank B. Ansted in charge. The papers for incorporation had been filed in Indianapolis several months earlier but the announcement was saved for the limelight of the automobile show.

Officers for the new corporation were Frank Ansted, president; George W. Ansted, Emery Huston and Frederic I. Barrows, vice presidents; James M. Heron, treasurer; and LeRoy A. Hanson, secretary. Other directors were William B. Ansted, president of Central Manufacturing; Charles C. Hull, president of the Rex Manufacturing Company; John C. Moore, chief engineer at Lexington; and Arthur A. Ansted, president of Indiana Lamp Company, all of Connersville. The one out-of-towner was Elmer J. Hess of Cincinnati, Ohio.[1]

Models offered for 1920 were the Series R, a carry-over from the previous year, and the new Series S that had been introduced in 1919 as a 1920 model. The Series R consisted of the Touring and the Tourabout, each listing for $1,785, and the Sedan at $2,285. The Series S offered the Touring, the Thorobred with a change of spelling, the Lex-Sedan (which replaced the convertible sedan, but still featured removable windows and center posts to create an open car with a fixed top), the Sedanette and the Coupe. Series S Prices ranged from $1,885 to $2,850,[2] but by February, prices had jumped to $2,185 for the Touring to $3,150 for the Sedanette and the Coupe. An interesting feature of the Lex-Sedan's removable windows this year was that all six side windows, front doors, rear doors and rear quarter windows were exactly the same size so one need not worry about which window went in which opening. They were all interchangeable!

One of the new features on the Series S for 1920 was 2-Way headlamps, Lexington's attempt at providing adequate lighting without blinding oncoming traffic. This system, developed by Samuel Arbuckle for the Indiana Lamp Company, did not change the intensity of the light, but the headlight reflectors were tilted by a vacuum control mounted on the dashboard so the light rays would be directed more toward the ground in congested areas. Arbuckle's idea produced an extremely

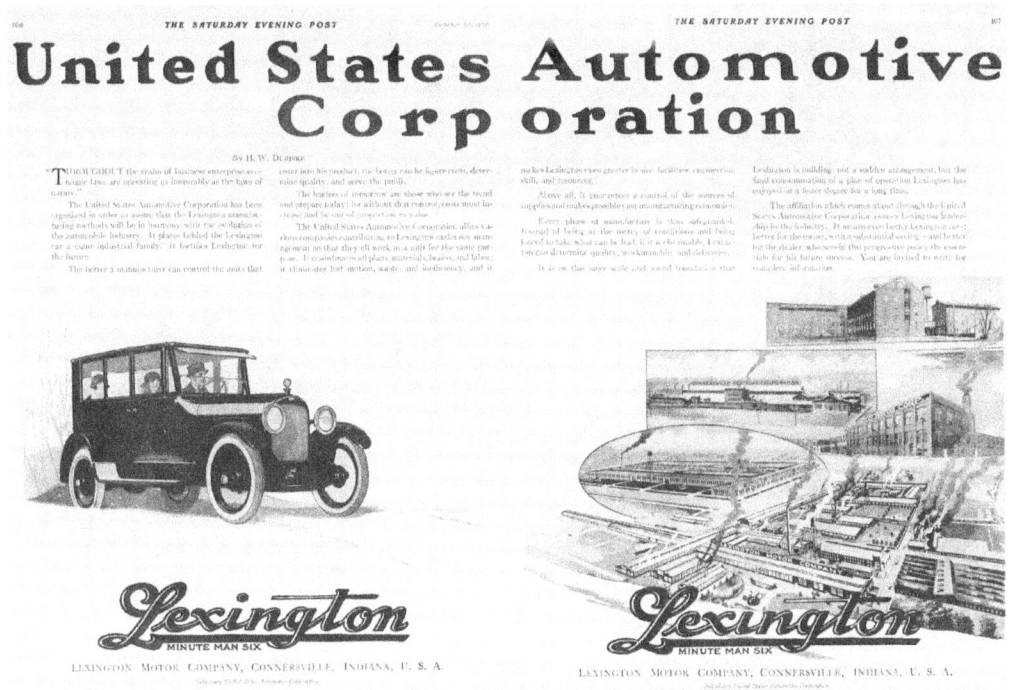

This ad announcing formation of the United States Automotive Corporation ran in the *Saturday Evening Post* on Oct. 30, 1920.

complicated and novel system of dimming the headlights using tubing, hoses and valves instead of a simple two-bulb headlamp. Another new item, the Lexi-gasifier, credited to chief engineer Moore, pre-heated the gasoline before it reached the intake manifold thus making the fuel burn cleaner. Gasoline quality suffered during and after the war causing problems with misfiring and poor performance. Whether the gasoline was of lower quality or not, Moore's Lexi-gasifier was a good idea that aided in fuel combustion. Also new that year was a change in the service brakes. They used external contracting shoes on sixteen inch rear wheel drums, and the brake rods were replaced with Cable-Brake, which was advertised to "grip both wheels equally for a skid-less stop."[3] Both series of cars used Continental engines and rode on 122 inch wheelbases, but the new Series S was considerably lighter in weight and with a 4.66 gear ratio in the differential, it was a spirited performer.

The 1920 model run was to be the banner year for Lexington as they capitalized on a booming economy in the latter part of 1919 and the first part of 1920. Wartime restrictions had been lifted, freeing manufacturers to use whatever materials they chose and produce vehicles in unrestricted quantity. Enough factory space had been added over the past few years to give room for increased production. Servicemen had returned home, making help more plentiful, and people seemed eager to buy. By March, storage space for newly finished automobiles was needed so badly that the vacant Moorish Tile Company facility in East Connersville was leased for vehicle storage until railroad cars became available for shipping, or until roads were in good enough condition to drive the cars to distributors.[4] Lexington

Top: **Preferred Stock certificate for the United States Automotive Corporation.** *Bottom:* **Common Stock certificate for the United States Automotive Corporation.**

sales for the year were 6,128, nearly double the automobile production of the previous year.[5]

Oftentimes customers would travel to Connersville by train, pick up their new car at the factory, and drive it home. One such purchaser in 1920 was Howard Engleka, who arrived from Berlin, Pennsylvania, got his Minute Man Six, and then drove to North Dakota where he had a homestead. In the fall, he drove back to Berlin where he raised goats and calves. The Lexington made trips back and forth for several years before being retired to a shed at Howard's home in Pennsylvania. After he had kept his prize for nearly sixty years, the relic was sold to R. Donald Williams, also of Berlin.[6] Whether or not this car is still in existence is not known at the present time.

When summer arrived, Lexington hosted the second annual Play Day celebration July 3–5, billed as Camp Lexington, with over 250 guests, most of whom were dealers or distributors for Lexington. The celebration was again held at Roberts Park in the north end of Connersville. The 1920 gathering was largely geared toward company business, although there were also activities to involve the entire community. A variety of entertainment included home made movies and various stunts. An afternoon baseball game between the Lexington Minute Men and the Indiana Lamp Company provided excitement. Evening entertainment featured musicians and vocalists from Chicago, and the Davis Brothers' dance tent was moved from downtown to the park so that "those who trip the light fantastic toe, can trip to their heart's content." At nighttime, a powerful searchlight mounted in a tree gave light in the park and also attracted outsiders to join the excitement. Then, of course, there was business for the dealer representatives with a tour of the Lexington factory where 27 new dynamometers had recently been installed.[7] The tour included Ansted Engineering, which was just beginning production of its new overhead valve engine, the Central Manufacturing Company where bodies were built, and other buildings in the USAC complex. During the dinner hour, guests of the company were entertained by Miss West, a talented singer, and Miss Ingersol, a dancer, both from Chicago. Later, the camp newspaper, *The Camp Chigger*, noted that during the "Egyptian Shimmy," Miss Rice was heard to remark, "Miss Ingersol is well named. I love to watch her movement." The real highlight for the distributors, however, was the unveiling of the Lexington Series T that was powered by the new Ansted engine. It would be considered a 1921 model. The gathering theme was a make believe military camp for the Lexington Minute Men, complete with Chet Beaumont, the bugler. Accommodations were on the spartan side for the dealer guests as there were 65 small tents pitched in the big enclosure just above the race track with cots for a not so soft slumber.[8] Since July 4 fell on a Sunday, Independence Day was to be celebrated on the following day. Everyone in the community was invited and welcomed to the Monday afternoon and evening programs. It was estimated that 20,000 people turned out to watch a hot-air balloon ascension and fireworks and to devour refreshments, all provided with compliments of the community's leading industry.[9]

The Series T was an entirely new automobile. It had a longer wheelbase of 128 inches and used the newly developed six cylinder overhead valve Ansted engine. This engine was an example of new technology in mechanical design, as it was a smaller unit that produced more power, developing 70 horsepower with a 224 cubic inch displacement. One comparison might be made with the prestigious Cadillac V-8. That well respected engine with 314 c.i.d. also developed 70 horsepower, but the new Ansted did it with 90 fewer cubic inches. One unusual feature of this engine was that the spark plugs were located in the engine block instead of in the head. Although the valves were in the head, the combustion chambers were in the block. The valves were large, being 1¾ inches in diameter with 7/16 inch of lift, and used a "rocking chair" rocker arm to obtain a higher lift with less noise. An especially

The 2-Way Headlamps were developed by Sam Arbuckle for the Indiana Lamp Company and were standard equipment on Lexingtons beginning in 1920. The Saturday Evening Post, *July 10, 1920.*

effective lubricating system forced oil through the heavy, stiff, hollow crankshaft and rod, and the main bearings had no groove and were practically shimless. The oil capacity was eight quarts with a bayonet gauge on the left side of the engine showing the oil level. Engine revolutions could run from 200 to 3,200 per minute, giving a high gear speed range of less than 6 to more than 60 miles per hour. A Rayfield carburetor provided the fuel mixture and a Gray and Davis starter cranked the engine. The three-speed transmission came from Warner Gear and a dry multi-disk clutch acted to separate the engine and transmission so gears could be shifted. The clutch consisted of five steel driving discs and six steel driven discs. The driving discs turned with the flywheel, whereas the driven discs turned with the transmission shaft. There were also ten molded asbestos fabric discs that floated alternately between the metal discs inside the clutch drum. Universal joints were non-metallic heavy leather pads bolted together and the rear axle was the traditional full-floating type.[10]

In July, it was announced that Frank Ansted had gained controlling interest in, and been named president of, a Newark, New Jersey, company that manufactured radiators. The company, which became the Ansted Radiator Company, was already well known for building radiators for race cars, including the Duesenbergs that had raced at the Indianapolis Motor Speedway and automobiles that had won first, second and third place at the Uniontown, PA, speedway.[11] Ansted also announced the purchase of the two story building at 10th and Eastern Avenue in Connersville that was to become a service center for repairing and refurbishing Lexingtons. Mechanical work was to be done on the bottom floor; the second floor had a trim shop for upholstering and top repair or replacement, and in back of the trim shop was a paint oven to aid in refinishing work.[12] Lexington owners could bring their cars in for a partial or complete renewal if they so chose.

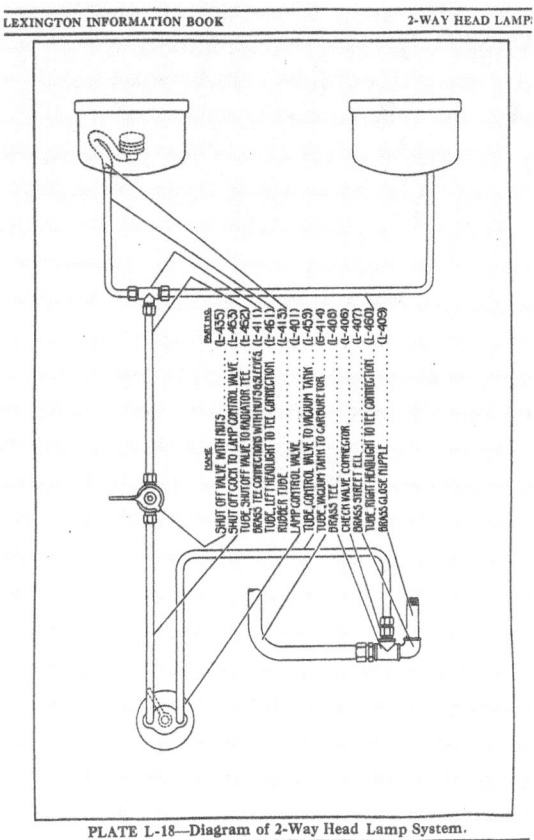

PLATE L-18—Diagram of 2-Way Head Lamp System.

The 2-Way Head Lamp System was far more complicated than headlights with a high-beam and a low-beam light bulb.

Lexingtons with the new Ansted engines began to show successes in various competitions in the latter part of 1920. On September 15, a Minute Man Six was one of twelve cars in an economy run held at the Virginia State Fair grounds at Norfolk. The Lexington placed first with 24½ miles per gallon, the highest figure of any of the cars entered. This achievement came right on the heels of the first and second place victories at Pikes Peak in early September, topping off a year when everything seemed to be going Ansted's way.

The economy in 1919 had seemed unstoppable, and 1920 had started off with much optimism. Lexington had seen substantial growth in sales and income, both from car sales and from parts and materials, during the past five years. Income from car sales had increased from $741,405 in 1916 to $9,969,108 for the year ending July 1, 1920. Sales of automobile repair parts and other items including war materials had increased similarly, from $963,771 in 1916 to $10,674,728 for the year ending August 31, 1920.[13]

Beginning in late spring 1920, however, manufacturers experienced a sharp slowdown. Some observers thought the auto industry was taking the brunt of rumors and speculations about a recession. One of the most often repeated rumors was that the steel companies were planning to supply the railroads plentiful quantities of finished steel products at the expense of the automobile industry. Another rumor was that many states were slacking in their plans to improve roads in response to railroad lobbies. Two specific events were that the Federal Reserve Bank of Kansas City refused to rediscount passenger car "paper" offered it by member banks, thus making it more difficult to obtain financing to buy automobiles, and labor strikes by steel, coal and railroad workers were causing uncertainty in automobile production, pricing and delivery throughout the country.[14] Manufacturers didn't know whether coal supplies would be maintained for heat and power, whether they would be able to get materials and parts, and if so, at what price, and would rail cars be available to deliver finished products. Lexington had, at times, experienced difficulties obtaining sufficient supplies of Continental engines for their cars, thus prompting them to develop their own Ansted engine that went on the market in July 1920. Other parts were generally available without delay because of the proximity of other supplying factories that were also located in Connersville.

The Sedanette

The Thorobred

The Touring Car

Top: **The 1920 Sedanette.** *Middle:* **The 1920 Coupe.** *Bottom:* **The 1920 Touring Car.**

Manufacturers had felt inflationary pressures since the United States had entered the war. By mid–1920, because of uncertainties, some were cutting back production while others were even cutting prices. However, in August, Willys-Overland

Opposite, top: **Large cities provided a substantial market for Lexington automobiles. This dealership was at 1850 Broadway, New York City.** *Bottom:* **A dealership at 2234 S. Wabash Ave., Chicago.**

6—*A New Corporation and Continued Expansion* 155

The Lexington Thorobred—a hill-eating, speedy, sport model for four passengers!

You Want a Car That Will Climb Hills—Here it is

The Moore Multiple Exhaust System and the Lexi-gasifier; the former increases Lexington's power more than 20 per cent by providing double-quick exit for burnt gases from the motor; the latter is the most effective device yet invented for vaporizing inferior gasoline before it enters the cylinders. (Cut A)

Showing the mechanism of the one-finger emergency brake: a band around the "propeller shaft" of the Lexington by which the driver can bring the car to an instant standstill, in an emergency, merely by a slight pressure of one finger on the brake lever. Women like this exclusive feature. (Cut B)

An example of Lexington refinement—vacuum-controlled 2-Way headlights which can be tipped up and down by turning a button on the dash. Lexington drivers can be courteous by lowering their lights and still take no risk, for the light is then bountiful where it is really needed. (Cut C)

Here are Lexington's springs—embodying entirely new principles. Above is the rear spring, with the exceptional length of 52 inches; below is the front spring, only 32 inches long. This combination hinges the front of the car around the front axle—and gives perfect riding ease. (Cut D)

Discs of especially prepared fabric, bolted together in such a way as to be very strong but very flexible, takes the place of the old-style, stiffer, troublesome metal universal joint. This method prevents transmission of road shocks from rear wheels to motor, and adds considerably to Lexington comfort. (Cut E)

For foot-breaking, Lexington has done away with the long, rattling rods running to the rear of the car and is using a powerful light steel cable to each wheel. How much more simple and sensible! The cable passes over a pulley which gives an absolutely equal pull on each rear wheel. (Cut F)

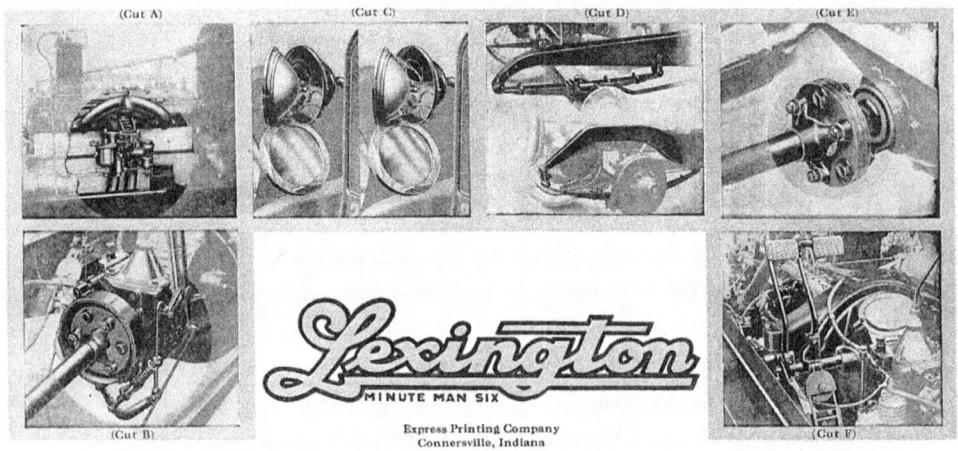

The 1920 Thorobred offered many desirable features.

and Reo made price increases from $50 to $100 per car. The next month, Frank Ansted took the bold step of increasing prices for the second time that year. The September 27 edition of the *News Examiner* boasted that Mr. Ansted had said that "at a time when there is talk of price reductions, and when those who see the surface only of economic conditions have been wondering, he has determined that a

The Lex-Sedan allowed for summer breezes or closed car comfort in winter. All of the side windows were identical in size and, therefore, were interchangeable. The Saturday Evening Post, August 7, 1920.

good article, worth more than it is being sold for, should be marked up, and he has done it."[15] With the recent publicity of the Pikes Peak victories and the company experiencing the best sales year in its history, it just seemed like the opportune time to reap the reward. The following day the newspaper carried another article supporting the price increase, stating that Mr. Ansted had received "congratulatory letters and telegrams from near and far" with a most significant one coming from William C. Durant, who was, at the time, president of General Motors Corporation.[16]

Frank Ansted made a serious miscalculation with this price increase, as had some other people in high profile positions. Durant himself also misjudged the severity of the economic slowdown and paid a heavy price. Durant had founded General Motors in 1908 when he was just 47 years old, but had been ousted as president a short two years later because he nearly drove the company bankrupt by overspending. He gained control of the presidency again in 1916 but now was ousted a second time during the panic of 1920-21, soon after he sent the congratulatory telegram to Frank Ansted. Durant continued his spending spree, gambling on questionable business ventures when the economic climate called for restraint. After being ousted from GM the second time, Durant founded his own company to market the Durant, Star, Flint, Princeton and other automobiles. For much of the automotive industry, a year that started on such a positive note ended with most factories running at far less than full capacity.

Henry Ford, on the other hand, chose to fight the slowdown with substantial price reductions of $105–$180 on his Ford Model T, making it possible to purchase a new Runabout for $395. This action not only astonished other Ford executives, but brought a hostile response from some other automobile manufacturers including Dodge Brothers, Maxwell-Chalmers, Hupp, Essex, Page and General Motors. Ford was also able to keep his factories working by forcing his dealers to accept cars they hadn't ordered while requiring cash payment upon delivery.[17]

A January 1921 article about the Lexington factory in *The Indianapolis Star* stated the plant was producing at 50 percent of capacity and employing 70 percent of its normal working force. Increased production was expected as soon as the demand for their product could justify it.[18]

The newly introduced overhead valve Ansted engine would continue to be successful in competition in 1921. On March 28, Otto Loesche drove a stock Lexington carrying four passengers up Gates Mill Hill, a steep and challenging incline near Cleveland, Ohio, that was more than one mile in length, passing a challenger along the way.[19] On May 4, a Lexington carrying seven passengers whose weight totaled 1,280 pounds climbed Eagle Rock Hill, New Jersey. This hill was 1.4 miles long and had a grade of 6–12 percent, with the steepest incline and a sharp turn near the summit. The Series T climbed the hill from a standing start in high gear. On May 9, in an economy contest in Philadelphia, a Minute Man Six ran 25.6 miles on a measured gallon of gasoline. On Fort George Hill in Manhattan, a Lexington pulled the hill from a standing start, in high gear, carrying five passengers and reaching the top at 25 miles an hour. In two separate runs up Snake Hill in Brooklyn, the Minute Man Six started in high gear carrying five passengers. On one run it reached the top at 60 miles per hour; on the other run, the driver held its speed to less than three miles per hour in high gear all the way to the top. On Miller Avenue Hill in Brooklyn, an Ansted powered Lexington made a high gear start and reached the top at 41½ miles per hour; the same car then ran 23½ miles on one gallon of gasoline, then reached 77 miles an hour running on Motor Parkway on Long Island.[20]

In September, at the Pikes Peak Hill Climb, Lexington was the winner in its class. On October 7, the newly introduced Lexington Lark outran the Dixie Flyer, which was considered to be the fastest train in the South. On a run between Atlanta,

Automotive Industries magazine gave an impressive write-up on production techniques at the Ansted Engineering Company in the Jan. 13, 1921, issue. 1—A cylinder block in the rough casting inspection jig. When the cylinders are received they are given a quick going over at the finish points with white cold water paint. This inspection jig in a very few minutes will go over each casting thoroughly and scribe the finish line of each important finished surface. This tells conclusively whether the cylinder block will machine. 2—The rough casting inspection jig without any casting in it, giving a good idea of its construction. 3—The first machine operation on the cylinder block. On the rough casting inspection jig and on the fixture for the first machine operation the location is from the cored holes of the cylinder barrels. This is contrary to usual practice and might be regarded as unnecessary, but is done to secure uniform cylinder walls and the balance of the machining on the cylinder block is brought to the barrels so there is no question of squareness on the entire job. This operation mills off the locating bosses on the side of the cylinder block. 4—In addition to the locating bosses there must be other locating points to fix the cylinder block for drilling and boring operations. This locating is done by means of two ½-in. reamed holes in the bottom of the cylinder block. These holes are show in this print. The operation of drilling them is done by a standard machine and fixture. 5—Milling top and bottom faces on a Davis rapid miller with a rotating table capable of carrying four blocks at a time. 6—End milling a block on a David rapid milling machine capable of handling 240 blocks a day because of its continuously rotating table carrying nine blocks.

Georgia, and Jacksonville, Florida, the Lark ran 374 miles and arrived in Jacksonville 90 minutes ahead of the Dixie Flyer. The distance covered by the Lexington, 374 miles, was 30 miles farther than the rail route and included terrible detours. The economical Ansted engine used just 23 gallons of gasoline, averaging nearly eighteen miles per gallon. Finally, on November 12, on Ensenada Beach, Mexico, a stock Lexington chassis with the Ansted engine ran a measured mile in 40.2 seconds for an average speed of 89.55 miles per hour.[21]

As each new year began, one prime thought on the minds of automobile industrialists was displaying their models prominently in the automobile shows. January 1921 was satisfying for the Lexington people, because, at the New York Automobile Show, Lexington's display was on the first floor just as one entered the main entrance of the Grand Central Palace. Only the manufacturers who had been top sellers the previous year were awarded first floor display spaces. On display were five models with their interiors specially done for the show. Artists Clarence Underwood, Alfred Leyendecker, Coles Phillips, and McNein had been asked to select a shade of material for the upholstery and supervise its completion. Each artist then placed his card on the car he had done, so his work could be identified. Reports were that thousands, especially women, were impressed, as a well-known Chautauqua lecturer, Joseph Severance, explained to the crowds the features of this Hoosier product.[22]

More national exposure of a positive nature came that same month with a feature article in the January 13 issue of *Automotive Industries* magazine. The article outlined the sequence of operations in the manufacture of the Ansted engine that was used in the Lexington. The article had numerous pictures of machinery used and spoke highly of the process.[23]

Just over a month later, on March 4, Lexington opened a magnificent new half million dollar, four story sales and service building in the heart of automobile row at 1142 North Meridian Street in Indianapolis. The building was built by the Hoosier Construction Company of Connersville, with J. Earl Faught as the superintendent of construction. A large delegation of company men from Connersville attended the opening. Special attractions were a life-size "Minute-Man" statue displayed on the mezzanine above the showroom and a large painting of the Pikes Peak race, both done by E. Pierre Wainwright, art director of the United States Automotive Corporation.[24] A sales promotion billed as "Thorobred Week" took place April 25–30. Every Lexington dealer in the United States and in foreign trade centers was encouraged to make special efforts to attract new customers.[25] The theme of this special promotion reflected the fine race horse tradition from the original Kentucky factory location. The new facility in Indianapolis participated in Thorobred Week by sponsoring a novel parade through the downtown streets. The parade was headed by the Indianapolis Military Band, followed by the new Lexington Thorobred with several fine horses from the Blue Ribbon Stables at the State Fair Grounds. At the new showroom, several stalls had been built to display thoroughbred horses alongside Thorobred and Minute Man Six automobiles.[26]

In early April, the United States Automotive Corporation purchased from Standard Parts Company of Cleveland the Spring and Axle Works of Connersville. This company was founded by E. W. Ansted in the 1890s to make springs and axles for horse-drawn vehicles, but had been changed over to serving the automobile industry with similar products. The Spring and Axle Works had been sold to the Cleve-

Thorobred Week was a sales promotion event sponsored by Lexington. Parades and unusual dealer displays were intended to attract customers. The Saturday Evening Post, *April 23, 1921.*

land company in 1916 shortly before E. W. Ansted's death. The facility was used for a time, but had been closed for four months before being purchased by the U.S.A.C.[27]

In July, the Fayette Paint and Trim Company was set up in the old Indiana Furniture Plant at South First and Eastern to paint and trim the new Lexingtons as they rolled out of the assembly plant on Eighteenth Street.

That same month, Ansted Engineering Company had announced that it was moving the manufacturing of small engine parts from the Teetor-Hartley plant in Hagerstown, Indiana, to Connersville. This would require additional employees and supposedly would enable increased production of the new engine. A very different version of that story was told at Hagerstown, where it was claimed that the factory building was being repossessed by the Indiana Piston Ring Company, formerly Teetor-Hartley. Frank and George Ansted had bought the engine plant in 1918 for $500,000 with $50,000 paid at the time and the remainder to be paid over the next three years. The Hagerstown company reported receiving only one other payment for $25,000 in the allotted period and therefore intended to take the building back, thus forcing the move.[28] The effort at repossession may have run into a snag, because two years later, the receiver for Ansted Engineering Company was given permission from Judge Himelick of the Fayette Circuit Court to remove certain machines and tools from the Hagerstown plant and install them at Connersville,[29] and in September of 1925, that same court gave Ansted Engineering permission to sell the Hagerstown plant. It was purchased by none other than the Indiana Piston Ring Company of Hagerstown, Indiana.[30]

Rumors had been circulating for some time that the Ansted Engineering was expecting a very large order for their new engine from a company outside of Connersville. These rumors were fueled even more when William C. Durant, who had started his own company after being ousted from General Motors, visited Connersville. It was learned that he planned to use the Ansted engine in his six cylinder Durant and Princeton automobiles, and in December, an announcement confirmed that Durant had placed an order for 30,000 Ansted overhead valve engines to be delivered over the next three years to his Durant factory at Muncie, Indiana. The work force, which amounted to approximately 300 at the time, was expected to be nearly doubled in order to meet the expected need. Durant also placed orders for springs with the Ansted Spring and Axle Works and for bodies with Central Manufacturing Company.[31]

Storm clouds were starting to gather as a patent infringement suit was filed in October by Alanson Brush, who several years earlier had built and sold the popular Brush cars. Brush alleged that the Ansted engine used in certain models of Lexington and Durant automobiles infringed on a number of his patents. Brush asked that the Lexington Company be made to account for the number of engines already sold and be restrained from further use and sale of cars equipped with the overhead valve engine. The law firm handling Brush's complaint was Williams, Bradbury, McCaleb & Pierce, who had just successfully completed a patent infringement suit against Stewart Warner.[32] The negative publicity hurt Lexington's credibility at a time when the company was already being challenged by a sharp recession.

The lineup for 1921 continued the Series S, offering the five-passenger Thorobred, five-passenger touring, five-passenger Lex-Sedan, four-passenger Coupe and five-passenger Sedan. One novel feature of the Lex-Sedan was a leatherette outside

Snead non-metallic universal joints were heavy leather pads that were bolted together. Automobile Industries, *April 21, 1921.*

sun shade over the windshield that could protect the driver from the bright rays of the sun, or when rolled up, a glass rain-visor was turned out.[33] The Series S continued to use the Continental engine with 3¼ inch by 4½ inch bore and stroke that developed 50 horsepower. The wheelbase remained at 122 inches and styling was unchanged. The new Series T offered the seven-passenger Touring, four-passenger

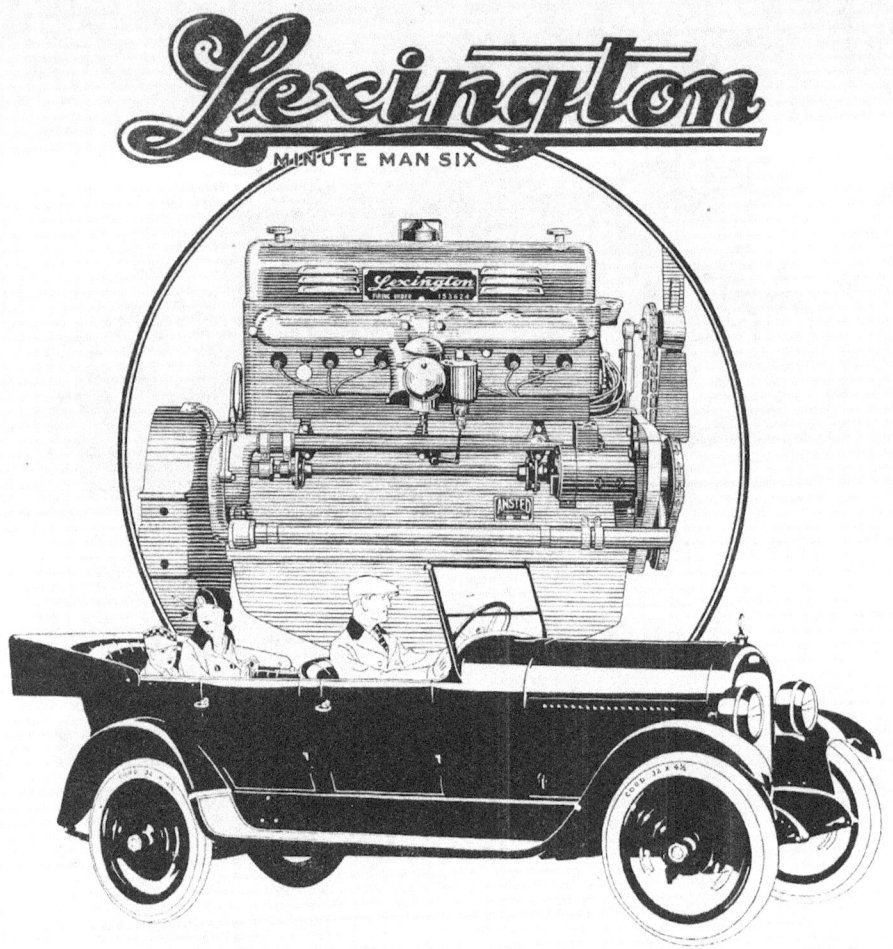

Cars with the Ansted engine won many performance contests during the early twenties. The highly advanced powerplant developed 70 horsepower with just 224 c.i.d. The Saturday Evening Post, May 21, 1921.

Seven-passenger Salon Sedan

CLOSED CARS ARE THE ultimate in motor transportation. This is particularly true of the Salon Sedan—the master motor car of the entire Lexington line. Price is at most a secondary consideration in purchasing equipage of this character. It must be so, for coach craftsmen are essentially artists, and artists must not be hampered by limitations of costs. However, the Lexington Salon Sedan is not extravagantly expensive—always remembering that you are buying something more than pounds of metal. It is a possession in which you will feel that pride of ownership which is rarely experienced.

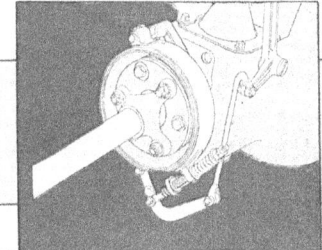

A one-finger emergency brake is appreciated by the ladies who drive—always perfectly equalized, always extremely powerful

The SEVENTY-SIX Car

The Seventy-Six was introduced on Christmas Day in 1920. It is doubtful that many dealers were swamped with customers on announcement day. This model pioneered drum type headlights that became quite popular in the 1920s.

Sedanette and the seven-passenger Salon Sedan. It used the new Ansted overhead valve engine which had a 3¼ inch by 4½ inch bore and stroke, developing 70 horsepower. The engine was about the same displacement as the Continental but pumped out considerably more power. This car rode on a 128 inch wheelbase. Wheels were artillery type (wood spoke) with wire or disk wheels as options. Late in 1920 and

The beautiful home once owned by Lexington president Frank Ansted is located at 1603 Virginia Ave. The 1921 Series Seventy-Six 7-passenger Salon Sedan is owned by the author. *Courtesy Alan Stanley.*

into 1921 new models were introduced in rapid succession. The "Revolutionary car" was introduced in the fall and was touted in company literature as a "new and novel experience in transportation." However, the specifications matched those of the recently introduced Series T including the 128 inch wheelbase, the Moore Multiple exhaust, the Lexi-gasifier and vacuum-controlled headlights. On Christmas Day, the new "Seventy Six" model rolled out of dealers' showrooms. It was also a Series T, but had the new drum type headlights, a feature that would become quite popular with other makes for the next few years. It was offered in a seven-passenger Touring, four-passenger Sedanette or seven-passenger Salon Sedan. The Seventy Six designation fit nicely with the Revolutionary Car and the Minute Man theme, but, in this case, it was translated to mean 70 horsepower with six cylinders.[34] Lexington became something of a style leader with their new headlights, and they were one of the earlier companies to offer disk or wire wheels as options, items that would also become popular industrywide.

A new limited production model, the Ansted-Lexington Roadster, came on the scene in April. This car was described as a custom-built two-passenger sport model. It had its own Ansted emblem on the radiator and hubs and was priced at $4,500. The Series T 128 inch wheelbase chassis with Ansted engine provided the foundation. The body was hand-hammered aluminum over a framework of seasoned ash with the interior finish of natural wood and wicker including a walnut dash and inlaid hardwood parquet floors. Contrary to the newest styling fad, its headlights were a teardrop design set lower between the front fenders with mounting brackets fastened to the frame instead of to the radiator as on other Lexingtons. The

This was the assembly line at the Lexington plant during the 1921 model year. *Courtesy* Connersville News-Examiner.

Ansted radiator shell was high, narrow and rounded, a cathedral type design somewhat similar to the Kissel, adding to the car's sporty appearance.[35]

Another model introduced mid-year was the Lark, a sporty four-passenger touring. It rode on the shorter 122 inch wheelbase but used the Ansted engine, giving it a more favorable power to weight ratio for snappy performance. It also had the new drum type headlights and matching smaller cowl lights. Adding to the sporting flair were six wire wheels as standard equipment. One spare wheel was carried on each running board at the side of the hood and was held in place by brackets fastened to the side of the frame, a popular feature later known as side-mounts. The Lark came in a choice of colors, Submarine Blue, Canyon Red, Pikes Peak Gray, Old-wine Maroon, Polo Brown or Canary Yellow, with upholstery to harmonize.[36]

By the year's end, Lexington had seen a drop in sales to 4,236 cars despite a price rollback in June from $100 to $600.[37] Other companies had similar sales setbacks during the year, but, for this small Eastern Indiana company, major expenditures had been incurred at a time when the economy was most unfriendly to the automobile industry.

As the year 1922 got under way, the economic panic was fading and a majority of motorcar manufacturers were bouncing back to increased production with a more optimistic outlook. Industrywide, January saw a 15.6 percent gain in automobile production over December of 1921.[38] The automobile shows attracted their

The Ansted Lexington had a hand hammered aluminum body with inlaid hardwood flooring. The radiator was tapered toward the top much like that of the Kissel.

The Ansted Lexington was a limited production custom-built sports roadster that listed for $4,500.

The "Trail Blazer" picture was created by E. Pierre Wainwright, art director for the U.S.A.C. Wainwright was from a prominent Connersville industrial family, but he preferred artistic work to machine trades. This theme is somewhat reminiscent of Jordan's popular "Somewhere West of Laramie" ads. *Courtesy Suzanne Wainwright Evans.*

usual onlookers with glitzy displays of the latest innovations and improvements. Lexington again had a preferred first floor space for the New York Automobile Show that was held, as usual, in Grand Central Palace, beginning January 7. It was reported that 92 different makes of automobiles were on display at this show. Lexington could take some comfort in knowing that, even though they had experienced difficulties with sales, they had again ranked well enough with the previous year's production to receive the preferred first floor location. Frank Ansted and his staff of executives stayed at the Biltmore Hotel, no doubt enjoying a week in the Big Apple.[39]

The Lark that was introduced in July 1921 proved to be a popular sporty model. Its Ansted engine along with a performance geared differential ratio of 5.1 offered plenty of excitement.[40] It had proved itself when it beat the Dixie Flyer train on its run between Atlanta, Georgia, and Jacksonville, Florida. The Thorobred also continued into 1922, riding on the same platform as the Lark but carrying plainer trim.[41] The Series T was still the flagship, riding on its 128 inch wheelbase, and was offered in a touring listing at $2,285 or the sedan at $3,350.[42]

The new Series U made its debut at the New York Automobile Show with the "U" referring to "Ultimate." It rode on a 122 inch wheelbase and was offered in a five-passenger touring with a selling price of $1,985, coming well-equipped including front and rear bumpers.[43] The shorter wheelbase models received the benefits

The Lark was introduced in mid–1921 as a car with sporty looks and snappy performance. Studebaker revived the Lark name for its popular compact cars in 1959. The Saturday Evening Post, *June 25, 1921.*

of a newly reworked frame with a combination front cross member and front motor support. Also, a 30-inch wide double triangular center cross-member was added and the rear frame section that carried spring shackles was made deeper and the rear cross-member became a protective shield for the gas tank. All of these improvements helped to strengthen the frame and prevent twisting.[44] The running boards,

In a race between the Lexington Lark and the Dixie Flier train, the Lark won with time to spare. *Courtesy Suzanne Wainwright Evans.*

which were an integral part of the frame system, were also changed slightly. They could now be unbolted and removed for repair or replacement if damaged. This was the first major change in the frame since 1917 as chief engineer John C. Moore kept working to improve problem areas. Both front and rear springs were lengthened, the front to 38 inches and the rear to 59 inches, to improve riding qualities. They were equipped with tightly laced boots to keep out water and preserve lubrication. To make the battery more accessible, it was moved from under the front seat to under the front floorboard. The 2-Way vacuum headlamp control was moved to the steering column and was activated by turning the horn button.[45]

All models used the 224 cubic inch displacement Ansted Model B engine, which had received several refinements. A new type two-ring piston that was to increase ring life and a thermostat controlling the water temperature at 140 degrees were important improvements. On the right hand side of the engine, the water pump had been moved forward and became belt- driven with an automatic belt-tightener, eliminating the shaft drive. The starter had been moved from the left to the right side of the engine and was attached to the bell housing. On the left side of the engine, the push-rods were completely enclosed but had removable plates, or windows, that permitted inspection and adjustment. The generator was also moved forward to be belt- driven for more efficient operation. Another improvement was an easier adjustment for the rear wheel brakes provided by an automatic locking turnbuckle adjustment located at the pedal.[46] Style-wise, Lexington continued to use drum type headlights as much of the industry followed suit.[47]

In April of 1922, the new Supreme was introduced using the Series T running gear with front and rear bumpers as standard equipment. Parking lights mounted

Lexington Leads Because It Lasts!

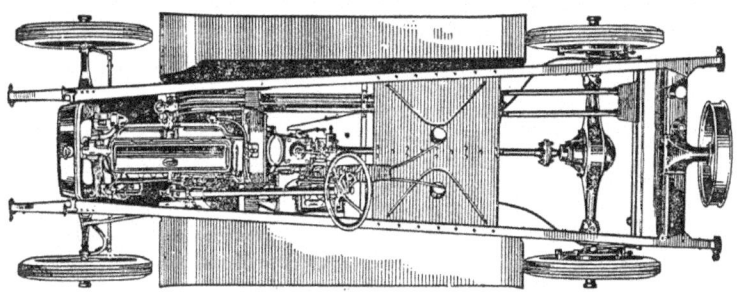

There Is No Other Car Built Like the New "U" Model Lexington. Something Entirely New

See Our Display at Our Sales Room—Its First Appearance in Indianapolis

There is only one safe way to buy a car in 1922—

Look beyond its beauty and ask this question—

"How well preserved will its chassis be in 1927 and later?" Also—"How well will it maintain its efficiency? How low will the upkeep be every hour and mile of those years?"

The new Series "U" Lexington meets those requirements in excess of previous standards—it establishes new standards!

It reflects everything which Lexington and its allied groups of factories have been trying to accomplish for years.

And this strictly high-grade car could not have originated in any other way except from our "factory-community" system that controls the source of supply and quality of workmanship.

See the new series "U" at our salesroom.

It has the famous Ansted Engine, amply proven to be the world's leading six-cylinder motor. It has many exclusive improvements. See this new car.

Series 'U'

$1985

MINUTE MAN SIX

LEXINGTON MOTOR SALES, 1142 Meridian St., North, Indianapolis, Ind.

The Series U was intended to mean "ultimate." It boasted a stronger frame and rode on a 122 inch wheelbase.

on the cowl matched the drum shaped headlights. Wood spoke wheels came standard, but wire or disk were available as options. The seven-passenger touring was priced at $2,285; also available was a seven-passenger sedan. Other than the longer stance, it had practically identical features to the Series U.[48]

Another spring introduction was the Series 22 with a five-passenger touring on a 123 inch wheelbase, listing for $1,745.[49] Specifications for this car were the same as the Series U except for a lower price and a one inch longer wheelbase. Advertising proclaimed the price was $240 less than any previous Lexington equipped with the Ansted engine and the Moore Multiple Exhaust.

It was probably a long, cold 1921-22 winter for most Lexington employees. The March 30, 1922, *Connersville News Examiner*, in a story headlined "Lexington Swings into Production," stated that activities in the final assembly department would resume on March 31, after a temporary halt in production. It was also stated that by the middle of the following week more men might be called back to work. Another article noted that "the factory has worked from hand to mouth for some weeks."[50] This almost certainly indicates a cash flow problem as business remained weak. The economy had not picked up at Lexington as it had at most other motorcar plants. Then, on March 29, just as work was resuming, a fire broke out and threatened heavy damage to the assembly department. Gasoline and oil in the pit beneath the motor testing block in the assembly room erupted into major flames about 11:15 p.m. and both divisions of the Connersville fire department worked more than an hour putting it out.[51]

Still, there was optimism as 21 investment bankers, plus W. R. Willet, general manager of the Durant plant in Muncie, toured the United States Automotive Corporation plants in Connersville on March 25. Predictions of increased production were given by Willet and by Charles C. Hanch, executive vice-president of the Lexington plant. Hanch brought some added prestige to his position as he was also a vice-president of the National Automobile Chamber of Commerce and was actively involved with that group trying to encourage standardization of many parts used in the manufacture of automobiles.[52] Hosting the delegation of bankers was good for publicity and public relations, but the hope of increased cash through bank loans did not materialize.

Ansted Engineering was running good production figures building the 70 horsepower overhead valve engines. One great testimony to this engine's capabilities came on March 31 when Tommy Milton set a new track record at the Los Angeles Speedway in a Durant Six. The car, with its Connersville made Ansted engine and with Milton at the wheel, took the second preliminary 25 mile sprint in 13 minutes 1.49 seconds for an average speed of 115.02 miles per hour and the final 50 mile event in 26 minutes 1.02 seconds for an even faster 115.2 miles per hour.[53] Many of these engines were shipped to Muncie, Indiana, for the new Durant Six model B22. The Durant car was built in the factory formerly owned by General Motors where the Sheridan automobile had been produced. Although it had a number of good features, sales for the six cylinder Durant did not meet expectations. Possibly its $1,650 price was too close to the cost of the much better known makes such as Buick, Hudson and Studebaker. Even the magic of the Durant name could not translate into major sales for his fine mid-price automobile. It was competing in a field saturated with quality products reeling from an economy that had not fully recovered. In July, Billy Durant did pay another visit to the Connersville indus-

A substantial price cut finally came with the Series 22, introduced in mid–1922. It would prove to be too little too late.

tries to place orders for bodies from Central Manufacturing and springs from the Spring and Axle Company.[54]

As warmer weather arrived, Lexington production picked up some, partly because of the reduced price of the newly introduced Series 22. There was evidence of foreign sales picking up also, as it was reported that a sales delegation was being

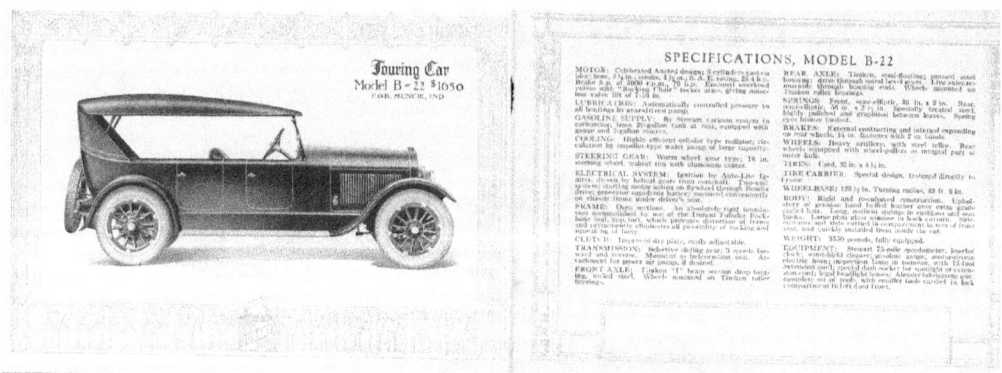

Durant literature for 1922 listed the celebrated Ansted engine as its power source.

sent to India after a manager in Calcutta had reported the Minute Man Six received favor whenever it was exhibited.⁵⁵ Closer to home and certainly more important in the export market, though, was Canada. On April 21 a shipment of 50 Lexington Supreme seven-passenger sedans left Connersville by the C.I. & W. Railroad bound for The Montreal Motor-Vehicle Company Ltd.⁵⁶ It was considered an order extraordinaire for this many high quality automobiles to be sent to one distributor.

An interesting event in Connersville occurred August 18, 1922, when a Minute Man monument was placed on a foundation of rocks in Lexington Park near the C.I. & W. Railroad depot on Eastern Avenue. This statue had a bronze gild and was cast by E. Pierre Wainwright, art director of the United States Automotive Corporation. Mr. Wainwright and Harry Griffin, a young architect, had laid out the plan for the park working with the improvement club.⁵⁷ Gaar Nurseries of Cambridge City had done the landscaping. Some years later the work of art disappeared in broad daylight as two men sawed the statue off at its ankles, loaded it into a small truck and left the scene.⁵⁸ No one seems to know what happened to the Minute Man or even what prompted their action, but one might assume they thought the bronze casting had salvage value. They must have been chagrined to find it made of plaster of Paris. On November 11, 2006, the park was rededicated as Veterans Memorial Park with a miniature Minute Man statue standing guard.

In spite of the glowing predictions of a soon to develop market, sales remained slow. Another blow to morale was the absence of Lexington entries in the Labor Day Pikes Peak Hill Climb. After placing first and second and winning the free-for-all in 1920 and their class in 1921, Lexington was absent from the event in 1922. Money was just not available to fund the race team on an extended trip. Sales were very disappointing. Not since 1914 had Lexington sold fewer cars in a year, as just 2,114 units left the Connersville plant in 1922.⁵⁹

With sales having taken a nose-dive from their level of just two years ago, various efforts were explored to raise money to pay bills and hopefully be prepared for increased production when the market allowed. On December 16, a special stockholders meeting was held and a certificate of amendment to the articles of incorporation of Lexington Motor Company was filed with the intent of increasing the capital stock from $3.7 million to $4.5 million. The document that explained the proposed increase was signed by company president Frank B. Ansted and sec-

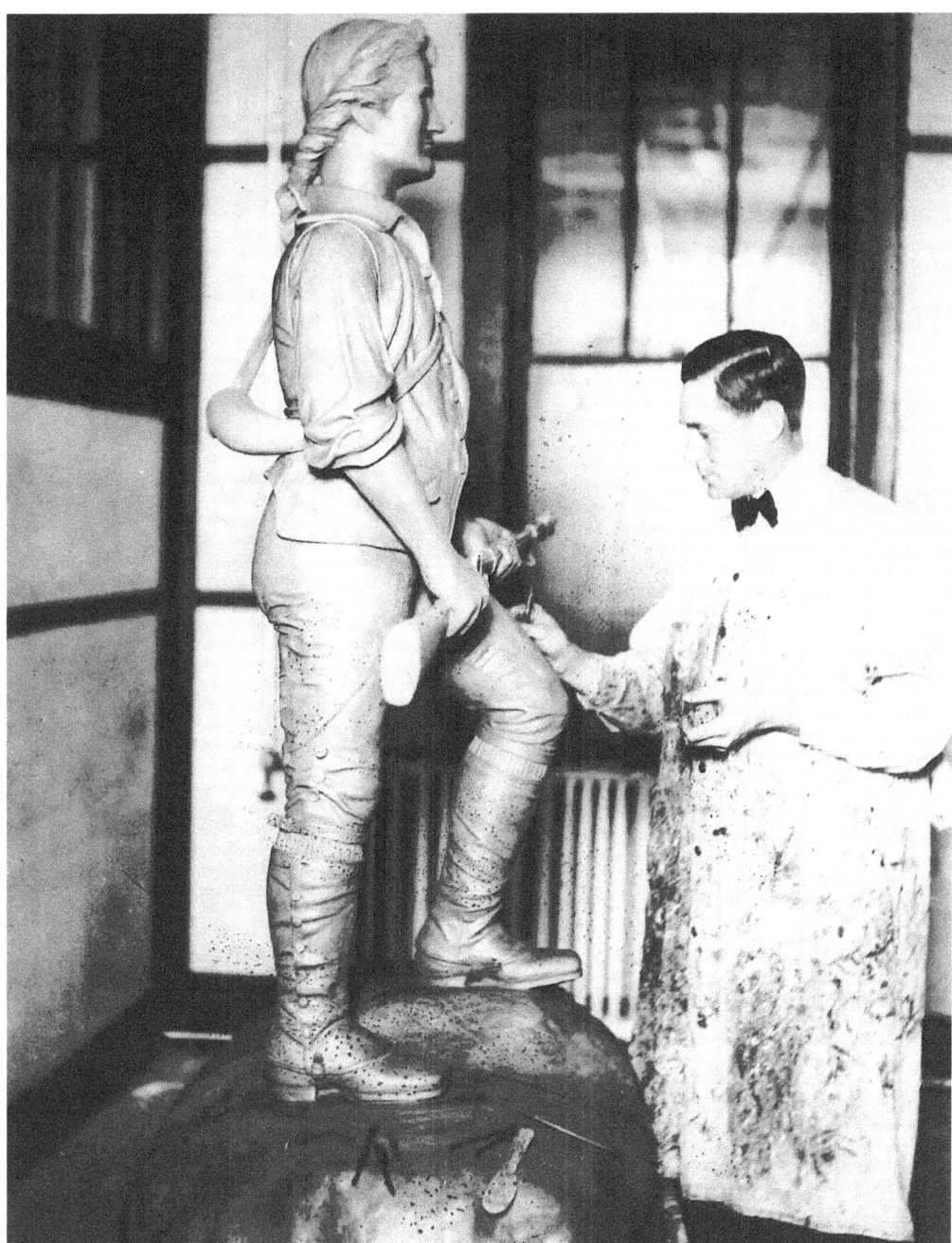

Sculptor E. Pierre Wainwright working on his Minute Man statue. *Courtesy Suzanne Wainwright Evans.*

retary Leroy A. Hanson.⁶⁰ There is no indication that any additional stock was sold or that this action generated any relief.

As the year 1922 was drawing to a close, cash flow became a more and more serious problem. Even the Ansted Engineering Company was running at slow speed after Durant had cut back on his order for engines. In April, Durant had made a loan of $369,000 to Lexington, but with a price for collateral that could have allowed a take-over of the corporation. This loan was a temporary bailout, but only temporary, because by year's end the Connersville company was seeking additional funds in order to stay open. They were borrowing from any source available, and in December they received $2,500 on a promissory note from a New York banking house. This loan was issued to the Continental Discount Corporation of Connersville, who signed it over to Lexington of New York, who in turn endorsed it over to the Lexington Motor Company of Connersville.[61] The local factory was unable to get any more loans through regular channels. The Continental Discount Corporation was made up of some of the same men who were involved with Lexington, but it was a completely separate company.

The year 1922 had been difficult for the automobile industry in general, and

This statue of the Minute Man was placed in Lexington Park in 1922, where it stood until mysteriously disappearing in the late 1930s. *Courtesy Fayette County Historical Museum.*

many names dropped off the list of manufacturers, including the Briggs & Stratton car, the Kenworthy, King, Meteor, Monroe, Oldfield, Piedmont, Regal, Saxon, Scripps-Booth and the Standard Eight to name just a few.[62] One company, Maxwell, on the verge of insolvency, was rescued by Walter P. Chrysler, who shortly after replaced that marque with an automobile bearing his own name. Another company, Lincoln, though just beginning production in 1920, was in receivership the next year and was sold at auction in February 1922 to Henry Ford. Ford saved the Lincoln name from going into oblivion. Lexington survived that terrible year, but was longing for better days.

7

Loss of Credit and Credibility

New Series 23 Lexingtons were announced July 19, 1922, in several new body styles: a new two-passenger Roadster for $1,695, a five-passenger Touring for $1,695, a seven-passenger Touring for 1,795, a five-passenger Lark Sport Model for $2,045, a five-passenger California Top for $1,995, a seven-passenger California Top for $2,095, a five-passenger Royal Coach for $2,145, a four-passenger Coupe for $2,345, a five-passenger Sedan with two taxi seats for $2,545 and a four-passenger brougham for $2,645.[1] In April of 1923, the Skylark Roadster was added to the line. It was a take-off of the regular roadster but promoted as "in a class all its own" and listed for $1,875.[2] All models rode on the 123 inch wheelbase with wire or disk wheels a $100 option except on the Lark, which had wire wheels as standard equipment. The California Top models replaced the Lex-Sedan featuring the fixed top with removable side windows for an open-air feel during warm weather.

Emphasis was placed on closed cars as sales for open cars had fallen off substantially. The four-passenger brougham was one example expected to attract sizeable sales. It looked trim on the outside, but had a spacious back seat with a high back and the two chairs in front gave Pullman-like ease. A rear trunk provided two removable suitcases for leisurely travel.[3] The introduction of the new models and substantially lower prices encouraged hopes of increased sales. Developing new models was possible for such a cash-strapped company because the bodies came either from their sister company, Central Manufacturing, also owned by the Ansted family, or the McFarlan Motor Company, also located in Connersville. Both companies were well known for producing quality products. Mechanically, the Series 23 was very much like the previous year's offering as all models were powered by the Ansted engine, which, with a few refinements, was now labeled the Model D. One improvement to assist with maintenance was an easy arrangement for oiling the clutch throw-out bearing using a tube that extended through the toe board.

In spite of its financial woes, it was reported that Lexington turned out 80 cars in January 1923, 80 in February, only 40 in March, and even fewer in April. During February, major creditors met in Chicago and formed a creditors' committee consisting of C. A. Dana of New York, I. I. Smith of Akron, Ohio, Henry Beneke of Chicago, and Charles Davis of Muncie. Mr. G. E. Shearhod was appointed controller. There was upheaval on Lexington's Board of Directors as four members, Charles Hull, A. O. Eberhart, Arthur Ansted and Frederic Barrows, resigned or were forced out and were replaced by the members of the creditors' committee, who were reported to be owed significant sums of money. Members of the board who did not resign at that time were Frank, George, and William Ansted. On April 10 a conference began in New York City involving company representatives, numerous creditors and various banking firms. Those representing the company were Frank,

The 1923 Princeton was a Durant "Master product" that was powered by an Ansted engine. Very few Princetons were actually built. *Courtesy Robert Smith.*

George and William Ansted, J. M. Heron, R. B. Belknap and Wilfred Jessup. The purpose of the gathering was to study the possibility of reorganization and to seek financial help. Of course, rumors were running rampant in Connersville that Henry Ford or General Motors wanted to buy the plant. There were also reports that creditors were trying to force Frank Ansted out as president of the company and this was causing dissension on the board. Mr. C. A. Dana, an attorney representing two companies considered to be the heaviest creditors, was chairman of the creditors' committee and acting chairman of the board of directors.[4] One of the creditors represented was Jacquea Manufacturing Company of Wilmington, Delaware, which claimed to have built and shipped to Lexington approximately 575 bodies in 1922 and had not received full payment.

The next day, April 11, the Jacquea Manufacturing Company filed suit in federal court in Indianapolis claiming that Lexington was insolvent and asked that a receiver be appointed.[5] As more information became available regarding the financial condition of the company, assets were listed at $1,794,000, including buildings and equipment. Liabilities came to $3,470,000, including first mortgage bonds of $1,500,000, merchandise owed to creditors totaling $1,250,000, bank liabilities of $220,000 and additional commercial paper liabilities of $500,000. Jacquea Manufacturing was just seeking $59,342.

The details of the loan that W. C. Durant had made the previous April indicated the seriousness of the financial condition facing Lexington, for the loan agreement had the potential of being a sellout to Durant. The agreement stated that the United States Automotive Corp. pledged $369,000 in notes payable to Durant on demand and pledged as security $500,000 worth of first mortgage bonds of the company and $975,000 in corporate bonds pledged to Durant. It was also alleged that Durant had been given the power to cause the assets of the U.S.A.C., including Ansted Engineering Co., to be sold at forced sale and other unsecured creditors could be prevented from sharing in the distribution of assets.[6]

Top: Open cars were still popular in 1923 for those who desired the lower price or the sporty appearance. *Bottom:* There were more choices available in closed cars than in open cars in 1923.

The hearing on insolvency was held on April 28. When the hearing ended, William P. Herod, an Indianapolis attorney, had been appointed as the receiver by Judge A. H. Anderson. Herod filed a $25,000 bond, then came to Connersville that afternoon and took charge. Durant received nothing. The Ansteds were out! This even included Frank's brother-in-law, Emery Huston. Herbert Clay replaced Emery as sales manager, and chief engineer John C. Moore, who had been with the company since day one, was replaced by G. C. Patrick. There had also been a complaint filed by the New York banking house that had lent the $2500 to the Continental Discount Corporation. The loan had been signed over to the Lexington Company. Attempts were to be made to settle that issue out of court.[7]

The lack of confidence within the Lexington management became more obvious in May when Frederic Barrows, who had been a vice-president of the United States Automotive Corporation until the reorganization, and had been connected with Lexington since 1912, submitted a bid to purchase the Premier Motor Corporation of Indianapolis. The purchase was arranged through the Fletcher Savings and Trust Company of that city, the receiver of Premier. Barrows was reported to have paid $250,000 in cash and lien notes.[8] The fact that he chose to try to salvage a company other than the one he had helped manage through the years shows the alienation that had occurred within Lexington management.

In the meantime, on April 23, a suit was filed in Fayette Circuit Court, asking that a receiver be appointed for the Ansted Engineering Company, makers of the Ansted engine. This suit was filed by the Wyman-Gordon Company of Worcester, Massachusetts, the Vonnegut Hardware Company of Indianapolis, the Cincinnati Screw Company of Loveland, Ohio, and the Wm. D. Gibson Company of Chicago. It was considered to be a friendly suit and a receiver was sought intending to preserve the assets of the company and to keep the plant in operation. It was alleged that the board of directors had resigned, most of whom were Ansteds, and there was no one with the authority needed to keep the plant running.[9]

The hearing for the engine plant receivership was held on April 27, one day before the U.S.A.C. hearing, with Judge E. Ralph Himelick appointing Arthur Dixon and Hyatt Frost co-receivers. Dixon was already familiar with company operations as he had been the vice-president and general manager the past four years. Frost was a local attorney and a member of the board of directors of the Fayette Bank and Trust Company. Their plan was to continue as a going concern seeking contracts to manufacture automobile parts.[10] One great loss of business came as William Durant cancelled his contract and stopped production of the Durant B22 six cylinder cars as he severed connections with the Ansted Engineering Company. Durant would not offer a six-cylinder engine in his cars for several years, but the losses he incurred with the reorganization of Lexington apparently soured him on having anything to do with the Ansted engine.

The remainder of the year did pick up slightly from the first quarter with a total of 1,330 Lexingtons being produced in 1923.[11] The receivership satisfied creditors enough that increased cash flow permitted more normal operation. In mid–August, John Phillips, from Wellington, New Zealand, visited the factory and signed a contract to handle Lexington's foreign sales.[12] Hopes for increased sales still existed, but the questions were whether the public had lost confidence in this small independent manufacturer and whether production could be increased enough for the company to become profitable.

Lexington used the Skylark designation fifteen years prior to the attractive Hupp Skylark and thirty years before Buick adopted it. This mid–1923 offering was a deluxe roadster intended to catch the fancy of the sporting set.

Lexington did enjoy limited successes in competition. Otto Loesche was again able to enter select events including the prestigious Pikes Peak Hill Climb. Otto again won first in his class, but bringing the Penrose trophy home a second time still eluded him. A Lexington also completed an unusual endurance test, running from Los Angeles to San Francisco with the transmission locked in second gear. A 1923 newspaper account noted that the feat was sponsored by Harold McIlvain, a California Lexington distributor. The Lexington covered 450 miles at an average speed of 29.03 miles per hour, taking 15 hours and 50 minutes. This was an interesting demonstration, but not one that attracted much interest with the general public.

The 1924 models were introduced in late October of 1923, known as the Minute Man or New Series. Body styles available were the five-passenger and seven-passenger touring, five-passenger and seven-passenger California Top, two-passenger roadster California Top, two-passenger Skylark roadster, five-passenger Lark Sport model, five-passenger Royal Coach, four-passenger Coupe, four-passenger Brougham and five-passenger Sedan with two taxi seats. These cars rode on the 123 inch wheelbase and were powered by the Ansted engine that had received additional refinements and was now known as the type F engine. Timing gears were eliminated in favor of a timing chain, bore was increased to $3\frac{5}{16}$ inches with stroke to $5\frac{1}{4}$ inches, jumping the horsepower to 75 from a 232 cubic inch displacement. Some other up-to-date features included a power driven tire pump, automatic windshield wiper, underhood light, and a liberal choice of paint colors.[13]

In January of 1924, the new Concord Six was introduced. This was a smaller, less expensive car that still carried the Lexington name and was powered by an Ansted engine. The Concord, with a 119-inch wheelbase, was offered in a five-passenger touring at $1,395 or sedan at $1,845. The Ansted engine used in the Concord was the Type M engine rated at 65 horsepower in standard form or 70

A mid-twenties Minute Man Six in Australia indicates the export trade still existed. The statue in the background is of King Edward VII. *Courtesy Mitchell Library, State Library of New South Wales.*

horsepower when equipped with the Moore Multiple Exhaust system, which was not a standard feature on the Concord. The frame did not have the more expensive integral metal running boards used on the Minute Man. Instead, it used the traditional wooden step-boards as did most of their competition. The frame was, however, reinforced with the double triangular center-cross member.[14] One new feature for 1924 was an anti-theft lock for the transmission. Both series of cars continued promoting long time features such as the Lexi-gasifier and both series offered disk wheels and balloon tires as options. Balloon tires were becoming quite popular because they were wider and offered a smoother ride by using lower air pressure. The vacuum controlled headlights were dropped in favor of the much less expensive dual filament bulb; however, Lexington did continue having the headlamps mounted on an adjustable radiator bracket instead of using a headlight bar as most other manufacturers did. Definite efforts were being made to cut production costs with the hope of becoming more competitive.

This 1924 California Top had removable windows but a fixed top. It replaced the Lex-Sedan that had similar features.

Optimistic expectations continued throughout the year. An article in the March 15 *News-Examiner* stated that Lexington had placed an order for 600 additional Ansted engines for delivery by the end of May, making the total contracted to date 1,300 engines. Engines were being produced at a rate of about ten a day. Ansted Engineering was also doing considerable work for Oakland and Buick manufacturing brake parts.[15] On July 31, a new Lexington dealership, headed by Dr. N. G. Wills, opened in Connersville. A noted speaker at the grand opening was plant receiver William Herod, who declared, "We have our heads more than above water. You need have no fear of losing the Lexington Company. It will be here when your children are grandparents."[16] Yet, earlier in the summer, Lexington had run an ad in the local newspaper headed "Come Now and Let Us Reason Together" with a biblical reference to Isaiah 1:18 outlining some of the ways the Lexington Motor Company contributed to the local economy. It even noted, "When we prosper, every individual in the city prospers. In the duller times, every individual is in some way

No pains have been spared to make the five-passenger and seven-passenger Touring Cars the utmost in individual transportation.

Ample leg room in both the front compartment and the tonneau is characteristic of all models of this New Series of the Lexington Minute Man Six.

Combined with high seat backs, and wide, deep cushions, the exceptional length of the springs affords riding comfort of unparalleled ease. Upholstery is of finest genuine leather.

In the smaller cut on this page you will note the locker in the back of the front seat. Here the storm curtains are stored, and there is room for other equipment as well. (This locker space is utilized for the two auxiliary seats in the seven-passenger.)

Every storm curtain is plainly marked so that they are readily attached when needed. Curtain rods are provided so that the door curtains may open with the wide, full-U doors on both sides and front and rear.

Handsome and substantial foot rests and robe rails complete the equipment.

All Lexington tops are tailored to fit individual cars on which they go out. Gypsy curtains button to top supports, secluding passengers without obstructing their view. These gypsy curtains also prevent a lot of dust from reaching passengers. A wide plate-glass window permits a clear view to the rear for the driver. See a Lexington Touring Car—!

The 1924 Minute Man Six Touring Car provided ample seating for seven when the auxiliary seats were used.

affected."[17] This clearly was still not a time of prosperity at Lexington as only 498 cars were produced.[18] In spite of the problems facing the company and a grim outlook for the future, there was tremendous excitement generated with the grand slam Pikes Peak victories and the celebration that followed giving a lift and creating hope within the community.

There were few things new for 1925. The Minute Man body styles were continued unchanged from the previous year with prices ranging from $2,195 for the touring to $2,895 for the sedan. They continued using the type F Ansted engine and a dual exhaust system; however, the Moore exhaust system was no longer mentioned in company literature. J. C. Moore had been ousted as chief engineer with the reorganization and his name was dropped from company advertising. Comparing prices of the 123 inch wheelbase Minute Man series against Buick shows the challenges facing Lexington. Both Buick and Lexington used six cylinder overhead valve engines and the Buick wheelbase of 128 inches was five inches longer than the Minute Man; however, the Buick touring could be purchased for just $1,700 and the sedan for $2,425. The 126 inch wheelbase Packard Six sedan was priced at $2,585 and the Hudson Super Six seven-passenger sedan was a bargain at $1,895.

The smaller 119 inch wheelbase Lexington Concord still offered the Touring and the Sedan but added the Special Touring and Special Sedan. The Special series was advertised as a limited production model with the sedan priced at $2,445. It included such niceties as nickel plating on the radiator shell, bumpers, head lights, cowl lights, and running board kick plates. The interior appointments included armrests, a heater and dome light. Options for the regular models focused on nickel plated trim, balloon tires and four choices of wheels: the standard wood spoke artillery, wire, steel disk or six spoked steel.[19] Again, competition was fierce as a Buick Master sedan with 120 inch wheelbase could be bought for $2,225 or the Studebaker Special Six sedan for just $1,895.[20] Within the past few years customers' preference in body styles had undergone a huge shift, so that closed cars dominated

Newly introduced for 1924, the Concord was a smaller car on a 119 inch wheelbase, powered by a smaller Ansted engine. Motor Age, *Jan. 3, 1924.*

the market by 1925. In the first three months of the year, Dodge Brothers delivered six closed cars for every open car and the ratio at Buick was nearly ten to one. The higher priced lines delivered almost exclusively closed cars, but even at Chevrolet closed car deliveries were about twice those of open cars.[21]

Lexingtons were displayed at the shows as usual. At the New York show, held

The car is a Lexington Concord; the statue in the background is the Minute Man as it stood in Lexington Park in Connersville. Motor, *January 1925.*

Top: The Coach. "The Lexington Minute Man Coach presents a compact, two door, family car of a pleasing design. The Brougham is of similar design equipped with a roomy trunk and body protecting bars at the rear." *Bottom:* The Sedan. This sedan came equipped with a body built by McFarlan, another Connersville manufacturer, known for producing very expensive automobiles.

in the Armory January 5–12, it was among approximately 60 makes on display. Lexington was relegated to a smaller space but remained on the main floor of the show area. At the Chicago show, Lexington displayed four cars, each with different wheels. Two of the cars had nickel trim and the bodies showed a variety of colors. Lexington was known for offering a wide selection of body colors and finishes. A new assistant general manager, C. H. Beaumont, came on board late in the year hoping to give the company the spark it desperately needed to become more competitive.[22] Only 339 cars were built that year.[23]

Ansted Engineering continued to produce the fine overhead valve engines used by Lexington. The plant was running far below capacity and still produced more engines than were used in new cars. By early September, with the approval of the Circuit Court, they were able to rid themselves of the Hagerstown plant in a sale to the Indiana Piston Ring Company of Hagerstown. They needed additional space for manufacturing their Perfect Circle piston rings that were gaining popularity. Therefore, the same people that Frank and George Ansted had purchased the factory from seven years earlier were back in full control of the building.[24]

Top: Skylark Roadster. The sporty Lark and Skylark continued to be offered in 1925. A popular option was balloon tires to provide a smoother ride. *Bottom:* Lark (balloon equipped). "Balloon tires add the final touch of comfort to the 'Lark.' Every Lexington is properly engineered to accommodate balloon equipment; making steering a matter of ease. Note the graceful lines."

Production did continue into the 1926 model year with a full line of automobiles. The Minute Man literature illustrated six different sedans: the Deluxe Sedan, Salon Sedan, Sedanette, Princess Sedan, Genteel Sedan and Suburban.[25] Open cars offered were a roadster, a touring and the Lark. The Minute Man series continued using the 123 inch wheelbase and was powered by the larger Ansted engine that developed 75 horsepower. The Concord was relabeled the 6–50 with a four-passenger Runabout or five-passenger Phaeton at $1,895, a five-passenger Sedan or five-passenger Landau at $2,245 or a four-passenger Landaulet. All 6–50s rode on the 119 inch wheelbase. The smaller Ansted engine remained the source of power, now with 3 5/16 inch bore and 4½ inch stroke and developing 70 horsepower. Modern updates included the use of hydraulic brakes on all four wheels as standard equipment. These were external contracting binders with 12-inch drums. The tire size dropped to 30 inches and balloon tires had become standard equipment, as had nickel-plated radiator shell, headlamps and cowl lamps.[26] Lexington continued to match the industry with improvements in appearance, performance and safety,

Literature prepared for the 1926 shows indicates the intention of producing the Minute Man Six; however, the smaller Series 6–50 dominated production.

but the magic of the Lexington name was gone. Only 186 cars were built for 1926 and most of those were the 6–50 model.

By the time the new year rolled around, the company was in its third year of receivership and production had continued to drop. The smell of death was in the air as one after another employee saw opportunities open with other companies and opted out of the Lexington picture. In January, Herbert L. Clay, sales and advertising manager, resigned to join the Stutz Motor Car Company of nearby Indianapolis.[27] On May 11, receiver William Herod tendered his resignation and petitioned the court for authority to sell the property. Different sets of creditors and holders of receiver certificates contended for priority of liens. Attorneys for holders of receivership certificates charged that the company had lost $350,000 and had incurred liabilities amounting to $150,000, and that Herod should be held responsible for the half million dollars.[28] June 11 was set as the date when priority liens were to be filed and the judge would then order that the property be sold.[29] George M. Barnard, an attorney from New Castle, was appointed to succeed William Herod by Judge Robert C. Baltzell of the Federal Court in Indianapolis. The court did order that Herod and his surety, the Fidelity Casualty Company, would not be discharged from accountability until an audit was completed.[30]

While the Lexington Motor Company was getting court permission to close, the Ansted Engine Company was already in the process of being auctioned out. Co-receivers Hyatt Frost and Arthur Dixon had been given a court order to liquidate the engine plant and foundry May 11, 12 and 13. Samuel T. Freeman and Company of Boston, was in charge of the auction.[31] A committee of local citizens made what proved to be the highest bid on the engine factory building, but there was reason to hope that more money could be realized and the bid was rejected. The Ansted engine service franchise was sold to the United Service Company of Detroit, Michigan, for $18,500. Machinery and equipment was sold in lots, bringing a total of $202,000, including the foundry real estate and equipment.[32] At that point, the

(A) Series 6–50 Phaeton. (B) Series 6–50 Landau. (C) Series 6–50 Runabout. (D) Series 6–50 Sedan. (E) Series 6–50 Landaulet.

Ansted real estate was vacant and ready for occupancy as soon as a suitable buyer could be found.

The Ansted Engineering Company next appeared in Kokomo, Indiana. A company by the name of the General Parts Corporation had been formed by a merger of the Apperson and the Haynes companies, both of Kokomo. They picked up the parts service for the Lexington and National cars as local manager L. L. Blake estimated that 25,000 Lexingtons and 10,000 Durants with Ansted engines were still in service and would need parts. The manufacture and distribution of parts was being done at a plant in Kokomo that had formerly been used for automobile production.[33] Fliers advertising parts for Lexington cars and listing Ansted Engineering Company of Kokomo, Indiana, were sent to known Lexington owners with the claim that in the past they had furnished replacement motors through the Lexington Motor Company, but had now severed connection with that organization and were making parts available direct to Lexington owners themselves. This company was supplying not only motor parts, but also a full line of service parts for all other Lexington units, such as clutches, transmissions, universal joints, axles, etc.[34] New replacement motors were available as well as various assorted parts for Lexington cars.

Production at the Lexington plant continued into the summer of 1926 under the new receiver, George Barnard, in hopes that there could be a re-organization of the business and that the manufacture of Lexington automobiles might continue in Connersville. Even after Ansted Engineering was closed, engines and component parts remained in stock and a few cars were assembled. A popular topic of speculative conversation among local citizens was the company's prospects for survival. During the several months previous, various attempts to sort out Lexington's affairs had failed. One plan after another was proposed, studied, and found to be impracticable. By that time, the dealer network had vanished and interested parties and the public were forced to abandon hope of continued production.

The Lexington inventory of completed automobiles and replacement parts was sold to a Chicago company. Their sales tactic involved rebadging several of the cars and selling them in the Los Angeles area as the 1927 Ansted.[35] Finding little success with this venture, that company sold the remaining cars at auction. The buyer was none other than the Ansted Engineering Company of Kokomo, Indiana. Left-over Lexingtons were advertised as new cars as late as 1928, nearly two years after the plant had closed. By late in the year 1926, both the Lexington plant and the service building at the corner of 10th and Eastern were vacant.

Frank Ansted and his son Dale are standing by a 1926 Lexington. The photo may have been taken in Los Angeles, where Frank settled after leaving Connersville.

Although the May auction produced no accepted bids for the Ansted Engineering property, two parties were interested in purchasing the plant: the Indiana Lamp Company of Connersville and the Auburn Automobile Company of Auburn, Indiana. This put the committee in a difficult position because an established local company was competing against a larger out-of-town concern for a facility that would allow expansion of manufacturing. Two local businessmen, B. M. Barrows and Ellis Ryan, had a business relationship with Errett Lobban Cord, president of Auburn. His company had shown a dramatic increase in production in the past two years and was looking for a location to add factory space. The city fathers at Auburn had not encouraged the plant expansion in that city, so at the urging of Barrows and Ryan, Cord visited Connersville on August 17 and was greeted by 25 community leaders. Cord inspected the engine plant and the Lexington facility and seemed pleased with the interest, enthusiasm and spirit of co-operation that he had observed. Before he left, he had made a tentative offer for both properties provided they could be acquired by the Bigger and Better Connersville Committee and then transferred to the Auburn Automobile Company.[36]

This committee was made up of representatives from the three local civic clubs, the Kiwanis, Rotary and Lions. It consisted of E. L. Rickert, chairman, E. R. Jeffrey, M. M. Shellhouse, Don P. Henthorn, H. M. Johnson, Fred D. Snyder, James M. Heron, Myron Levinson, and Harry A. Wainwright. The committee was not in a position to sell either of the factories because they did not own them. The Ansted property was in the hands of Hyatt L. Frost and Arthur Dixon, receivers, and the Lexington building was in the hands of George L. Barnard, receiver. The situation was made all the more complex because the Ansted receivership was in the Fayette Circuit Court and the Lexington receivership was in federal court. There were claims on both properties, both real and personal, on behalf of mortgage bondholders, receivers' certificate holders, common creditors, and the local, state, and federal governments for corporate taxes, income taxes, excise taxes before receivership, excise taxes during receivership, local assessments, and so on.

The situation was further complicated because the sprinkler systems were

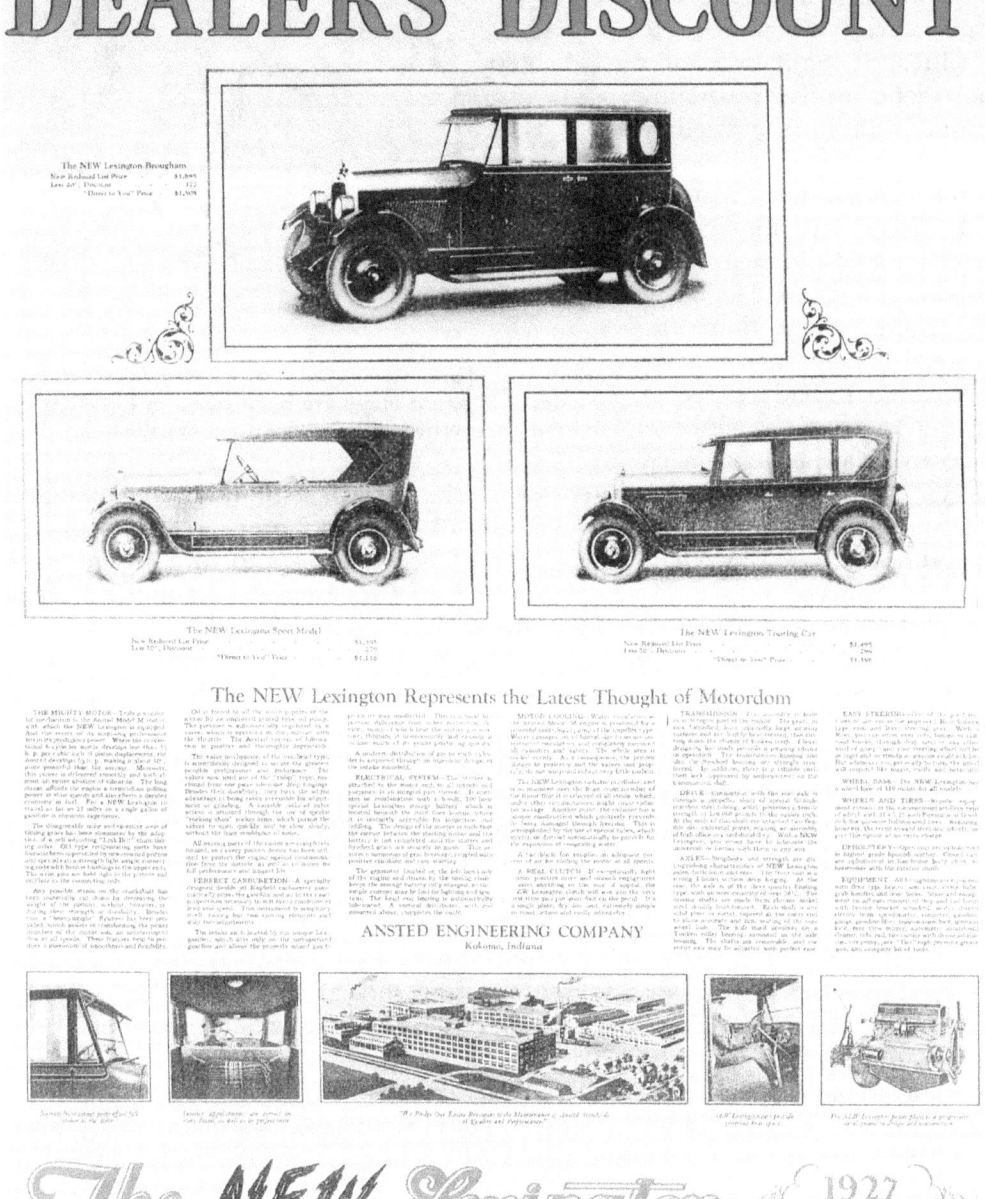

1927 Series Lexingtons were being offered for sale by the Ansted Engineering Company. The company was no longer located in Connersville, but instead in Kokomo, Indiana.

installed under contracts that gave the vendors the right to remove them if not paid for. Thus, there was a claim for $32,000 on these systems. Negotiations between the committee and the parties involved resulted in a sum of $8,000 being paid to satisfy the sprinkler system claim. A more difficult issue to settle for Lexington involved back federal taxes from a period before the company filed for receivership in 1923.

Several times a solution seemed to be at hand when another delay would arise in settling the back taxes. These records were finally cleared through a compromise settlement with $92,000 in government claims wiped off for $100.

The Bigger and Better Connersville Committee found that it was necessary to obtain $30,000 from business and individual donations to supplement the Auburn offer on both properties. This money was promptly raised by committees under the direction of C. C. Hull and H. M. Johnson as 190 contributors donated toward that cause. On September 15, 1926, the Ansted property was offered for sale by the court. Judge E. Ralph Himelick of the Fayette Circuit Court accepted the $40,000 bid. E. I. Richert received the property on behalf of the Bigger and Better Connersville Committee in the interest of the Auburn Automobile Company. This plant was turned over to Auburn on October 26, 1926. Auburn immediately began using the building for storing Auburn car bodies that had been made by Connersville's Central Manufacturing, until they could be shipped north for assembly at the plant at Auburn.

The Lexington real estate had not been vacated at that time. The remaining machinery and personal property was disposed of during November and the property was offered for sale at auction on November 27. The federal court provided that the property should be sold free and clear of any and all liens, encumbrances, claims, charges, debts, and demands, save and except special assessments and the city, state, and county taxes, payable in 1927. There were several prospective bidders at the sale, but the only actual bid was that made by the Committee. It was accepted and the sale was approved by the federal court several days later.[37] The Auburn Automobile Company was eager to take possession of the property, which was expected to be available within a few weeks. Those few weeks turned into nearly six months as the transfer to Auburn finally took place on May 23, 1927.

During all of this time the Auburn Automobile Company had deposited the money to back up its purchase offer in the First Trust and Savings Bank of Chicago. It was turned over to the Committee by Auburn's attorney, Judge J. E. Ross, of Fort Wayne, as the property was being transferred to the new owner.[38]

Selecting an out-of-town company over Connersville's own Indiana Lamp Company, which had shown steady growth over the past nearly two decades, was a difficult decision. Auburn won out because of its intention to purchase not only the engine plant, but also the Lexington plant, whereas the Lamp Company wanted only the Ansted Engineering Company facility. Auburn had been doing business in Connersville for several years also and had spent one and a half million dollars there in the past 18 months, purchasing bodies from the Central Manufacturing Company. Auburn immediately announced its intention to expand its manufacturing process and to eventually build their six cylinder automobiles in Connersville. Spirits were hopeful again in this east-central Indiana city.[39]

Auburn did, in fact, use these properties for automobile production as six-cylinder Auburn closed cars began rolling off of the assembly line in 1929, and by 1934, their entire automobile production was moved to the Connersville plant. The crowning jewel for these buildings may have been the production of the Cord 810 and 812 during 1936 and 1937 by the Auburn Automobile Company. By that time, even their main offices had been moved to Connersville.

In September of 1927, the service facility building at 10th and Eastern Avenue was finally sold for $12,000 to J. L. Kenley, owner of the Betsy Ross Bakery. This sale

New leftover Lexingtons were still being offered for sale in 1928.

was also handled by the Bigger and Better Connersville Committee under the leadership of E. L. Rickert. One more step had been taken in the process of liquidating properties formerly owned by the U. S. A. C.[40] That building is still very much in use in 2006 as a retail store, Wells Warehouse.

Since 1910, Lexington had been a regular exhibitor at the car shows, but it

The *Dawn* of NEW POWER for Lexington Motor Cars

OUT of the night of waning usefulness that has settled over many service-worn Lexington automobiles, there comes a glorious day of motor efficiency, of economy, of driving pleasure and satisfaction. By the mere exchange of old, work-impaired Ansted motors for new ones, there are restored to these cars all the attributes of power and performance which they possessed the day they left the factory.

And how moderate is the cost of this transformation! Just think! At hardly more than it would stand you if you were to have your present engine overhauled, you can now replace it with the latest type Model M Ansted motor. Brand new, designed for maximum, smooth-flowing power, amazing flexibility and splendid fuel economy, this 65 horsepower master of motors, is precision built and fully guaranteed. Furthermore, it will fit any and all Lexington cars manufactured since 1920.

Shipped direct from our factory, the new motor comes to you completely assembled and thoroughly tested. The change from your old, service-worn power plant to our new and perfect one can be made very quickly, and the price we ask is only the return of your used engine to us, plus a cash difference of...... $167⁵⁰

When you consider the fact that the Ansted Model M motor was built to retail at $550, you will appreciate more than ever the tremendous savings made possible through our direct-to-owner service.

Our Model U22, T22, T21 and ST21 friends will be glad to know that we are able to offer them *rebuilt* Ansted motors, complete and ready to install, at a reduction from the old price of $265 to the low figure of.. $119⁷⁵

NOTE—*These Model U22, T22, T21 and ST21 motors are, of course, not the Model M described at the left, but are exact duplicates of those now in the cars. They are entirely rebuilt and block tested right here in our plant, are guaranteed as to quality and workmanship, and insure to any Model U22, T22, T21 or ST21 the return of its original power and good service.*

We shall be pleased to send detailed specifications or whatever other information is desired about any Ansted motor ever built.

ANSTED ENGINEERING COMPANY. Kokomo, Indiana

Complete engines and replacement parts were also available from Ansted Engineering Company or Kokomo.

Complete engines and replacement parts were available from Ansted Engineering Company of Kokomo.

would not display any offerings in the 1927 shows. Other names had also disappeared during 1926: Ajax had become the Nash light-six, Cleveland had become the Chandler light-six, and Case, Gray, and Roamer had come to an end. There were still 46 other makes of automobiles on display that year at the National Automobile Show in New York City.[44]

The Lexington was a fine automobile offering good value for the money. They were known for a high quality finish that was available in a variety of colors. Pete Rigor, who turned 100 years of age in 2006, remembered, "Those were beautiful cars but there were just too many chiefs."[47] It was one of the first American automobiles, if not the first, to deal with the problems of exhaust back-pressure through the use of dual exhausts. Under Moore's system, no two cylinders exhausted through the same pipe at the same time. In 1917 and again in 1922, the company addressed the problem of the flexing frame that caused jammed doors when cars were parked on uneven surfaces or allowed doors to bounce open when driving over rough roads. Extra wide running-boards, made entirely of metal that curved up at each end to join front and rear fenders, were part of the integral frame structure and became one of Lexington's trademarks. Although Lexington is often considered to have been an assembled car, the fact is that most of the major component parts were made in factories owned by the United States Automotive Corporation or controlled by the Ansted family. Lexington's Ansted engine was manufactured specifically for Lexington in an adjoining factory that was part of the U.S.A.C. Then there was the Central Manufacturing Company, makers of bodies, Connersville Foundry for gears and transmission cases, Ansted Spring and Axel Company, and the Indiana Lamp Company, all under the control of the Ansted family. During the 1920s, the "assembled" designation does not seem appropriate.

Lexington was a leader in advertising. As early as 1911, full color brochures promoted the choices of finish afforded Lexington customers. Color accents began appearing in their magazine advertising as early as 1909 with full color ads placed occasionally in nationally circulated magazines such as *Leslie*'s, *Life* and the *Saturday Evening Post* by the late teens. Lexington also gave subtle support to women's suffrage through their advertising at a time when that issue was at its peak. Unique advertising items included cloth pennants in varying colors and sizes with the Lexington logo, a toy "pop-gun" used to get children on their side, and a neat little advertising game consisting of a round metal case with a glass top. Underneath the glass cover was a small metal car and a little garage. The object was to manipulate the case until the car slipped into the Lexington garage. This company's advertising showed unusual creativity, but the cost, per vehicle sold, would have been astronomical compared with the larger manufacturers who sold tens of thousands of vehicles compared to Lexington's thousands.

With all of the qualities that Lexington had to offer, a number of factors led to the company's failure. At the forefront was financial impropriety with continued purchases on credit without proper planning to pay back the debts. Then came the miscalculation of raising prices during an economic slowdown, the construction of an extravagant facility in Indianapolis and purchases of other companies that kept a financial strain on the company. There were seemingly more vice-presidents and other well paid executives, mostly from the controlling family, than could be justified for the size of the operation. The lack of efficiency of operation by not using modern production methods also kept costs high while production was modest at best.

However, this was also a time when many small automobile manufacturers had their backs to the wall because of increased competition from the giants in the industry. It was either get bigger or go out of business. Frank Ansted chose the route of expansion.

Frank Ansted was, after his father's death, probably the most influential man in the community. He had proven himself to be an able salesman when he managed the Indiana Lamp Company and had made significant gains at Lexington. His skills at fund raising were put to use when he helped sell $65,000 in country club stock in less than a day, and he supported other community projects. Lexington was the generous provider of goodies during the Play Days at Roberts Park, and he backed the building of homes that his employees could purchase on low payment plans.[43]

John C. Moore shared his talents with other companies besides Lexington. He designed the Moore auxiliary transmission for the Tractor Train Company to improve the performance of the Model T Ford.

Robert F. Williams, who turned 102 years old in March of 2006, knew Frank Ansted, but not as a friend. Robert remembered Frank as "quite an operator." He was a real benefactor for Connersville because of the empire he built and helped bring down. Frank had engineered the idea of having a Pullman rail car parked on a siding in Connersville. People could board the car and a train from Cincinnati would pick it up while Chicago bound patrons slept, arriving the next morning to do their business, then sleep on the return trip back to

A promotional matchbook case produced for Gore-Lexington Motor Sales Co. in Huntington, West Virginia.

The Lexington factory sat empty from the fall of 1926 until May of 1927 when the Auburn Motor Company took possession of the property. Auburn first used the building to store car bodies, but Auburn Six closed cars were rolling off of the assembly line by 1929. *Courtesy Fayette County Historical Museum.*

Fayette County. Frank was born into wealth. The older generation had acquired money but was far more conservative.[44]

After being ousted as company president in 1923, Frank B. Ansted left town within a few months, settling in the Los Angeles, California, area. He apparently did not sever ties with Lexington because, the following year, the Ansted Lexington Company was offering new and used Lexingtons for sale in their two Los Angeles locations; Fegueroa at 16 and 6449-51 Sunset Boulevard. Frank B. Anstead died there October 27, 1933, at the young age of 48 years. He was survived by his wife Isabel and their son Dale.[45] Frank had led the company through major expansion, but had failed to make provision to pay creditors in a timely fashion. Even though he was chairman of the board of Fayette Bank and Trust in Connersville, the sources of operating capital had dried up for his ailing company.

From 1892, when E. W. opened a factory to make springs and axles for buggies, until the 1920s, the Ansteds were one of Connersville's leading families. Yet the only monument to the Ansted family is the impressive mausoleum in Dale Cemetery where several family members are buried. There is a nice portrait of E. W. Ansted hanging in Fayette Memorial Hospital in recognition of his contribution to that organization; however, no buildings or streets honor the family that was, for several years, responsible for providing employment to many persons in this Eastern Indiana community.

John C. Moore was the real innovator who kept Lexington on the cutting edge mechanically. Although he was a machinist by trade and there is no record that he ever had any formal training that would aid in designing or building automobiles, he had a vision for building automobiles and a desire to improve their performance. He was one of the company's founders in 1908 and remained loyal to them through the years until eventually being replaced as chief engineer by G. C. Patrick after the company had gone into receivership in 1923. Moore also used his talents for other companies in the Connersville area. One such company was the Lincoln Manufacturing Company. It began operations in 1920 as the Tractor-Train Company of Indiana and made accessories to improve the performance of the Model T Ford. John Moore designed the Improved Moore Transmission, later known as the Lincoln Utility Transmission, to double the pulling power of the Ford truck.[46] A lighter duty unit was also available for the car. John continued to reside in or near his adopted Hoosier city until he passed away at age 81 on May 28, 1951.[47]

For nearly twenty years, new Lexington automobiles were available to the motoring public. This small company that was responsible for only a minuscule percentage of American automobile production still left its mark in the record books for outstanding accomplishments. It was received with enthusiasm in its home city of Lexington, Kentucky, and brought many good years of prosperity and growth to its adopted city in Indiana. Connersville was in a period of marked growth as the 1920 census reported 9,901 residents compared to 6,836 just ten years earlier. Fayette County also experienced a similar percentage of growth during the same decade. The 17-year period from 1910 to 1927 may very well be called the Lexington Age in Connersville. Several other business firms and industries preceded the Lexington and were here longer, but none have equaled the pomp and pageantry that, in good times, gave the community good reason to celebrate.[48]

8

Lexington Lives On

The Lexington automobile made its own impact on the motoring world. When the factory was silenced and the Lexington automobile seemed to be gone forever, also missing was a certain amount of pizzazz, with no more victories at Pikes Peak to celebrate or new automobiles lined up awaiting shipment. There would be no more Minute Man Musters in Roberts Park or optimistic newspaper reports of big orders for the company to fill. But that hasn't been the total end for this marque.

Recently there has been a "Mr. Lexington." He is Eric vonGrimmenstein, president of Van Ausdall and Farrar, a business-equipment company that was located at 12th and Meridian streets in Indianapolis. The building at the Meridian Street location had been restored to the original grandeur it enjoyed when built as a Lexington dealership. Eric deals daily with sales and service of high-tech office equipment, but he also became the caretaker of several Lexington automobiles that had been well preserved, had been restored or were in the process of being restored.

An announcement made by Lexington in early June 1920 told of plans for a large building to be built at 900 Meridian Street in Indianapolis. Plans called for the building to be 70 feet wide and to extend the full block from Meridian to Illinois Street, a distance of nearly 300 feet, with entrances on both streets. The contract to build the four story building had been awarded to the Hoosier General Construction Company of Connersville. The announcement claimed that the ground had already been purchased and a large old house was being demolished at the location so this building could be erected at an estimated cost of $200,000.[1]

The grand opening of Lexington's fine new building was held about nine months later and three blocks up the street at 1142 North Meridian, March 3–5, 1921. The building was built by the Connersville company as originally planned with J. Earl Faught as the superintendent of construction. Although not on the location originally announced, dimensions of this four story building were still 70 feet frontage on Meridian, but extending West 220 feet, not all the way to Illinois Street. Structural materials in the new building included concrete, steel and brick with the front being finished in brown terra cotta. The design included many large windows to maximize the benefits of daylight to aid illumination.

The centerpiece of the interior was the first floor showroom, which was bordered by two staircases with a walkway that led to a mezzanine where various offices were located. On the ground floor in back of the showroom was a second room where a Lexington chassis and an unfinished body were on display. Farther back was the shipping department and an emergency service station was at the rear. The second floor was the used car display area with a storage room and a machine shop in the rear. The entire third floor was used for new car storage and the fourth floor for service and refinishing.[2] An electric powered elevator, large enough to accom-

The grand opening for this magnificent sales and service facility was held in early March of 1921. The winning Pikes Peak race cars were also on display. Hoosier Motorist, *April 1921*.

modate an automobile, made it easy to move vehicles from one floor to another. Two entrance drive-throughs led to the ground floor service areas; both faced Meridian Street, one at the south end of the building and the other at the north end. The company planned to build a service shop at some future date using the remaining land on the Illinois Street side of the building.

A large delegation from Connersville attended the celebration. One of the dignitaries was E. Pierre Wainwright, a local artist and the art director at the United States Automotive Corporation. Pierre had two of his masterpieces on display. In the center of the mezzanine stood a life-size statue of the Minute Man of Lexington overlooking the Lexington Minute Man automobiles that were on display in the showroom below.[3] Another of Wainwright's works was a four foot by three foot oil painting of the 1920 Pikes Peak race where Lexingtons had placed first and second. The winning cars, number seven and number six, were also on display in front of the building. Leather-bound notebooks were given to guests as souvenirs. The celebration went on into the evening hours with a band concert and dancing. Here was one of the nicest automobile sales and service facilities in the Midwest, built and equipped at a cost of more than half a million dollars. Charles D. Finney was the president of the Lexington Motor Sales Company; Olin Peck was sales manager, William Meuser district sales manager, Charles Irvin used car manager and Wilbur May superintendent of service.[4]

The restored building at 12th and Meridian St. in Indianapolis where Lexingtons were on display from the late 1990s until 2005 will soon serve other interests. *Photograph by author.*

This fine new facility surely aided the sales effort in central Indiana, but it opened at about the worst possible time, right in the midst of the sharp recession of 1920–21. Lexington sales had reached their peak the previous year but within two years, the parent company was in the hands of a receiver. Still, the building had its days of glory before deteriorating along with the Midtown neighborhood of which it was a part.

During the 1930s, various firms used and possibly abused this fine structure. Beginning in 1941 and for the next 55 years, the building served as the headquarters of Rough Notes, publisher of an insurance trade magazine and various other items. Over the course of years, the beauty of the building was hidden. The windows were blocked up and painted and the Romanesque archways were bricked in, making it look more like a mausoleum than a business. Inside, the chandeliers had been replaced with fluorescent strip lighting. The dual staircases and the walkway across the front of the mezzanine had been removed. Plaster scrollwork was painted anonymous white, dulling the graceful forms of ribbons, flowers and leaves.[5] Even the address changed as it presently is listed as 1200 North Meridian Street.

In 1996, the business next door to the north, Van Ausdall & Farrar, needed additional space for their increasing sales of business machines. Their first interest in acquiring the building was strictly to use as a warehouse. But as company president Eric vonGrimmenstein looked the building over, recognized what remained of the grandeur of the original showroom and with his interest in restoring antiques, he could visualize the possibilities of returning the building to its original splendor.

The showroom was all decked out for the grand opening. Hoosier Motorist, *April 1921*.

A grand staircase is the focal point of the restored showroom at 1200 N. Meridian. *Photograph by author.*

Not realizing at the time that there had been two staircases, he directed the construction of a center grand staircase to the mezzanine with local artisans re-creating original design moldings on the walls and on the side of the staircase.[6] The original 50 foot wide showroom was expanded to 70 feet by including the areas once used for service entrance drive-throughs. Chandeliers replaced the fluorescent strip lighting to spread their warm glow throughout the room.[7]

Not satisfied with just "fixing the place up," when vonGrimmenstein learned the building started life as a Lexington automobile sales facility, he decided that it would again display these rather rare automobiles alongside the high-tech business machines that had made this company so successful. He started tracking down information on this Indiana made car and even made a trip to Connersville to visit with local historian Henry Blommel, who has since passed away. Eric claims that antique automobiles are not his hobby, but he developed a passion for anything Lexington, hunting down and acquiring advertisements, manuals, literature and automobiles, to the point that he could justifiably be named "Mr. Lexington." Eric provided substantial assistance to this author by generously sharing some of the information and ad copies used in this book. The $1.4 million spent for purchasing and restoring this fine structure that is a piece of automobile history seemed to be money well spent, at least from the automobile historian's point of view. But, in July of 2004, Eric recognized the need to change his priorities related to Lexington and has since disposed of most of his collection of cars and materials. In the interest of efficiency, the building at 1200 North Meridian was placed on the market and the new owner is Shiel Sexton Company. As of November 2006, the plan is to keep the four story part of the old Lexington building, although the warehouse at the rear may be razed, and the Lexington name may be retained with the property development. It is hoped that this beautifully restored structure that was a part of Indiana automobile history will be saved and continue a useful existence.

9
A Gallery of Surviving Lexingtons

Approximately 25 Lexingtons that range from fairly complete to mint condition have been accounted for. Some have been beautifully restored, and others are in the process of being brought back, but all of them carry on the legacy of this once well known marque. Some of the survivors are pictured on the following pages.

1911 Lexington. This is the oldest known Lexington survivor. It is owned by Mike Gibbens of San Rafael, California. In the 1920s, it was owned by a farmer in

The oldest Lexington known to have survived is this immaculate 1911 model. It was stored in the top of a barn for decades. *Courtesy Mike Gibbens.*

Top: This double-roadster body type was not shown in Lexington literature. Could it have been an experimental model? *Bottom:* The Rutenber engine had individual castings for each cylinder making repairs easier. *Courtesy Mike Gibbens.*

This unusual power train arrangement had a short drive shaft between the large flywheel and the transmission. *Courtesy Mike Gibbens.*

central California. When he stopped using it, it was put up in the top of a barn. When the farmer died, his son inherited the farm but wouldn't consider selling the car. Bill Harrah wanted to buy it and even sent other people to try to acquire it, but they were turned away by the unfriendly farmer who usually carried a gun. Around 1980, the farmer was having trouble with his tractor and needed to replace it. A person who knew about the rare car in the top of the barn brought a used tractor out to the farm for him to look at. When asked what he wanted for the tractor, the sales person said he wanted the Lexington in the barn, whereupon the farmer went back into the house. When he emerged nearly an hour later with his son, both carrying guns, he told the salesman to get the car and get off of the property.

This car is rare for many reasons. Besides being the oldest known surviving Lexington, it is a double roadster, a body style not shown in period literature. It has a center shift instead of an outside shift as shown in 1911 Lexington literature; however, the transmission cover has "Lexington" cast into it and does not appear to have been altered. The rear axle ratio is a low one, around three to one, and it has a double drop frame from back to front. The frame showed no signs of having been tampered with when it was cleaned before being painted. Mr. Gibbens believes that this car may have been an experimental model or may have been used in early racing.[1]

1916 Minute Man Six. This 1916 Lexington is owned by Sturgis St. Peter of Barnstable, MA. A Minute Man Six with a two-passenger speedster body, its serial num-

Top: This 1916 Lexington Minute Man Six with a two-passenger speedster body is owned by Sturgis St. Peter of Barnstable, Massachusetts. The running gear has been completely rebuilt, primed, painted and pinstriped. *Bottom:* The bucket seats, aluminum aircraft fuel tank, removable luggage trunk, twin spare tire carrier and other features suggest that this car was modified in the 1920s. *Courtesy Sturgis St. Peter.*

ber is 3050. Power is supplied by a Continental engine, number 7w5016. It was probably sold new by C. Ashton Cox of Wollaston, Massachusetts. Mr. St. Peter suspects that the car was "hot rodded" in the twenties because it has leather bucket seats, a thirty gallon aluminum aircraft fuel tank, motor man's runningboard truck, removable luggage trunk, twin spare tire carrier, and dual direction marker lights, all of which are correct for this time period. St. Peter was in the process of doing a complete restoration in the winter of 2005.

1917 Minute Man Six. Originally a touring car, this 1917 Lexington Minute Man Six with serial no. 6312 was converted into a tow truck in the mid–1920s. It is now owned by Todd Goudeau of Youngsville, Louisiana. His father bought the tow-car from the original gas station owner/operator in 1962, and stored it away. Todd's older brother restored this relic, but put a truck bed on it instead of the wrecker boom. Todd purchased the car-truck in 2004. It has spent its whole life in Louisiana.

1919 Series S Minute Man Six Touring. The serial number of this car, owned by Jan Rune of Karlstad, Sweden, is S20492 and the Continental engine number is 103–7R-11591. Two gentlemen from Karlstad made this story possible: Igemar Ols-

Originally a touring car, this 1917 Lexington Minute Man Six was converted into a tow truck and later fitted with a pickup bed during restoration. *Courtesy Todd Goudeau.*

son, a historian, credited with the research, and Mats Heder, who translated his findings. This Series S was one of five Lexingtons that arrived in Karlstad in the spring of 1920, imported by the Huzell Hardware store. This car was first registered to Oscar J. Carlstrom, the sales manager at the hardware store, and was most likely used as a demonstrator. About three weeks later, the car was sold to Mr. Per Persson of Likenas. Per Persson was a landowner living on an estate called Langav about 170 km north of Karlstad. He made his living on farming and forestry. Mr. Persson and his wife, Lena, raised a large family, having 12 children, ten of whom were daughters. The two sons, Ivar and Sven, went to Karlstad to study and most likely they convinced their father to buy a motorcar. At the time that Mr. Persson purchased the Lexington, he was 63 years old. He didn't have a driver's license so when the car was delivered in Karlstad, Per and his two sons took the opportunity to get their licenses at the same time. While taking his driving test with the inspector, Per accidentally ran over and killed a dog on a bridge over the Klaralven River in downtown Karlstad. In spite of the accident, Per got his license; however, he was apparently so shaken by the incident that he never drove a car again. The Persson car was registered with Swedish registration number S534. Since he didn't drive, he hired others to drive for him. When Per passed away in 1925, the car was taken over by his son Sven, who was then 24 years old and a trained forester. After their father's death, the sons bought out their sisters and took over the estate. Sven used the Lexington as his personal car until late in 1928 when he traded it in on a new Volvo OV4. The value of the aging touring car must not have been very great because the dealer left the car in a barn on the estate through the winter. During the winter of 1928–29 the block froze up and cracked on the left side, all the way from the front to the rear. When it was discovered the next spring, the dealer considered the car

This photo, taken in about 1922, shows the Minute Man Six owned by Mr. Per Persson. At the wheel is Mr. Ossian Karlstem, a well-known local motorman or chauffer. *Courtesy Mats Heder.*

Top: The original Swedish license number, S534, was replaced with a new issue in the 1970s; however, the original plate is used for special occasions. *Bottom:* This type of trunk was called an America trunk because emigrants going to America often carried their belongings in this type of container. *Both photographs courtesy Mats Heder.*

Jan Rune is shows the Lexington Motometer he purchased at Hershey in 1986. The price was twice as much as for other makes because of its rarity. *Courtesy Mats Heder.*

scrap and asked if it could be left there. There was plenty of space available at Langav so the Minute Man was abandoned. At some point, the block was repaired, probably by a local blacksmith. But who fixed it or when is not known. The crack can clearly be seen even now, but the repair has caused no problems since. The crack probably saved the car. If the car had been sold as a cheap used car in 1929, it most likely would have had a rather short life as most Lexingtons in Sweden had been scrapped by 1930. In 1938, Sven had a son, christened Jan. Jan became interested in mechanical things and started talking about fixing up the old Lexington while just a teenager. However, other plans came in between, such as marriage and his studies in mechanical engineering. In 1965 the estate was sold, but the old relic was not forgotten. It was moved to a new resting place until 1976 when Jan built a new house in Karlstad and made a space for his grandfather's Lexington in his garage. In the late 1970s and into the 1980s, Jan worked on refurbishing his keepsake. The general condition of the car was good in spite of all the years of storage. The body was lifted off of the frame and all parts were cleaned and painted. There wasn't any rust. The body was repainted the original color, black, and the leather upholstery just needed cleaning to be useable. The brakes were overhauled, but the engine, gearbox and rear axle are still in their original condition. The original carburetor was lost long ago so Jan fitted a Stromberg carburetor instead. A local enthusiast also helped by providing a vacuum tank for the fuel system that had also disappeared over the years. When visiting Hershey in 1986, Jan found a vendor with an impressive assortment of Motometers for different cars. Jan needed one for his Lexington, but the vendor's asking price was twice as high as those for other cars. When Jan asked why the difference, the vendor replied, "You will never see another one." Jan took him at his word and the Motometer now resides proudly on top of the radiator of his car. In 1984 the Lexington was finally back on the road again after sitting idle for many years. It is now in excellent running condition and is frequently seen taking part in local meetings for old cars in the Varmland area. When Jan's father, Sven, owned the car, he had two silver plates attached to the dashboard. One had been engraved with the name of his father, Per, and one with his name. Jan has added two more silver plates, one with his own name and one with the name of his daughter Maria Persson. Already, plans are that the next name to be added on the dashboard will be Maria's son Joakim, who has already shown great interest in the antique Lexington and is learning to drive it. One day, Joakim will be the 5th generation in the same family to own this remarkable car.[2]

1919 Lexington Touring. The owner of serial number 14338 is Ray Clark of Nicholasville, KY. In 2003, he purchased the car from David Estes, who had owned it for 13 years. David drove his Continental engine powered Minute Man Six on several Glidden tours including one at Salisbury, Maryland, in 1993 just after he had overhauled the engine. A few parts fell off during the tour, but those were reattached and the car performed flawlessly in the level coastal area. After getting back to his home state of Kentucky, David found that the car wouldn't climb hills. The problem was the location of the electric fuel pump. When that was corrected, hills were no problem. Mr. Estes also took his Lexington on Glidden tours to Redding, Pennsylvania, Detroit and Georgia. A previous owner of the car had been Craig Markle, Jr., of Haverford, Pennsylvania. David Estes enjoyed owning and driving it until he moved to a smaller home and decided to sell it.

The 1919 Touring owned by Ray Clark.

1920 Series S Thorobred. Serial number 22014, model 6 ST, is owned by Bill Baker of Nicholasville, Kentucky. Mr. Baker has driven his Thorobred on several

Top: This 1920 Lexington is owned by Bill Baker of Nicholasville, Kentucky. He has driven the car on various tours including the Hoosier Heritage Tour that made a stop in Connersville. *Courtesy Bob Barnard. Bottom:* This photo of the 1920 Series S Thoroughbred now owned by Bill Baker was taken in 1963 as Connersville was celebrating its sesquicentennial. The car owner at that time, Wesley Schickli, is standing behind local historian Henry Blommel. The building in the background was, at one time, the Lexington factory. *Author's collection.*

tours including the Hoosier Heritage Tour that made a stop in Connersville. Bill purchased this car from Wesley Schickli, who had owned the car for approximately 35 years after buying it from a man in Plattsburg, New York, in 1962. When he got it to his home in Louisville, Kentucky, he had it repainted and had new side curtains made for it. Wesley looked for a Lexington for a long while before finding this one. He wanted this particular make because it had been his father's favorite car. At one time his father had owned a 1921 Minute Man Six with the Ansted engine. This car is the smaller Thorobred powered by a Continental engine. Wesley had his car shining like new in time to drive it to Connersville for their 1963 sesquicentennial parade. Mr. Schickli enjoyed driving the car but remembered one time he got into trouble with it. He had been invited to show the Lexington in Cincinnati. On the way, coming into Madisonville, some young fellows pulled up alongside and said, "Hey old man, do you want to race?" Wesley related, "I don't know why I did it but I took off fast and kept ahead of them for a while until I blew the fiber timing gear." After they got the car back to Louisville, he had a new one made from aluminum.[3]

1920 Series S Thorobred Model 6ST. Serial number 24441 is owned by the Indianapolis Motor Speedway Museum. It has a Continental engine with serial number 181–7P-370. The car was originally owned by William Ansted, who managed the Central Manufacturing Company in Connersville. Ansted was also a member of the Board of Directors of the Lexington Motor Company.

The 1920 Series S Thorobred owned by the Indianapolis Motor Speedway Museum. *Photograph by author.*

1920 Series S Model 6ST. Serial number 22233 has been in the process of restoration for a longer period of time than it usually takes. The original owner may have been Ann B. Payne of Woodland Hills, California. She was quite elderly when she sold it on June 9, 1963, for $180.00 to Harvey E. McLaughlin of Encino,

Top: Serial number 22233 seen in the 1960s. *Bottom:* Serial number 22233 is now housed in the Fayette County Historical Museum in Connersville, where restoration work continues. *Photograph by author.*

California. A body and fender mechanic from the old school, McLaughlin worked with lead when filling or smoothing body panels. He started the restoration working on small parts. His health declined and in 1986 the car was obtained by Ray Gordon of Ojay, California, who intended to continue the restoration. The Thorobred occupied a space in Gordon's garage until 2004, at which time Gordon gave major assistance toward seeing that the car was returned to the city of its origin. It has the Continental engine and is generally complete except for runningboards and hubcaps. The forty-year restoration is being continued by the current owner, the Fayette County Historical Museum, Connersville, Indiana.

1920 Minute Man Six. This Continental powered car is owned by the Auburn Cord Duesenberg Museum at Auburn, Indiana. The color combination would have been typical of the choices offered customers. Prior to the museum obtaining the car, it had been owned for forty years by Bill Lyford of Bensonville, Illinois.

This 1920 Lexington Minute Man Six is owned by the Auburn Cord Duesenberg Museum. *Courtesy Eric vonGrimmenstein.*

1920 Thorobred. Now owned by Ray Clark of Nicholasville, Kentucky, this car's Continental engine was rebuilt during the time it was owned by Eric von Grimmenstein. Clark purchased the car in November 2004. (See photograph on top of page 220.)

The sporty motif of this 1920 Lexington Thorobred owned by Ray Clark is enhanced by the six wire wheels and the side mounted spares. *Photograph by author.*

1920 Lexington Minute Man Six. John Rehberg of Springfield, Nebraska, purchased this touring car in the spring of 2005 from Stanley Francis of Howard, Col-

This 1920 Lexington Minute Man Six, owned by John Rehberg, may be made into a Pikes Peak type racecar. *Courtesy Eric vonGrimmenstein.*

orado, who obtained it several years ago while attending the swap meet at Chickasha, Oklahoma. The serial number is 23180 and the car is generally complete with the Continental engine. John purchased the car with the intention of eventually making it into a Pikes Peak type race car.

1921 Lexington Seventy-Six Series T Seven Passenger Salon Sedan. Serial number 30208, Model 6 T S S, engine number COY 10339, was purchased new by George W. Smith, 2135 N. 4th St., Columbus, Ohio. The purchase price was $2,850. Mr. Smith had lived on the East Coast where he co-owned some dance halls, but moved to Columbus to determine if he and his partner should open a dance hall that far west. His partner in the dance hall business was J. T. Murphy, who marketed Murphy's Oil Soap. After arriving in Columbus, George fell in love with and married a skater and, therefore, built Smith's Skating Rink. Right behind it in a second building, he built a dance hall. He used the Lexington to drive back East to check on his holdings there. Emmet Bibler and some other men who worked at the rink borrowed the Lexington to go on a fishing trip to Michigan. When they returned, Emmet started to hand the keys to George, but George said, "Just keep it." George bought a new car every year or so. Emmet drove the big sedan until 1935. He then stored it in leaky garages until 1989 when it was sold. Ron Margello of Dublin, Ohio, Emmett Bibler's grandson, had always wanted the big Lexington. As a young boy he would sit behind the wheel imagining he was the driver. After graduating from high school he asked if he could have the car, but was told he was too young. He tried several times later on to convince his grandfather to let go of the family heirloom, so was horrified when he learned the car had been sold. He tracked down the buyer and bought it back for twice what his grandfather had sold it for. Ron

The 1921 Seventy-Six Series T Seven-Passenger Salon Sedan now owned by the author.

Top: The original interior remains intact. *Bottom:* An underhood view of Ansted engine number COY 10339.

and his wife, Peg, restored the car mechanically and cosmetically, but left the interior original. They drove it occasionally until they sold it at the 2000 Fall Kruse auction at Auburn, Indiana.[3] Eric von Grimmenstein, president of Van Ausdall & Farrar Inc., bought the car and displayed it in the company's showroom in midtown Indianapolis. This fine example of the top-of-the line sedan has returned to its home city, Connersville, since being purchased by the author, Richard Stanley, in the fall of 2004. The car is presently on display at the Fayette County Historical Museum.

1921 Touring. Not pictured is a 1921 Lexington Touring missing the back half of the body, that is owned by the Smith family of Sebastopol, California. George H. Smith acquired the car from Peter Allino of Petaluma, California. George passed away in 2002, but his son, Guy, is familiar with the car.

1922 Minute Man Six Touring. Owned by Bill Baker of Nicholasville, Kentucky, this car is mostly complete except for the interior. Bill purchased this car with the intention of making a Pikes Peak race car out of it. It had come from Missouri.

The 1922 Minute Man Six Touring owned by Bill Baker. *Courtesy Eric vonGrimmenstein.*

1922 Lexington Lark. This very rare car is owned by Leonard Sullivan of Yisilia, California. At one time this car was part of the famous William Harrah collection and was thought to be the only Lark in existence. (See photograph on page 224.)

The 1922 Lexington Lark owned by Leonard Sullivan. *Courtesy Eric vonGrimmenstein.*

1922 Minute Man Six Seven-Passenger Touring Model 6 T22. Eric von Grimmenstein acquired this car, serial number 31220 and motor number BOX 102831,

Another survivor is this 1922 Lexington Minute Man Six seven-passenger touring, now on display in Connersville at the Fayette County Historical Museum. *Photograph by author.*

in 2001 from Stanley and Cecil Josey of North Carolina. He originally intended to restore the car, but after deciding to sell the old Lexington dealer building, he assisted in getting the Lexington back to its place of origin. Therefore, in 2004, the Minute Man changed hands again and is now owned by the Fayette County Historical Museum. It is being restored by the Whitewater Technical Career Center.

1922 Minute Man Six Five-Passenger Touring Model 6 UTC. Serial number 35402 is owned by David Bottom of Lexington, Kentucky. Power is supplied by an Ansted engine with serial number 3180. The earliest known owner was W. B. Day of Mt. Sterling, Kentucky, who owned the Minute Man Six for 26 years and supposedly brought the car to Mt. Sterling from Indiana. Mr. Day died in 1968 at age 75 and the Lexington, reported to have been in perfect condition, was sold at auction along with several other antique cars in March of 1969. The next owner was Bob Thomason, also of Mt. Sterling, who likewise kept the car for an impressive 26 years before selling it to William Poe of Paris, Kentucky, in 1995. David Bottom acquired this well preserved Minute Man in 2004, returning the car to the city where the first of this marque was built.

This fine running 1922 Lexington Minute Man Six Five-Passenger Touring model is owned by David Bottom of Lexington, Kentucky. *Photograph by author.*

1922 Lexington Supreme Series U22 Seven-Passenger Sedan. Originally owned by William Ansted, this Ansted-powered car, serial number 363815ED7, is now owned by the Indianapolis Motor Speedway Museum. (See photographs on top of page 226.)

Top: This Lexington Supreme Series U22 Seven-Passenger Sedan, owned by the Indianapolis Motor Speedway Museum, is in pristine condition inside and out. *Photograph by author. Bottom:* William Ansted managed Connersville's Central Manufacturing Company, which built bodies used by Lexington and several other automobile manufacturers. After the family moved to Indiana's capital city, his son, William Jr., became an Indianapolis 500 racecar owner. A. J. Foyt drove Ansted's car to first place finishes in the 1964 and 1967 500 mile races. This picture of Foyt (right) with William Ansted, Jr., was taken after the 1964 win. William Sr.'s 1922 Supreme seven-passenger sedan is in the background. *Courtesy* The Connersville News-Examiner.

1922 Series U Touring. Now in Indianapolis, Indiana, after being purchased by Eric von Grimmenstein during the spring of 2004, this beautifully restored specimen came from California.

Top: This 1923 Lexington Series U is now in Indianapolis, Indiana, after being purchased by Eric vonGrimmenstein in 2004. The Ansted engine has serial no. CA 2769. *Photograph by author.* *Bottom:* From the unique storage compartment behind the front seat to the glistening dash and steering wheel, the quality of the restoration shines through. *Photograph by author.*

1923 Minute Man Six Touring. Owned by John J. Mawhinney of Ft. Myers, Florida, serial number 38876 has the Ansted engine. Jon's father purchased this car in 1951 from the Gage family in Hamilton, Ontario, Canada, and used it to go on Sunday drives for ice cream. It has never been in an accident or had major repairs. John bought the car in 2003 from his father's estate and had it shipped to Florida where he resides.

The 1923 Lexington Minute Man Six touring car owned by John J. Mawhinney of Ft. Myers, Florida. *Courtesy Paul Mawhinney.*

Minute Man Five-Passenger Coach. This car is approximately 1923 vintage and was last known to have been located in Minnesota. It appears to be a nice example of a two-door closed car from the twenties.

The present owner and location of this five-passenger Minute Man Coach are unknown. *Courtesy Eric vonGrimmenstein.*

1923 Lexington Roadster. This two-passenger car powered by an Ansted engine is owned by Bernard Wolfson of Clarksburg, Maryland.

This sporty two-passenger 1923 Lexington roadster is owned by Bernard Wolfson of Clarksburg, Maryland. *Courtesy Bernard Wolfson.*

1924 Minute Man Six Model VTC5. Serial number 40530 is owned by Milton Bacon of Gardnerville, Nevada. Mr. Bacon purchased this car, along with an extra

This 1924 Lexington Minute Man Six is owned by Milton Bacon of Gardnerville, Nevada, and is on display in the Minden Automotive Museum. *Courtesy Milton Bacon.*

Ansted engine, from the George Smith estate. Mr. Smith had several old cars which he displayed in the Western Museum and at times used as movie props. This car appeared in the movie *Blue Wonder*, where it looked very nice, and in the remake of the movie *Bonnie and Clyde* that was never released. Mr. Smith had acquired the car from Peter Allino of Petaluma, California. Mr. Bacon has had his Minute Man Six since mid–2004 and it is on display in his Minden Automotive Museum.

1924 Lexington Concord Boattail Speedster. Owned by the Indianapolis Motor Speedway Museum, this snappy red car has the Ansted series M engine number 6508. The body has apparently been modified for competition as no such body type was listed in company literature.

The 1924 Lexington Concord Boattail Speedster owned by the Indianapolis Motor Speedway Museum. *Courtesy Ken Lane.*

Pikes Peak Number 7 Race Car. The Number 7 Lexington, serial number 16585, that won the 1924 Pikes Peak Hill Climb is a survivor. The serial number indicates

Top: 45 Lexington Number 7, the 1924 Pikes Peak winner, in front of the building at 815 Central Ave., Connersville, that opened in 1916 as a Lexington dealership. The author and his two sons are pictured: left to right, Andrew, Richard and Alan Stanley. *Courtesy* The Connersville News-Examiner. *Bottom:* Pikes Peak winner No. 7 was displayed at the Fayette County Historical Museum in Connersville while on loan from the Pikes Peak Hill Climb Museum. *Photograph by author.*

The beautiful Penrose trophy on display at the Fayette County Historical Museum in Connersville. *Photograph by author.*

that the car may have been built in 1920 and rebuilt from year to year as it continued to be used in competition. The short wheelbase race car, in unrestored condition and nearly complete with its original paint and upholstery, was rescued by the New York Lexington dealer, who later sold it to the duPont family. Eventually it became the property of the Pikes Peak Hill Climb Museum at Colorado Springs, Colorado. While it was on loan to the Fayette County Historical Museum in Connersville, it was sold to another museum and had to be returned. The present owner is the El Pomar Foundation of Colorado Springs, Colorado. This foundation was funded through the Penrose fortune.

Ansted-powered Durants. A few Durant cars with Ansted engines are known to survive, including two B22 models pictured below.

Left: One of the few surviving Durant cars with an Ansted engine is this 1922 B22 with motor number DV 10444. The car is owned by Oscar Borufsen, who lives in Virginia. He purchased it as a basket case and restored it himself. He most recently rebuilt the Ansted engine in 2004. It has the original Rayfield carburetor with air cleaner and vacuum fed fuel system. *Above:* Another Durant B22 with an Ansted engine is owned by Ralph and Ruth Balla. They purchased this car from a neighbor who had owned it since it was new. *Both photographs courtesy Robert Smith.*

Appendix
Lexington Models

Year	Model	Engine	Cyl	Hp	Wb	Notes	Serial Nos.
1909	A	Rutenber	4	40–50	120"	1st car April 3.	Number plate on
	B	Rutenber	4	40–50	120"	Outstanding in	dash under hood,
	C	Rutenber	4	40–50	116"	1909 Glidden Tour.	left front spring, left rear kick-up.
1910	A	Rutenber	4	40–50	120"	Company	
	B	Rutenber	4	40–50	120"	moved to	
	C	Rutenber	4	40–50	116"	Indiana.	
	D	Rutenber	4	30–35	116"	Disappointing performance in Glidden Tour.	
1911	A	Rutenber	4	50	122"		
	D	Rutenber RA	4	40	117"		
	DF	Rutenber RA	4	40	117"		
	E "40"	Rutenber RA	4	40	117"		
	F	Rutenber RA	4	40	122"		
1912	DF Master	Rutenber RA	4	40	118"	Presto-Start and	
	E Standard	Rutenber X	4	40	118"	electric lights on	
	G Perfect Six	Rutenber	6	55–60	133"	all models. Dual	
	K Popular	Rutenber "27"	4	30	116"	exhaust first used. Entered Indy 500 race.	
1913	D	Rutenber	6	55–60	129"	Company	
	G	Rutenber	4	40	118"	reorganization—	
	Howard C	Continental	6	60	130"	Ansted family in control. Steering wheel moved to left side.	
1914	Howard D	Continental	6	60	130"		101–199
	Lexington H	Rutenber	4	40	114"		2101–2500
1915	KA MinuteMan	Teetor-Hartley	4	40	115"	Minute Man first used.	
	L Thoroughbred	Continental	6	50	128"	Thoroughbred first used.	1000–1350
	Six Supreme	Continental	6	60	130"		
1916	6-N Thoro.	Continental	6	50	132"	V-shaped radiator.	1500–1600
	6-O	Continental	6	40	116"		3000–4000
1917	6-O open cars	Continental	6	40	116"		4001–8000
	6-OO closed	Continental	6	40	116"		
	3-P	Continental	6	50	144" 130"	Touring Clubster	2000–2100
1918	6-O	Continental	6	40	116"		
	R	Continental 7-W	6	50	122"	Major frame revamp.	5001–11500
1919	R-19	Continental 7-W	6	50	122"	U.S. Automobile Corp formed;	12000–17296
1920	R	Continental	6	50	122"	2-way headlights;	
	S	Continental	6	50	122"	1st & 2nd at Pikes Peak	18000–23499

233

Year	Model	Engine	Cyl	Hp	Wb	Notes	Serial Nos.
1921	S	Continental	6	50	122"		23500–26500
	ST	Ansted	6	70	122"		
	T	Ansted	6	70	128"		30000–31200
1922	S	Continental	6	50	122"		26500–26592
	T	Ansted	6	70	128"		31200–31308
	U	Ansted	6	70	122"	Frame strengthened.	35001–38000
	Series 22	Ansted	6	70	123"		
	Lark	Ansted	6	70	122"		
1923	Series 23	Ansted D	6	70	123"	Receiver appointed.	36801–38999
1924	Minute Man	Ansted F	6	75	123"	1st, 2nd & 3rd at Pikes Peak;	39000–40249
	Concord	Ansted M	6	70	119"	smaller Concord introduced.	50000–50299
1925	Minute Man	Ansted F	6	75	123"		40250–40649
	Concord	Ansted M	6	70	119"		50300–50799
1926	Minute Man	Ansted F	6	75	123"		40650–up
	6–50	Ansted M	6	70	119"	4 whl. hydraulic brakes.	50800–up
1927	Auburn took possession May 23					Leftover cars sold as "new" into 1928.	

Notes

Chapter 1

1. "J. C. Moore, 81, Dies; Was Engineer with Lexington Motor Co.," p. 1.
2. "The Postbellum Period: 1865–1900," *The Best of Scott County*, p. 241.
3. "John C. Moore," *Lexington City Directory*, 1908.
4. Apple, *Scott County Kentucky: A History*, p. 290.
5. *Allied Companies*, pp. 1–4.
6. Articles of Incorporation, Fayette County, Kentucky, 12/2/08.
7. "Motor Company Files Articles of Incorporation," p. 6.
8. "Automobiles to Be Built in This City," p. 5.
9. Articles of Incorporation, Kentucky, Secretary of State, 12/15/08.
10. "Passing of Col. Kinzea Stone," p. 304.
11. Gantz, "Kinzea Stone," pp. 2234–2236.
12. "Site for Car Factory Purchased," p. 1.
13. "Site Purchase for Factory," p. 4.
14. "Mammoth Rink May Be Used as Factory," p. 6.
15. "No Deal for Rink," p. 7.
16. "New Auto Purchased," p. 3.
17. "Error in Survey," p. 1.
18. "The Lexington Car Name of New Auto," p. 10.
19. "Motor Car Co. Removes Offices from Hernando Bld.," p. 8.
20. "Lexington Car Name for New Automobile," p. 5.
21. "Lexington Motor Car Co. Factory Is Being Rushed," p. 8.
22. Gray, *Alloys and Automobiles*, pp. 114–116.
23. "43 Cars Sold by Lexington Motor Co.," p. 8.
24. "The Lexington Motor Car Manufacture Will Begin Tuesday," p. 7.
25. *Ibid.*
26. "Motor Co. Removes Offices to Plant," p. 3.
27. *Ibid.*
28. "Newcomer from the Bluegrass Region," p. 32.
29. "The Lexington Try to Get One," p. 54.
30. "Southern Auto Plant Wants to Locate Here," p. 1.
31. Ebert, Tentative Rutenber Motor Model List, Nov. 2000.
32. "The Rutenber 1909 Models," p. B-21.
34. Ebert, correspondence, Oct. 26, 2003.
35. "Rutenber Motors Absolutely Guaranteed," March 2, 1912.
36. "The Lexington New Automobile on Streets," p. 14.
37. "The Lexington Orders Received for Automobile," p. 3.
38. Gantz, "Kinzea Stone," pp. 2234–2236.
39. "New Auto Purchased," p. 3, c. 5.
40. Vance, interview, April 11, 2005.
41. "Lexington Car Co. Will Entertain," p. 10.
42. "Motor Car Co. to Entertain Commercial Club," p. 6.
43. "Lexington Car Plant Is Inspected," p. 10.
44. "No Entry of Lexington Motor Car Co. Will Be Made," p. 7.
45. "Auto Business is Holding Full Sway," p. 6.
46. "Lexington Entered in Hill-Climbing Contest," p. 2.
47. "No Entry of Lexington Motor Car Co. Will Be Made," p. 7, c. 4.
49. "The Lexington Automobile Is Registered," p. 3.
50. "Lexington Auto Test," p. 9.
51. "Packard Wins 50 Mile Auto Race," p. 5; "Reception By Lexington Motor Car Co.," p. 5, c. 1.
52. "Explosion Injures J. C. Coates," p. 1.
53. "Autos Turn at Denver," p. 1.
54. "Glidden Tour on Honk!" p. 1.
55. "Glidden Tour Will Contain a Lexington," pp. 1, 3.
56. "Glidden Tour on Honk!" p. 1.
57. "Detroit Gives Gliddenites Enthusiastic Send-off," p. 3. 48. "Our Challenge to Educate the Show Me's," p. 9.
58. "Clean Score for Moore," p. 11.
59. "The Lexington Still Has a Perfect Record," p. 4.
60. "The Lexington Still Has Perfect Score," p. 3.
61. "How Minneapolis Extended a Real Welcome," p. 123.
62. "The Lexington Still Has a Perfect Record," p. 4.
63. "Clean Score Retained," p. 7.
64. "A Lexington Auto Bought by James Helm," p. 1.
65 "Glidden Tourists Easily Make Schedule Tuesday," p. 1.
66. *Ibid.*
67. "Lexington Still Running with Perfect Score," p. 1.
68. "The Summing Up of The Tour," p. 209.
69. "Penalized Last Lap of Run," p. 1; "The Lexington Still Has a Perfect Record," p. 4.
70. "Twenty-four of Thirty Contestants Finished the Run," p. 209.
71. "Local Autoists Back from Glidden Tour," p. 7.
72. "Cup Races Held During Fair," p. 5.
73. "Automobile Races," p. 2.
74. "The Auto Parade," p. 4.
75. "Lexington Auto Test," p. 9, c. 2.
76. "No Contempt Intended," p. 2.
77. "Automobiles Damaged $200 Worth by Gasoline Fumes Igniting," p. 2.
78. "Explosion Injures J.C. Coates," p. 1, c. 2.
79. "Dr. Bryan Says He Has Not Sold His Motor Car Co. Stock," p. 5.
80. "Dr. Brian Sells His Auto Company Stock," p. 3.
81. "E. D. Johnston Elected President of Company," p. 1.
82. "May Move to Indiana," p. 3.
83. "Lexington Factory Is Secured Beyond Doubt," p. 1.
84. "Auto Company Plans for Moving Factory," p. 10.
85. "Motor Car Co. Is in Better Condition Than Was Expected," p. 5.
86. "Motor Company Will Be Retained in City," p. 7.
87. "Motor Car Company Will Not Move Away," p. 1.

88. "Motor Company Owner Comes to Close Deal," p. 8.
89. *The 1910 Lexington*, p. 4.
90. *Ibid.*
91. "New York Wants Lexington Cars," p. 1.
92. "Motor Company Moves Its Stock," p. 3.
93. "Lexington Product in Big Auto Show," p. 3.
94. "New York Wants Lexington Cars," p. 1, c. 1.

Chapter 2

1. "Southern Auto Plant Wants to Locate Here," p. 1.
2. "Lexington Plant May Be Landed," p. 1.
3. "Lexington Motor Car Plant Is Inspected," p. 10
4. "Annexed Skating Rink at Lexington," p. 1.
5. "Mr. Coats Writes," p. 1.
6. "Commercial Club Directors Meet," p. 1.
7. *Ibid.*
8. "Deal for Landing Lexington Plant," p. 1.
9. "Rites Wednesday for A. E. Leiter, 74, Veteran Merchant," p. 1.
10. "Lexington Plant Almost Assured," p. 1.
11. "Lexington Plant Can Be Secured," p. 1.
12. "Everybody Come to Mass Meeting To-Night but Leave Money at Home," p. 1. 13. "Lexington Men Already Here," p. 1.
14. "Size of New Plant Now Determined," p. 1.
15. "Lexington Men to Come on Monday," p. 1.
16. "Lexington Secured Beyond Doubt," p. 1.
17. "Lexington Motor Co. Let Contract," p. 1.
18. "E. D. Johnston Elected President of Company," p. 1.
19. Barrows, "E. D. Johnston," *History of Fayette County*, pp. 942–944.
20. "Lexington Factory Is Secured Beyond Doubt," p. 1.
21. "Bond for Deed," pp. 416–417.
22. "Committee Will Submit Contract," p. 1.
23. "Walls Are Rising on New Factory," p. 1.
24. "Lexington Soon to Be a Hoosier," p. 1090.
25. "Lexington Men to Come on Monday," p. 1.
26. "Annexed Skating Rink at Lexington," p. 1.
27. "Work Going On at Lexington Plant," p. 1.
28. "Lexington Plant May Soon Move," p. 1.
29. "Where Will These Men Be Housed?" p. 1.
30. Goetz, personal interview, Feb. 2002.
31. "Lexington Plant Now Dismantled," p. 1; "Lexington Plant Machinery Here," p. 1.
32. Goetz, personal interview, Feb. 2002.
33. "Fully a Hundred Men Now at Work," p. 1.
34. "Frank B. Ansted Brings Home Beautiful 7-Passenger Touring Car," p. 1.
35. "Lexington Wins in Missouri Contest," p. 2.
36. "Lexington Car Wins Connecticut Contest," p. 2.
37. "Lexington Car Wins Kansas Magazine Cup," p. 1.
38. "Lexington Cars Leave Connersville Today," p. 10.
39. "Lexington Cars Sent to Cincinnati from Connersville, Ind.," p. 1.
40. "Lexington Cars for Glidden Tour," p. 6.
41. "Fatal Auto Accident," p. 1.
42. "Seventeen Entries for Glidden Tour," p. 10.
43. "Map of States and Cities Through Which Tour Goes," p. 1076.
44. "The Glidden Tour Start Made Today," p. 8.
45. "Ten Thousand Saw Tourists Start," p. 1.
46. "Glidden Tour Will Start From Cincinnati Tuesday," p. 3.
47. "Lexington Cars for Glidden Tour," p. 6.
48. "Glidden Tour Will Start from Cincinnati Tuesday," p. 3.
49. "Glidden Tourists Meet Few Accidents on the First Day," p. 1.
50. "Lexington Cars Sent to Cincinnati from Cornersville, Ind.," p. 1.
51. "Glidden Tourists Meet Few Accidents Meet Few Accidents on the First Day," p. 1.
52. "Ten Thousand Saw Tourists Start," p. 1.
53. "Fatal Auto Accident," p. 1.
54. "Glidden Tourists Meet Few Accidents on the First Day," p. 1.
55. "Glidden Tour Will Start from Cincinnati Tuesday," p. 3.
56. 'Worst Day in Any Tour, Says Moore," p. 1.
57. "Wrecked Is Lexington No. 110 in the Glidden Tour," p. 2.
58. "Nine Days of Glidden Besmirched Records," p. 1122.
59. "Gliddenites Protest Against the Records," p. 4.
60. "Ten Are Left in Glidden Tour," p. 1.
61. "Glidden Tour Winners," p. 1124.
62. Ebert, correspondence, Oct. 26, 2003.
63. "Lexington Auto Goes to Europe," p. 1.
64. "Better Cars and Not Too Cheap," p. 1.
65. Kimes, *The Standard Catalog of American Cars,* 3rd ed., p. 861.
66. "Motor Cars for 10–11," p. 8.
67. "Lexington This Very Moment You Are Reading," pp. 125–128.
68. "Details of Passenger Automobiles on the American Market for 1911," pp. 86–87.
69. "Lexington Gasoline Cars," p. 179.
70. "Beautiful Car Appeared on Streets Today," p. 1.
71. "Lexington What Mr. L. E. Russell Thinks of His," p. 6.
72. "Story of the Lexington Truck," p. 6.
73. 'Superintendent at the Lexington Comes from Packard," p. 1.
74. "Coats, Fred N.," *Coron's Directory of the City of Connersville*, p. 61.
75. "Lexington Factory to Build Large Addition," p. 1.
76. Kimes, *The Standard Catalog of American Cars,* 3d. ed., p. 861.
77. *Lexington,* 1912.
78. "Elucidating the Lexington Line," p 576—579.
79. *The Lexington,* Nov. 20, 1911.
80. *Lexington,* 1912.
81. *The Lexington,* Nov. 20, 1911.
82. *Lexington,* 1912.
83. *Ibid.*
84. Williams, *My Life During The 20th Century,* p. 63.
85. "Lexington Car Qualifies," p. 1.
86. "Accidents Befall Local Cars," p. 1.
87. Kimes, *The Standard Catalog of American Cars,* 3d. ed., p. 861.
88. "Connersville Seeks to Hold Lexington," p. 1310.
89. Barrows, "Frederic I. Barrows," *History of Fayette County,* p. 1096.

Chapter 3

1. "Open Cars for Five Passengers," p. 83.
2. "Fayette County Swept by Terrible Flood," p. 1.
3. "Railroads Recovering from Flood," p. 19.
4. "Lexington Company to Make a Thousand Cars," p. 1.
5. "Central Car Company Is Founded by Local Men," p. 1.
6. "Articles of Association," pp. 436–437.
7. "Automobile Incorporations," p. 397.
8. "Article of Association of Howard Motor Car Company," pp. 441–444.

9. "Howard Car on Market," pp. 404–405.
10. "The New Series D Howard in Detail," p. 8.
11. "Howard Motor Co. Increases Capital," p. 1.
12. Barrows, "E. W. Ansted," *1917 History of Fayette County*, pp. 672–673.
13. Hubbard, *A Little Journey to Connersville*, 1914.
14. Barrows, "E.W. Ansted," *1917 History of Fayette County*, pp. 672–673.
15. Barrows. "Frank Ansted," *History of Fayette County*, pp. 715–717.
16. *Ibid.*
17. "Howard Six Makes Debut in Chicago," p. 1.
18. "Howard Six Has Double Exhaust Line," pp. 1132–1133.
19. "Howard Six Has Double Exhaust Line," pp. 1132–1133.
20. Kimes, *Standard Catalog of American Cars 1805–1942*, 3d ed., p. 861.
21. "Articles of Incorporation," pp. 524–525.
22. "You Find In Lexington-Howard Cars These Three Essential Selling Requisites," p. 55.
23. "The New Howard Six and the Lexington Four," pp. 218–222.
24. "Howard Has a Six," p. 61.
25. "The New Howard Six and the Lexington Four," pp. 218–222.
26. "You Find in Lexington-Howard Cars These Three Essential Selling Requisites," p. 55.
27. "Two Carloads of Howards Go Out," p. 1.
28. "The New Series D Howard in Detail," p. 8.
29. "Test Cars Raise the Public Wrath," p. 1.
30. "Lexington Four and Howard Six Have Novel Exhaust," pp. 32–33.
31. "Double Exhaust Shows Efficiency," p. 790.
32. "Engineering Aspects of Chicago Show," pp. 294–295.
33. *Ibid.*
34. "The New Howard Six and the Lexington Four," pp. 218–222.
35. "You Find in Lexington-Howard Cars These Three Essential Selling Requisites," p. 55.
36. "Lexington Criterion of Its Class," p. 34.
37. "Oh You Lexington Booster," p. 4.
38. Kimes, *Standard Catalog of American Cars 1805–1942*, 3d ed., p. 861.
39. *Ibid.*
40. "Lexington Thoroughbred Six—$1875," pp. 2–3.
41. "Lexington Has New Six," p. 1243.
42. *Lexington Series—Number 3 The Minute Man Four*, pp. 1–4.
43. *All About a New Light Six*, pp. 1–4.
44. "We Say This to Dealers," pp. 95–96.
45. "This Advertisement Tells You Facts About a Greater Six-Cylinder Car," pp. 72–73.
46. *The New Six Supreme*, pp. 1–4.
47. "Car Company Has Rush of Business," p. 1.
48. "The Six-Cylinder Lexington Car," p. 37.
49. "Indianapolis Is New Inland Field," p. 1.
50. "Lexington Gets Old Friend Back," p. 1.
51. "Lights and Music to Blend Tonight," p. 1.
52. "Motor Men Here and Are to Stay," p. 1.
53. "Woodruff, of the Lexington, Changed," p. 2.
54. "Death Angel Calls Prominent Young Man," p. 1.
55. "Indiana Auto Makers Again Discuss Merger," p. 9.
56. "Lexington Sales Are Running High," p. 1.
57. "Lights and Music to Blend Tonight," p. 1.
58. "Motor Men Here and Are to Stay," p. 1.
59. Tatman, Interview, Feb. 2004.
60. "Lexington Howard Co. Increase Capital," pp. 229–231.
61. " Lexington Makes Important Move," p. 1.
62. "A Summary of Principal Factory Additions," p. 1099.
63. "Lexington Annex Is Started Today," p. 1.
64. *The New Lexington Thoroughbred Six Series 6-N*.
65. "Lexington Minute Man Six," p. 1485.
66. "How a Lexington Crossed a Swamp," p. 6.
67. "Along the White Way at Richmond Auto Show," p. 10.
68. "Lexington Train Leaves the City," p. 1.
69. "Annex Doubles Power of Plant," p. 1.
70. Kimes, *Standard Catalog of American Cars 1805–1942*, 3d ed., p. 861.

Chapter 4

1. *Lexington Minute Man Six The Fashion Car for 1917*, pp. 1–12.
2. *Lexington Series 6-O-17 and 6-OO-17 Operation and Maintenance Manual*, pp. 19, 29.
3. "Lexington In Two 6-Cylinder Chassis," p. 612.
4. "Lexington Touring—6-P," *Handbook of Automobiles*, pp. 144–145.
5. *Lexington the Thoroughbred Six*, 1917.
6. "Lexington in Two 6-Cylinder Chassis," p. 612.
7. *Ibid.*
8. *Moore Multiple Exhaust System*, pp. 1–4.
9. *Lexington*, 1917, p. 2.
10. "Out of These Ten Big Factories," p. 51.
11. "Drive-Away Made a Handsome Start," p. 1.
12. "A New Drive-Away Shortly to Start," p. 1.
13. "Fifteen Cars of New Lexingtons," p. 1.
14. "Lexington Lands Large War Order," p. 1.
15. Manson, "Aussie Lexingtons," Dec. 3, 2002 (unpublished).
16. "Business Genius Gone," p. 1.
17. Walters, "Fayette Memorial Hospital Was a Private Sanitarium," p. 309.
18. "Lexington Howard Breaking Ground," p. 1.
19. "Three Lines Forward Moving," p. 1.
20. "Lexington Makes a Mighty Increase," p. 1.
21. "Articles of Association of Lexington Motor Company," pp. 472–475.
22. Kimes, *Standard Catalog of American Cars 1805–1942*, 3rd Ed., p. 861.
23. "Lexington Model Unveiled Today," p. 1.
24. "New Design in 1918 Lexington," p. 17.
25. "Lexington One–Finger Emergency Brake," p. 99.
26. *Lexington the Minute Man Six*, "Series O," 1918, pp. 1–4.
27. "Lexington Minute Man Six the Perfect Six," Oct. 25, 1917.
28. "Tomorrow Is Day of All Big Days," p. 1.
29. "Lexington Lands Fresh Rope Order," p. 1.
30. "Lexington to Build Government Trucks," p. 1.
31. "A Real Whale Is Landed by the Lexington," p. 1.
32. "Lexington Lands Another Big Order," p. 1.
33. "Lexington Makes a Start on Trucks," p. 1.
34. "Steel Wall Around Lexington Factory," p. 1.
35. Crowell, *America's Munitions*, p. 217.
36. Walters, "The Connersville, a World War I Steel Freighter," pp. 331–332.
37. Kimes, *Standard Catalog of American Cars 1805–1942*, 3d ed., p. 861.
38. "McFarlan Cars Are Driven to Seaside," p. 1.
39. "Lexington Leads the Entire State," p. 1.
40. Kimes, *Standard Catalog of American Cars*, 1st ed., p. 1137.

41. "Ansted Brothers Turn a Big Deal," p. 1.
42. "A New Annex for Lexington Plant," p. 1.
43. "Lexington Annex Is Leaping South," p. 1.
44. "Lexington Building Nearly Completed," p. 1. .
45. "F. B. Ansted Contracts for Supplies," p. 1.
46. Crowell, *America's Munitions*, p. 217.
47. Schlereth, *U. S. 40: A Roadscape of the American Experience*, p. 10.
48. "Nineteen Nineteen Touring Season to Be Record Breaker," p. 49.
49. "Minute Man Route Will Play a Part," p. 1.
50. "Lexington Immediate Delivery of New Models," p. 43.
51. "Lexington Men Given Glad Hand," pp. 1, 3.
52. "Ten Thousand People Came to Take Part in Celebration," pp. 1, 3.
53. "Hemp Is Ready for the Crowd," p. 1.
54. "Ten Thousand People Came to Take Part in Celebration," pp. 1, 3.
55. "F. B. Ansted Is Nationally Noted," p. 2.
56. "Lexington Plans a Testing Track," p. 1.
57. "Great New Buildings to Be Erected" p. 1.
58. "Shipping Floor Soon to Be Built," p. 1.
59. Walters, "The One Hundred-Foot Lexington Smokestack," p. 410.
60. Brown, personal interview, "Lexington Smokestack," Sept. 30, 2004.
61. "Thirty Each Day Lexington's Goal," p. 1.
62. *Ibid*.
63. "A Frightful Fire at the Lexington," p. 1.
64. Olsson, Heder, "Lexington in Sweden," 2004 (unpublished).
65. Olsson, Heder, "Lexington in Sweden," Dec. 6, 2002 (unpublished).
66. *Lexington Motor Cars*, 1919, pp. 1–16.
67. "Lexington Costly Molded Fenders," p. 4.
68. Kimes, *Standard Catalog of American Cars 1805–1942*, 3d ed., p. 861.

Chapter 5

1. "Auto Race to Be Held May 29th," p. 2.
2. "Lexington Car Loses," p. 4.
3. "Lexington in 100 Mile Run at Elgin," p. 1.
4. "Glidden Tour Cars Stop Here," p. 1.
5. "Lexington Car Qualifies for the Big Speedway Race," p. 1.
6. "Youngster Won Speedway Helmet," p. 1.
7. "Marion Made Motor Works Well in Race," p. 8.
8. "500-Mile Sweepstakes Run Off at the Indianapolis Speedway," pp. 1231–1235.
9. Gebby, "National at Indy," p. 25.
10. "Knight Used Rutenber Motor," p. 1.
11. "The Rutenber Motor," p. 984.
12. "Twenty-One Cars Have Qualified," p. 1.
13. "The Rutenber Motor," p. 984.
14. Fox, "1911," *The Illustrated History of the Indianapolis 500*, p. 24.
15. Nolan, "Ralph De Palma," p. 265.
16. "Dawson in a National Wins Thrilling 500-Mile Indianapolis Race," pp. 983–984.
17. Davidson, "Indy Incidents," pp. 44–46.
18. "Accidents Befell Local Race Cars," p. 1.
19. "Knight Gets New Motor for His Auto," p. 6.
20. "Harry Knight Met Death Yesterday," p. 1.
21. "Harry Knight Meets a Tragic Death on Track," p. 1.
22. "Driver Knight and His Helper Killed in Race," p. 3.
23. "Motor Racing at Victoria Park Course, Sydney," pp. 20–21.
24. "Buick Wins!" p. 58.
25. "Motor Car Racing," p. 6.
26. Manson, correspondence to Richard Stanley, August 4, 2004.
27. "Turner—Record Master," p. 40.
28. "Home Made Auto Is Victor in Sweden," p. 1.
29. "History of the Pike's Peak Hill Climb," p. 1.
30. "Lexington Wins, Pike's Peak Is Captured," p. 1.
31. "Lexington Ready for Hill Climb," p. 1.
32. "Lexington Wins, Pike's Peak Is Captured," p. 1.
33. "Afterthoughts upon the Triumph at Pike's Peak," p. 5.
34. "Lexington Ready for Hill Climb," p. 1.
35. "The Majestic Setting of the Pikes Peak Hill Climb," p. 29.
36. "Lexington Wins, Pike's Peak Is Captured," p. 1.
37. "Otto Loesche Wore a Redskin Charm," p. 1.
38. "Lexingtons Win Race to Top of Pike's Peak in Blinding Blizzard," p. 1.
39. "Lexingtons Come Home from Trial," p. 1.
40. "Celebration for Lexington Party Tuesday Evening," p. 1.
41. "Otto Loesche," p. 1.
42. "Important Announcement!" p. 1.
43. "Lexington Ready for Hill Climb," p. 1.
44. Bauer and Corbett interview, May 3, 2004.
45. "Otto Loesche," p. 1.
46. "Lexingtons Win Race to Top of Pike's Peak in Blinding Blizzard," p. 5.
47. "Lexington Ready for Hill Climb," p. 1.
48. "Lexington Wins, Pike's Peak Is Captured," p. 1.
49. "Avenues to Be Clear," p. 1.
50. "Parade Meant for Everyone," p. 1.
51. "Honor to the Two Victors," p. 1.
52. "Lexingtons Come Home from Trial," p. 1.
53. "Penrose Cup Here and Will Be Seen," p. 1.
54. "Pike's Peak Race Pictures," p. 6.
55. "Lexington Turns Hills to Smiles," p. 1.
56. "Racing Crew Off for Pike's Peak," pp. 1, 4.
57. "Local Racers Are First and Second in Speed Trials," p. 1.
58. "Loesche Is Winner[;] Breaks Own Record in Pike's Peak Race," pp. 1, 13.
59. "Loesche Is Amid Admiring Throngs," p. 1.
60. "Lexington Car in Pikes Peak Event," p. 14.
61. *Ibid*.
62. "23 Cars Entered in Annual Hill Climb," p. 1.
63. "Lexingtons Win First and Second," p. 1.
64. "Honor Members of Lexington Team," p. 1.
65. "Four Local Cars in Pike's Peak Event," p. 6.
66. *Ibid*.
67. "Flemming, "The King-of-the-Hill Dream," pp. 24–25.
68. "Robert Rudd Dies of Broken Back," p. 1.
69. Bauer and Corbett interview, May 3, 2004.
70. Flemming, "The King-of-the-Hill Dream," pp. 24–25.
71. "Lexington Wins at Pike's Peak; Loesche Breaks World Record," p. 1.
72. Goetz, personal interview, Feb. 2002.
73. "Lexington Wins at Pike's Peak; Loesche Breaks World Record," p. 1.
74. "Novel Fireworks for Victory Day," pp. 1, 5.

75. Blommel, "The Mighty Minute Man," p. 36.
76. Clymer, "Winners of Former Pikes Peak Races," p. 29.
77. Flemming, "The King-of-the-Hill Dream," pp. 24–25.
78. Snyder, correspondence to Eric vonGrimmenstein, July 1, 1995.
79. Gould, *For Gold & Glory*, p. 202.
80. Adams, correspondence to Richard Stanley, July 12, 2005.
81. Bauer and Corbett interview, May 3, 2004.
82. "Lexington Car Loses," p. 4.
83. "Four Local Cars in Pike's Peak Event," p. 6.
84. "Victory Day to Set High Mark," p. 1.
85. Smith, personal Interview, Feb. 20, 2004.
86. "Pike's Peak Home-coming Celebration," parody poem (unpublished).

Chapter 6

1. "A Powerful Concern with Several Units," p. 1.
2. "Passenger Car Prices and Weights," p. 399.
3. *Lexington Minute Man Six Motor Cars*, 1919, pp. 1–16.
4. "Tile Plant on East Side Leased by Lexington Motor Company," p. 1.
5. Kimes, *Standard Catalog of American Cars 1805–1942*, 3d ed., p. 861.
6. Williams, correspondence to Richard Stanley, Dec. 26, 2004.
7. "Another Fourth at Roberts Park with Lexington as Host," p. 1.
8. *The Camp Chigger*, pp. 1–4.
9. "Enormous Throng Assembles at Park," pp. 1–2.
10. *Lexington Information Book*, p. 124.
11. "Ansted Radiator," p. 1.
12. "Lexington Service Repair Department Has Fine New Building and Fittings," p. 8.
13. *United States Automotive Corporation Stock as an Investment*, pp. 2–6.
14. "Is the Motor Car Industry Being Attacked?" p. 25.
15. "Lexington Makes Announcement of Advance in Price," p. 1.
16. "Lexington Given Shower of Words of Commendation," p. 1.
17. Nevin, *Ford Expansion & Challenge 1915–1933*, p. 153.
18. "Lexington Plans Spoken of in Star," p. 1.
19. "Local Car Climbs Tremendous Hill," p. 1.
20. "Can Any Stock Car Equal These Certified Records?" p. 111.
21. *The Miraculous Ansted Engine*. 1922, pp. 1–4.
22. "Connersville Was There with Bells at the Auto Show," p. 1.
23. "Cylinder Blocks Manufactured in an Efficient Manner," pp. 72–77.
24. "Lexington Show Opens New Offices," p. 1.
25. "Lexington's Sales Era Opens Monday," p. 1.
26. "A Novel Display in the Inland Window," p. 2.
27. "Ansted Takes Plant Back," p. 41.
28. Meyer, *One Man's Vision*, p. 64.
29. "Approves Petition of Co-Receivers," p. 1.
30. "Indiana Piston Ring Co. Buys Teetor-Hartley Building—To Move to it," p. 1.
31. "Ansted Engineering Has Order for 30,000 Engines," p. 1.
32. "Brush Charges Ansted Motor Is Infringement," p. 737.
33. *The Revolutionary Car*, pp. 1–8.
34. *Lexington Minute Man Six Motor Cars The Seventy-Six Car*, 1921.
35. *Ansted-Lexington*, pp. 1–4.
36. *Announcing The Lark*, pp. 1–4.
37. Kimes, *Standard Catalog of American Cars*, 3d Ed., p. 861,
38. "Some Points About the 'U,'" p. 32.
39. "Local Cars Get Prominent Place at Automobile Show," p. 1.
40. "Announcing the Lark," pp. 1–4.
41. "At the Shows—Lexington Open Models," p. 33.
42. "Specifications of Current Passenger Car Models," p. 48b.
43. "Announcing Series 'U,'" p. 111.
44. "Some Points About the 'U,'" p. 32.
45. *Ibid*.
46. "Lexington Service Repair Department Has Fine New Building and Fittings," p. 8.
47. *A Wonderful New Lexington Series 22*.
48. "Specifications of Current Passenger Car Models," p. 48b.
49. "A Wonderful New Lexington Series 22."
50. "Lexington Swings into Production," p. 1.
51. "Motor Plant Is Scene of Blaze," p. 1.
52. "Bright Future for Lexington," p. 1.
53. "Ansted Engine Wins New Mark," p. 1.
54. "Big Boost for Local Industry," p. 1.
55. "Boom in Sale of Lexingtons," pp. 1, 8.
56. "Lexington to Ship Autos to Montreal," p. 1.
57. "Minute Man Statue in Depot Park Reflects Credit on Local Artist," pp. 1, 6.
58. Walters, "The Unsolved Case in Lexington Park," pp. 488–489.
59. Kimes, *Standard Catalog of American Cars 1805–1942*, 3d ed., p. 861.
60. "Increase of Capital Stock," pp. 140–141.
61. "Status of Auto Firm Outlined," pp. 1, 7.
62. Burness, *Cars of the Early Twenties*, p. 36.

Chapter 7

1. "Lexington Series 23," pp. 1–8.
2. "The Skylark: A New Lexington in a Class All Its Own," pp. 1–8.
3. "Two New Lexington Ideas," p. 32.
4. "Status of Auto Firm Outlined," pp. 1, 7.
5. "Asks Receiver for Local Firm," p. 1.
6. "Status of Auto Firm Outlined," pp. 1, 7.
7. "Receiver Named for Motor Plant," p. 1.
8. "Barrows Figures in Premier Deal," p. 1.
9. "Seek Receiver for Local Firm," pp. 1, 5.
10. "Two Named in Receiver Case," p. 1.
11. Kimes, *Standard Catalog of American Cars 1805–1942*, 3d ed., p. 861.
12. "Lexington Car in Pikes Peak," p. 14.
13. "Lexington Minute Man Six Models for 1924."
14. "Announcing Lexington Concord Six," p. 77.
15. "Orders Placed for 600 More Motors," p. 1.
16. "Outlook Good for Lexington—Herod," p. 1.
17. "Come Now and Let Us Reason Together," p. 4.
18. Kimes, *Standard Catalog of American Cars 1805–1942*, 3d ed., p. 861.
19. "Lexington," 1925, pp. 1–8.
20. "Prices and Weights of Current Passenger Car Models," pp. 44–45.
21. "Detroit New Car Deliveries for March Take Big Jump," p. 43.
22. "Men of the Industry and What They Are Doing," p. 122.
23. Kimes, *Standard Catalog of American Cars 1805–1942*, 3d ed., p. 861.
24. "Indiana Piston Ring Co. Buys Teetor-Hartley Building—To Move to It," p. 1.

25. "At the Shows Lexington Minute Man Six Closed Cars," 1926.
26. "Lexington Motor Cars New Series 6–50," 1926.
27. "Men of the Industry and What They Are Doing," p. 122.
28. "Sale of Lexington Ordered by Court," p. 908.
29. *Ibid.*
30. "New Castle Man Is Named Receiver," p. 1.
31. "Catalog Is Out for Sale of Plant," p. 1.
32. "Ansted Plant Sale Total at $202,000," p. 1.
33. "Car Service Merger," p. 18.
34. *Parts for Lexington Cars,* 1927, pp. 1–4.
35. Blommel, "Lexington and Ansted Engineering Company," p. 15.
36. "Property Sale Holds Interest," p. 1.
37. Rickert, *Record of the Transactions of the Lexington Motor Co., & Ansted Engineering Co.*
38. *Ibid.*
39. "Final Action Taken in Auburn Project," p. 1.
40. "Former Lexington Property Is Sold," p. 1.
41. "Six 1926 Show Cars Not in 1927 Exhibit," p. 672.
42. Rigor, personal interview, Jan. 8, 2004.
43. "An Apostle of the Joy of Working," pp. 33, 64.
44. Williams, R. F., phone interview, July 1, 2004.
45. "Frank B. Ansted Is Taken by Death," p. 1.
46. Walters, H. Max, "The Tractor Train, Lincoln Brakes and a Two Post Timer," pp. 425–427.
47. "J. C. Moore, 81, Dies; Was Engineer with Lexington Motor Co.," p. 1.
48. Walters, H. Max, "The Lexington Motor Car Company," p. 256.

Chapter 8

1. "Local Company is Given a Contract," p. 1.
2. "New Lexington Home to be Open Thursday," p. 18.
3. "Minute Man' Chief Attraction at Show," p. 1.
4. "New Home of Lexington," pp. 19–20.
5. "Building on the Past," p. 1.
6. vonGrimmenstein, Eric, personal interview, January 14, 2004.
7. "City business district on the rebound," pp. E-1, 2.

Chapter 9

1. Gibbens, Mike, unpublished material (survey).
2. Olsson, Igemar, and Mats Heder. "Lexington in Sweden" (unpublished).
3. Schickli, Wesley. Telephone interview, Dec. 14, 2004.
4. Margello, Ron, and Peg Margello. Unpublished material, Sept. 22, 2004.

Bibliography

Newspaper Articles

"Accidents Befell Local Racing Cars." *The Evening News* (IN). May 31, 1912, p. 1.
"Afterthoughts Upon the Triumph of the Lexingtons at Pikes Peak." *Connersville News-Examiner* (IN). Sept. 7, 1920, p. 5.
"Along the White Way at the Richmond Auto Show." *The Richmond Item* (IN). March 25, 1916, p. 10.
"Annex Doubles Power of Plant." *The Evening News* (IN). November 14, 1916, p. 1.
"Annex Skating Rink at Lexington." *The Evening News* (IN). Jan. 21, 1910, p. 1.
"Another Fourth at Roberts Park with Lexington as Host." *Connersville News-Examiner* (IN). June 14, 1920, p. 1.
"Ansted Brothers Turn a Big Deal." *The Evening News* (IN). April 4, 1918, p. 1.
"Ansted Engine Wins New Mark." *Connersville News-Examiner* (IN). April 6, 1922, p. 1.
"Ansted Engineering Has Order for 30,000 Engines; Double Force in February." *Connersville News-Examiner* (IN). December 16, 1921, p. 1.
"Ansted Plant Sale Total at $202,000." *Connersville News-Examiner* (IN). May 14, 1926, p. 1.
"Ansted Radiator." *Connersville News-Examiner* (IN). July 14, 1920, p. 1.
"Approves Petition of Co-Receivers." *The News-Examiner* (IN). July 30, 1923, p. 1.
"Asks Receiver for Local Firm." *Connersville News-Examiner* (IN). April 11, 1923, p. 1.
"Auto Business Is Holding Full Sway." *The Lexington Herald* (KY). June 20, 1909, p. 6.
"Auto Company Plans for Moving Factory." *The Lexington Herald* (KY). October 7, 1909, p. 10.
"The Auto Parade." *Lexington Leader* (KY). August 9, 1909, p. 1.
"Auto Race." *Lexington Leader* (KY). May 4, 1909, p. 2.
"Automobile Men Arrive Tomorrow." *The Evening News* (IN). May 26, 1915, p. 1.
"Automobile Races to Be a Big Feature of the Opening Day of the Blue Grass Fair." *Lexington Leader* (KY). August 7, 1909, p. 2.
"Automobiles Damaged $200 Worth by Gasoline Fumes Igniting in a Freight Car." *Lexington Leader* (KY). June 30, 1909, p. 2.
"Automobiles to Be Built in This City." *Lexington Herald* (KY). December 4, 1908, p. 5.
"Autos." *Lexington Leader* (KY). August 1, 1909, p. 19.
"Autos Turn at Denver." *Lexington Leader* (KY). July 25, 1909, p. 1.
"Avenues to Be Clear." *Connersville News-Examiner* (IN). September 11, 1920, p. 1.
"Barrows Figures in Premier Deal." *Connersville News-Examiner* (IN). May 22, 1923, p. 1.
"Beautiful Car." *Connersville Times* (IN). November 16, 1910, p.1.
"Better Cars and Not Too Cheap." *The Evening News* (IN). August 13, 1910, p. 1.
"Big Boost for Local Industry." *Connersville News-Examiner* (IN). July 8, 1922, p. 1.
"Boom in Sale of Lexingtons." *Connersville News-Examiner* (IN). April 24, 1922, p. 1.
"Bright Future for Lexington." *Connersville News-Examiner* (IN). March 27, 1922, p. 1.
"Buick Wins!" *The Argus (Melbourne, Australia)*. Nov. 15, 1921, p. 58.
"Building on the Past." *The Indianapolis Star*." July 7, 1999, pp. E-1, E-5.
"Business Genius Gone[;] City's First Citizen Called Across Divide." *The Evening News* (IN). June 20, 1917, p. 1.
"The 'Car Beautiful'[:] 'The Lexington.'" *The Lexington Herald* (KY). May 9, 1909, p. 3.
"Car Company Has Rush of Business." *The Evening News* (IN). April 24, 1915, p. 1.
"Car Service Merger." *The Kokomo Daily Tribune* (IN). June 12, 1926, p. 18.
"Catalogue Is Out for Sale of Plant." *Connersville News-Examiner* (IN). May 1, 1926, p. 1.
"Celebration for Lexington Party Tuesday Evening." *Connersville News-Examiner* (IN). Sept. 9, 1920, p. 1.
"Central Car Company Is Founded by Local Men." *The Evening News* (IN). Jan. 17, 1913, p. 1.
"City Business District on the Rebound." *The Indianapolis Star*. June, 28, 1998, pp. E-1, E-2.
"Clean Score for Moore." *Lexington Leader* (KY). July 13, 1909, p. 11.
"Clean Score Retained." *Lexington Leader* (KY). July 22, 1909, p. 7.

"Commercial Club Directors Meet." *The Evening News* (IN). September 4, 1909, p. 1.

"Committee Will Submit Contract." *The Evening News* (IN). November 13, 1909, p. 1.

"Connersville Was There with Bells at the Auto Show." *Connersville News-Examiner* (IN). January 18, 1921, p. 1.

"Deal for Landing Lexington Plant." *The Evening News* (IN). September 20, 1909, p. 1.

"Death Angel Calls—Prominent Young Man." *The Evening News* (IN). Dec. 13, 1915, p. 1.

"Dr. Bryan Sells His Auto Company Stock." *The Lexington Herald* (KY). September 22, 1909, p. 3.

"Dr. Bryan Says He Has Not Sold His Motor Car Co. Stock to Mr. Johnson (Johnston)." *Lexington Leader* (KY). Oct. 5, 1909, p. 5.

"Drive-Away Made a Handsome Start." *The Evening News* (IN). March 1, 1917, p. 1.

"Driver Knight and His Helper Killed in Race." *The Indianapolis Star*. July 5, 1913, p. 1.

"E. D. Johnston Elected President of Company." *The Evening News* (IN). October 9, 1909, p. 1.

"Engine Company Swinging Forward." *The Daily Examiner* (IN). March 19, 1919, p. 1.

"Enormous Throng Assembles at Park." *Connersville News-Examiner* (IN). July 6, 1920, p. 1.

"Error in Survey Responsible for Motor Car Co. Property Encroaching on C. & O." *Lexington Leader* (KY). January 22, 1909, p. 1.

"Everybody Come to Mass Meeting To-Night but Leave Money at Home." *The Evening News* (IN). October 1, 1909, p. 1.

"Explosion Injures J. C. Coats." *Lexington Leader* (KY). December 8, 1909, p. 1.

"F. B. Ansted Contracts for $2,000,000 Worth of Supplies." *The Daily Examiner* (IN). March 14, 1919, p. 1.

"F. B. Ansted Is Nationally Noted." *The Daily Examiner* (IN). Jan. 27, 1919, p. 2.

"Factory Sold, E. W. Ansted Acquires McFarlan Carriage Plant." *The Evening News* (IN). Dec. 31, 1913, p. 1.

"Fatal Auto Accident." *Lexington Leader* (KY). June 14, 1910, p. 1.

"Fayette County Swept by Terrible Flood." *The Evening News* (IN). March 23, 1913, p. 1.

"Fifteen Cars of New Lexingtons." *The Evening News* (IN). March 30, 1917, p. 1.

"Final Action Taken in Auburn Project." *Connersville News-Examiner* (IN). May 23, 1927, p. 1.

"Former Lexington Property Sold." *Connersville News-Examiner* (IN). September 22, 1927, p. 1.

"43 Cars Sold by Lexington Motor Company." *Lexington Leader* (KY). February 28, 1909, p. 8.

"Four Local Cars in Pikes Peak Event." *Connersville News-Examiner* (IN). August 2, 1924, p. 8.

"Frank B. Ansted." *The Evening News* (IN). May 3, 1910, p. 1.

"Frank B. Ansted Is Taken by Death." *Connersville News-Examiner* (IN). October 28, 1933, p. 1.

"A Frightful Fire at the Lexington." *The Evening News* (IN). June 19, 1919, p. 1.

"Fully a Hundred Men Now at Work." *The Evening News* (IN). June 8, 1910, p. 1.

"Gen. Chrisman Is Coming Home." *The Daily Examiner* (IN). July 1, 1919, p. 1.

"Glidden Tour Cars Stop Here." *Lexington Leader* (KY). June 14, 1910, p. 1.

"Glidden Tour on Honk!" *Lexington Leader* (KY). July 12, 1909, p. 1.

"The Glidden Tour Start Made Today." *The Evening News* (IN). June 14, 1910, p. 8.

"Glidden Tour Will Contain a Lexington Car and Supt. Moore Will Drive It." *Lexington Leader* (KY). July 1, 1909, p. 1.

"Glidden Tour Will Start from Cincinnati Tuesday." *The Lexington Herald* (KY). June 12, 1910, p. 3.

"Glidden Tourists Easily Make Their Schedule Tuesday and Are Off for Kansas." *Lexington Leader* (KY). July 28, 1909, p. 6.

"Glidden Tourists Meet Few Accidents on the First Day." *The Lexington Herald* (KY). June 15, 1910, p. 1.

"Glidden Tourists Will Be Here Next Tuesday and Two Lexingtons Will Be in Line." *Lexington Leader* (KY). June 8, 1910, p. 6.

"Gliddenites Protest Against the Records." *Lexington Leader* (KY). June 27, 1910, p. 4.

"Great New Buildings About to Be Erected." *The Evening News* (IN). July 28, 1919, p. 1.

"Harry C. Knight Meets a Tragic Death on Track." *Marion Leader-Tribune* (IN). July 5, 1913, p. 1.

"Harry Knight Met Death Yesterday." *The Evening News* (IN). July 5, 1913, p. 1.

"Home Made Auto Is Victor in Sweden." *Connersville News-Examiner* (IN). March 21, 1921, p. 1.

"Honor Members of Lexington Team." *Connersville News-Examiner* (IN). Sept. 14, 1923, p. 1.

"Honor to the Two Victors." *Connersville News-Examiner* (IN). Sept 15, 1920, p. 1.

"How a Lexington Crossed a Swamp." *The Evening News* (IN). April 20, 1916, p. 1.

"Howard Firm Makes Increase In Capital." *The Indianapolis Star*. September 28, 1913, p. 33.

"Howard Motor Co. Increases Capital." *The Evening News* (IN). Sept. 25, 1913 p. 1.

"Howard Six Makes Debut in Chicago." *The Evening News* (IN). Feb. 6, 1913 p. 1.

"Important Announcement!" *The Evening News* (IN). February 26, 1913, p. 6.

"Indiana Auto Makers Again Discuss Merger/" *The Indianapolis News*. Dec. 24, 1915, p. 9.

"Indiana Piston Ring Co. Buys Teetor-Hartley Building—To Move to It." *Hagerstown Exponent* (IN). September 10, 1925, p. 1.

"Indianapolis Is New Inland Field." *The Evening News* (IN). Nov. 2, 1915, p. 1.

"J.C. Moore, 81, Dies; Was Engineer with Lexington Motor Co." *Connersville News-Examiner* (IN). May 28, 1951, p. 1.

"Knight Gets a New Motor for His Auto." *The Marion Chronicle* (IN). July 17, 1912, p. 6.

"Knight Used Rutenber Motor." *Marion Daily Leader* (IN). June 3, 1911, p. 1.

"The Lexington[:] First Picture of the Splendid Touring Car That Will Soon Be Turned Out from Local Automobile Factory." *Lexington Leader* (KY). Feb. 17, 1909, p. 10.

"Lexington Annex Is Leaping South." *The Evening News* (IN). Dec. 9, 1918, p. 1.

"Lexington Annex Is Started Today." *The Evening News* (IN). August 17, 1916, p. 1.

"Lexington Auto Goes to Europe." *The Evening News* (IN). July 22, 1910, p. 1.

"A Lexington Auto Is Bought by James S. Helm and It Is a Beauty." *Lexington Leader* (KY). August 24, 1909, p. 1.

"Lexington Auto Test." *Lexington Leader* (KY). May 19, 1909, p. 9.

"Lexington Auto Entered in Hill Climbing Contest Lookout Mountain Club." *Lexington Leader* (KY). April 14, 1909, p. 2.

"The Lexington Automobile Is Registered" *Lexington Leader* (KY). May 31, 1909, p. 3.

"Lexington Building Nearly Completed." *The Daily Examiner* (IN). Feb. 11, 1919, p. 1.

"Lexington Car in Pikes Peak Event." *Connersville News-Examiner* (IN). August 17, 1923, p. 14.

"Lexington Car Loses." *Lexington Leader* (KY). Aug. 27, 1910, p. 4.

"Lexington Car Name for New Automobile." *Lexington Leader* (KY). Jan. 13, 1909, p. 5.

"The Lexington Car, Name of New Auto." *The Lexington Herald* (KY). January 13, 1909, p. 10.

"Lexington Car Qualifies for the Big Speedway Race." *The Evening News* (IN). May 27, 1912, p. 1.

"Lexington Car Wins Connecticut Contest." *The Lexington Herald* (KY). May 29, 1910, p. 2.

"Lexington Car Wins In Missouri Contest." *The Lexington Herald* (KY). May 18, 1910, p. 2.

"Lexington Car Wins Kansas Magazine Cup." *The Lexington Herald* (KY). January 1, 1911, p. 1.

"Lexington Cars at Fair." *Lexington Leader* (KY). August 6, 1909, p. 5.

"Lexington Cars for Glidden Tour." *The Evening News* (IN). June 11, 1910, p. 6.

"Lexington Cars Leave Connersville Today." *The Lexington Herald* (IN). June 10, 1910, p. 10.

"Lexington Cars Sent to Cincinnati from Connersville, Ind. to Get in Glidden Tour." *Lexington Leader* (KY). June 13, 1910, p. 1.

"Lexington Company to Make a Thousand Cars." *The Evening News* (IN). Oct. 4, 1912, p. 1.

"Lexington Costly Molded Fenders." *The Daily Examiner* (IN). January 25, 1919, p. 4.

"Lexington Factory Is Secured Beyond Doubt." *The Evening News* (IN). Nov. 10, 1909, p. 1.

"Lexington Factory to Build Large Addition." *The Evening News* (IN). August 10, 1911, p. 1.

"Lexington Gets Old Friend Back." *The Evening News* (IN). Sept. 15, 1915, p. 1.

"Lexington Given Shower of Words of Commendation." *Connersville News-Examiner* (IN). Sept. 28, 1920, p. 1.

"Lexington Howard Breaking Ground." *The Evening News* (IN). July 25, 1917, p. 1.

"Lexington in 100 Mile Run at Elgin." *The Evening News* (IN). August 27, 1910, p. 1.

"Lexington Lands Another Big Order." *The Evening News* (IN). Nov. 5, 1918, p. 1.

"Lexington Lands Fresh Rope Order." *The Daily Examiner* (IN). July 17, 1918, p. 1.

"Lexington Lands Large War Order." *The Evening News* (IN). Dec. 17, 1917, p. 1.

"Lexington Leads the Entire State." *The Evening News* (IN). April 25, 1918, p. 1.

"Lexington Makes a Mighty Increase." *The Evening News* (IN). August 30, 1917, p. 1.

"Lexington Makes a Start on Trucks." *The Evening News* (IN). Dec. 14, 1918, p. 1.

"Lexington Makes Announcement of Advance in Price." *The News-Examiner* (IN). Sept. 27, 1920, p. 1.

"Lexington Makes Important Move." *The Evening News* (IN). May 12, 1916, p. 1.

"Lexington Men Already Here." *The Evening News* (IN). Oct. 4, 1909, p. 1.

"Lexington Men Given Glad Hand." The Evening News (IN). May 31, 1919, p. 1.

"Lexington Men to Come on Monday." *The Evening News* (IN). Oct. 2. 1909, p. 1.

"Lexington Model Unveiled Today." *The Evening News* (IN). Sept. 15, 1917, p. 1.

"Lexington Motor Car Co Factory Is Being Rushed." *Lexington Leader* (KY). February 4, 1909, p. 8.

"Lexington Motor Car Company Let Contract." *The Evening News* (IN). October 29, 1909, p. 1.

"The Lexington Motor Car Manufacture Will Begin Tuesday." *Lexington Leader* (KY). March 15, 1909, p. 7.

"Lexington Motor Car Plant Is Inspected." *The Lexington Herald* (KY). June 12, 1909, p. 10.

"Lexington Motor Car Still Running with Perfect Score in the Glidden Tour." *Lexington Leader* (KY). July 29, 1909, p. 1.

"Lexington Motor Car Will Entertain." *The Lexington Herald* (KY). June 10, 1909, p. 10.

"The Lexington New Automobile on Streets." *Lexington Leader* (KY). April 4, 1909, p. 14.

"Lexington Not to Enter Big Merger." *The Evening News* (IN). Dec. 17, 1915, p. 1.

"The Lexington Orders Received for Automobile Made Here from Distant Points." *Lexington Leader* (KY). May 21, 1909, p. 3.

"Lexington Plans a Testing Track." *The Evening News* (IN). April 24, 1919, p. 1.

"Lexington Plans Spoken of in Star." *Connersville, News-Examiner* (IN). Jan. 29, 1921, p. 1.

"Lexington Plant Almost Assured." *The Evening News* (IN). September 17, 1909, p. 1.

"Lexington Plant Can Be Secured." *The Evening News* (IN). September 28, 1909, p. 1.

"Lexington Plant Inspected by the Rotarians in Mass." *Connersville News-Examiner* (IN). September 25, 1920, p. 1.

"Lexington Plant Machinery Here." *The Evening News* (IN). April 13, 1910, p. 1.

"Lexington Plant May Be Landed." *The Evening News* (IN). September 2, 1909, p. 1.

"Lexington Plant May Soon Move." *The Evening News* (IN). April 6, 1910, p. 1.

"Lexington Plant Now Dismantled." *The Evening News* (IN). April 18, 1910, p. 1.

"Lexington Product in Big Auto Show." *The Lexington Herald* (KY). January 26, 1910, p. 3.

"Lexington Ready for Hill Climb." *Connersville News-Examiner* (IN). August 13, 1920, p. 1.

"Lexington Sales Are Running High." *The Evening News* (IN). Sept. 3, 1915, p. 1.

"Lexington Service Repair Department Has Fine New Building and Fittings." *Connersville News-Examiner* (IN). Sept. 15, 1920, p. 8.

"Lexington Show Opens in Offices." *Connersville News-Examiner* (IN). March 4, 1921, p. 1.

"The Lexington Still Has a Perfect Record." *Lexington Leader* (KY). July 20, 1909, p. 4.

"The Lexington Still Has a Perfect Score." *Lexington Leader* (KY). July 17, 1909, p. 3.

"Lexington Swings into Production." *Connersville News-Examiner* (IN). March 30, 1922, p. 1.

"Lexington to Build Government Trucks." *The Daily Examiner* (IN). August 9, 1918, p. 1.

"Lexington to Ship Autos to Montreal." *Connersville News-Examiner* (IN). April 18, 1922, p. 1.

"Lexington Train Leaves the City." *The Evening News* (IN). June 15, 1916, p. 1.

"Lexington Turns Hills to Smiles." *Connersville News-Examiner* (IN). May 7, 1921, p. 1.

"Lexington[,] What Mr. L. E. Russell, of Los Angeles, Thinks of His." *The Evening News* (IN). December 31, 1911, p. 6.

"Lexington Wins at Pikes Peak; Loesche Breaks World Record." *Connersville News-Examiner* (IN). Sept 2, 1924, p. 1.

"Lexington Wins Pikes Peak is Captured." *Connersville News-Examiner* (IN). Sept. 7, 1920, p. 1.

"Lexington's Sales Era Opens Monday." *Connersville News-Examiner* (IN). April 23, 1921, p. 1.

"Lexington's Show Opens in Offices." *Connersville News-Examiner* (IN). March 4, 1921, p. 1.

"Lexingtons Win First And Second." *Connersville News-Examiner* (IN). Sept 4, 1923, p. 1.

"Lights and Music to Blend Tonight." *The Evening News* (IN). May 26, 1916, p. 1.

"Local Autoists Back from Glidden Tour Pleased with Record Made by the Lexington Car." *Lexington Leader* (KY). August 4, 1909, p. 7.

"Local Car Climbs Tremendous Hill." *Connersville News-Examiner* (IN). March 31, 1921, p. 1.

"Local Cars Get Prominent Place at Automobile Show." *Connersville News-Examiner* (IN). Jan. 4, 1922, p. 1.

"Local Company Is Given a Contract." *Connersville News-Examiner* (IN). June 2, 1920, p. 1.

"Local Company Will Be Retained in City." *The Lexington Herald* (KY). November 5, 1909, p. 7.

"Local Racers Are First and Second in Speed Trials." *Connersville News-Examiner* (IN). Sept. 2, 1921, p. 1.

"Loesche Is Amid Admiring Throngs." *Connersville News-Examiner* (IN). Sept 10, 1921, p. 1.

"Loesche Is Winner[;] Breaks Own Record in Pikes Peak Race." *Connersville News-Examiner* (IN). Sept. 4, 1921, pp. 1, 13.

"Mammoth Rink May Be Used as Factory for Lexington Motor Car Co." *Lexington Leader* (KY). December 18, 1908, p. 6.

"Marion Made Motor Works Well in Race." *The Marion Chronicle* (IN). June 1, 1911, p. 8.

"McFarlan Cars Are Driven to Seaside." *The Evening News* (IN). April 8, 1918, p. 1.

"Minute Man Chief Attraction at Show." *Connersville News-Examiner* (IN). Feb. 28, 1921, p. 1.

"Minute Man Route Will Play a Part." *The Evening News* (IN): April 11, 1919, p. 4.

"Minute Man Statue In Depot Park Reflects Credit on Local Artist." *Connersville News-Examiner* (IN). August 21, 1922, p. 1.

"Mr. Coats Writes." *The Evening News* (IN). September 23, 1909, p. 1.

"Motor Car Co. Is in Better Condition Than Was Expected—Will Remain in Lexington." *Lexington Leader* (KY). Nov. 4, 1909, p. 5.

"Motor Car Co. New Automobile Manufacturing Concern to Entertain the Commercial Club." *Lexington Leader* (KY). June 10, 1909, p. 6.

"Motor Car Co. Removes Offices from Hernando Building to Trust Structure." *Lexington Leader* (KY). Jan. 22, 1909, p. 8.

"Motor Car Company Will Not Move Away." *The Lexington Herald* (KY). November 9, 1909, p. 1.

"Motor Car Racing." *Sydney Morning Herald* (Australia). June 30, 1919, p. 10.

"Motor Cars for '10–11." *The Evening News* (IN). September 17, 1910, p. 8.

"Motor Co. Files Articles of Incorporation." *Lexington Leader* (KY). December 3, 1908, p. 6.

"Motor Co. Removes Offices to Plant" *Lexington Leader* (KY). March 2, 1909, p. 3.

"Motor Company Moves Its Stock." *The Lexington Herald* (KY). January 24, 1910, p. 3.

"Motor Company Owner Comes to Close Deal." *The Lexington Herald* (KY). November 13, 1909, p. 8.

"Motor Company Will Be Retained in City." *The Lexington Herald* (KY). Nov. 5, 1909, p. 7.

"Motor Men Here and Are to Stay." *The Evening News* (IN). May 29, 1915, p. 1.

"Motor Plant Is Scene of Blaze." *Connersville News-Examiner* (IN). March 30, 1922, p. 1.

"A New Annex for Lexington Plant." *the Evening News* (IN). June 19, 1919, p. 1.

"New Auto Purchased." *Lexington Leader* (KY). February 26, 1910, p. 3.

"A New Drive-Away Shortly to Start." *The Evening News* (IN). March 15, 1917, p. 1.

"New Lexington Home to Be Open Thursday." *The Indianapolis Star*. March 2, 1921.

"The New Series D Howard In Detail." *The Evening News* (IN). Nov. 1, 1913 p. 8.

"New York Wants Lexington Cars." *The Evening News* (IN). January 17, 1910, p. 1.

"Newcastle Man Is Named Receiver." *Connersville News-Examiner* (IN). May 12, 1926, p. 1.

"No Contempt Intended." *Lexington Leader* (KY). June 29, 1909, p. 2.

"No Deal For Rink." *Lexington Leader* (KY). December 21, 1908, p. 7.

"No Entry of Lexington Motor Car Co." *Lexington Leader* (KY). April 15, 1909, p. 7.

"A Novel Display in the Inland Window." *Connersville News-Examiner* (IN). April 28, 1921, p. 2.

"Novel Fireworks for Victory Day." *Connersville News-Examiner* (IN). Sept. 12, 1924, pp. 1, 5.

"Oh You Lexington Booster!" *The Evening News* (IN). August 8, 1914, p. 3.

"Orders Placed for 600 More Motors." *Connersville News-Examiner* (IN). March 15, 1924, p. 1.

"Our Challenge to Educate the Show Me's." *The Lexington Herald* (KY). May 9, 1909, p. 3.

"Otto Loesche." *Cincinnati Enquirer*. Jan 9, 1975, p. 1.

"Otto Loesche Wore a Redskin Charm." *Connersville News-Examiner* (IN). Oct. 27, 1920, p. 1.

"Outlook Good for Lexington-Herod." *Connersville News-Examiner* (IN). August 1, 1924, p. 1.

"Packard Wins the 50-Mile Auto Race." *The Lexington Herald* (KY). June 6, 1909, p. 5.

"Parade Meant for Everyone." *Connersville News-Examiner* (IN). September 12, 1920, p. 1.

"Penalized Last Lap of Run." *Lexington Leader* (KY). July 31, 1909, p. 1.

"Penrose Cup Here and Will Be Seen." *Connersville News-Examiner* (IN). Oct. 25, 1920, p. 1.

"Plant of the Lexington Car Co. Likely to Go to Connersville." *Lexington Leader* (KY). October 1, 1909, p. 3.

"A Powerful Concern with Several Units." *Connersville News and Examiner* (IN). Jan. 12, 1920, p. 1.

"Property Sale Holds Interest." *Connersville News-Examiner* (IN). August 26, 1926, p. 1.

"Racing Crew Off for Pikes Peak." *Connersville News-Examiner* (IN). July 27, 1921, p. 1 & 4.

"A Real Whale Is Landed by the Lexington." *The Evening News* (IN). Oct. 4, 1918, p. 1.

"Receiver Named for Motor Plant." *Connersville News-Examiner* (IN). April 30, 1923, p. 1.

"Reception by Lexington Motor Car Co." *Lexington Leader* (KY). June 11, 1909, p. 5.

"Rites Wednesday for A. E. Leiter, 74, Veteran Merchant." *Connersville News-Examiner* (IN). October 27, 1947, p. 1.

"Robert Rudd Dies of Broken Back." *Connersville News-Examiner* (IN). August 19, 1933, p. 1.

"Rutenber Motors Absolutely Guaranteed." *The Marion Chronicle* (IN). March 2, 1912, p. 1.

"Score Perfect." *Lexington Leader* (KY). July 24, 1909, p. 1.

"Seek Receiver for Local Firm." *Connersville News-Examiner* (IN). April 23, 1923, p. 1.

"Seventeen Entries for Glidden Tour." *The Lexington Herald* (KY). May 11, 1910, p. 10.

"Shipping Floor Soon to Be Built." *The Evening News* (IN). April 16, 1919, p. 1.

"Site for Car Factory Purchased by Recently Organized Lexington Motor Company." *Lexington Leader* (KY). December 16, 1908, p. 1.

"Site Purchase for Automobile Factory." *The Lexington Herald* (KY). December 17, 1908, p. 4.

"Size of New Plant Now Determined." *The Evening News* (IN). October 6, 1909, p. 1.

"Southern Auto Plant Wants to Locate Here." *The Evening News* (IN). August 30, 1909, p. 1.

"Status of Auto Firm Outlined." *Connersville News-Examiner* (IN). April 12, 1923, p. 1.

"Steel Wall Around Lexington Factory." *The Daily Examiner* (IN). June 25, 1918, p. 1.

"Story of the Lexington Truck." *The Evening News* (IN). September 4, 1911, p. 6.

"Superintendent at the Lexington Comes from the Great Packard Auto Factory." *The Evening News* (IN). Sept. 7, 1911, p. 1.

"Ten Are Left in Glidden Tour." *The Evening News* (IN). June 27, 1910, p. 1.

"Ten Thousand People Came to Take Part in Celebration." *The Daily Examiner* (IN). July 5, 1919, p. 1.

"Ten Thousand Saw Tourists Start." *The Evening News* (IN). June 15, 1910, p. 1.

"Test Cars Raise the Public Wrath." *The Evening News* (IN). Oct. 5, 1914, p. 1.

"Thirty Each Day Lexington's Goal." *The Daily Examiner* (IN). March 18, 1919, p. 1.

"Three Lines of Forward Moving." *The Evening News* (IN). January 23, 1917, p. 1.

"Tile Plant on East Side Leased by Lexington Motor Company." *Connersville News and Examiner* (IN). March 16, 1920, p. 1.

"Tomorrow Is Day of All Big Days." *The Daily Examiner* (IN). July 3, 1919, p. 1.
"Twenty-One Cars Have Qualified." *The Evening News* (IN). May 28, 1912, p. 1.
"23 Cars Entered in Annual Hill Climb." *Connersville News-Examiner* (IN). August 25, 1923, p. 1.
"Two Carloads of Howards Go Out." *The Evening News* (IN). December 11, 1913, p. 1.
"Two Named in Receiver Case." *Connersville News-Examiner* (IN). May 27, 1923, p. 1.
"Victory Day to Set High Mark." *Connersville News-Examiner* (IN). Sept. 10, 1924, p. 1.
"Walls Are Rising on New Factory." *The Evening News* (IN). November 20, 1909, p. 1.
"Where Will These Men Be Housed?" *The Evening News* (IN). March 3, 1910, p. 1.
"Woodruff, of the Lexington, Changed." *The Evening News* (IN). May 25, 1915, p. 2.
"Work Going On at Lexington Plant." *The Evening News* (IN). February 7, 1910, p. 1.
"Worst Day in Any Tour, Says Moore." *The Evening News* (IN). June 18, 1910, p. 1.
"Wrecked Is Lexington No. 110 in The Glidden Tour and Is Ordered Back to the Factory." *Lexington Leader* (KY). P. 4.
"Youngster Won Speedway Helmet." *Marion News-Tribune* (IN). Sept. 4, 1910, p. 1.

Other Articles

"A-C-D Museum Receives Rare 1920 Lexington." *Antique Automobile*. March-April 1994, pp. 18–19.
"Announcing / Lexington Concord Six." *Motor Age*. January 3, 1924, p. 77.
"Announcing Series 'U.'" *Motor*. Feb. 1922, p. 111.
"Ansted Takes Plant Back." *Motor West*. May 1, 1921, p. 41.
"An Apostle of the Joy of Working." *Motor*. Nov. 1921, pp. 33, 64.
"At the Shows—Lexington Open Models." *Cars & Parts*. June 1967, p. 33.
"Automobile Incorporations." *The Automobile*. January 23, 1913, p. 397.
Blommel, Henry. "The Mighty Minute Man." *Antique Automobile*. Nov.-Dec. 1969, pp. 32–36.
"Brush Charges Ansted Motor Is Infringement." *Automotive Industries*. October 13, 1921, p. 737.
"Can Any Stock Car Equal These Certified Records?" *The Saturday Evening Post*. September 10, 1921, p. 111.
"Connersville Seeks to Hold Lexington." *The Automobile*, December 23, 1912, p. 1310.
"Cylinder Blocks Manufactured in an Efficient Manner." *Automotive Industries*. January 13, 1921, p. 72–77.
Davidson, Donald. "Indy Incidents." *Special Interest Autos*. May-June 1975, pp. 44–46.
"Dawson in a National Wins Thrilling 500-Mile Indianapolis Race." *The Horseless Age*. June 5, 1912, pp. 983–984.
"Details of Passenger Automobiles on the American Market for 1911." *The Automobile*. January 5, 1911, pp. 86–87.
"Detroit Gives Gliddenites Enthusiastic Send-Off." *The Automobile*. July 15, 1909, p. 3.
"Detroit New Car Deliveries for March Take Big Jump." *Motor Age*. April 16, 1925, p. 43.
"Double Exhaust Shows Efficiency." *The Automobile*. April 9, 1914, p. 790.
"Elucidating the Lexington Line." *The Automobile*. Oct. 5, 1911, pp. 576–579.
"Engineering Aspects of Chicago Show." *The Automobile*. January 26, 1914, pp. 294–295.
"500-Mile Sweepstakes Run Off at the Indianapolis Speedway." *The Automobile*. June 1, 1911, pp. 1230–1235.
Flemming, Janice. "The King of the Hill Dream." *Indianapolis Star Magazine*. May 15, 1983, pp. 24–25.
Gantz, Tracy. "Kinzea Stone." *The Blood Horse*. April 26, 1980, pp. 2236–2244.
Gebby, Jerry. "National at Indy." *Antique Automobile*. Nov.-Dec. 1968, p. 25.
"The Glidden Tour Is On." *The Automobile*. June 16, 1910, p. 1076.
"Glidden Tour Winners." *The Automobile*. July 7, 1910, pp. 3–4.
"History of the Pikes Peak Hill Climb." *History of the Pikes Peak Hill Climb Official Souvenir Program. 1964*
"How Minneapolis Extended a Real Welcome." *The Automobile*. July 22, 1909, p. 123.
"Howard Has a Six." *The Automobile*. January 1, 1914, p. 61.
"Howard Motor Car on Market." *The Automobile*. February 6, 1913, p. 404–405.
"Howard Six Has Double Exhaust Line." *The Automobile*. May 29, 1913, p. 1132.
"Immediate Delivery of New Models." *The Saturday Evening Post*. January 4, 1919, p. 43.
"Is the Motor Car Industry Being Attacked?" *Motor Age*. May 6, 1920, p. 25.
"The Lexington: Try to Get One." *Cycle and Automobile Trade Journal*. May 1909, p. 54.
"Lexington Criterion of Its Class." *Motor*. January 1914, p. 34.
"Lexington Four and Howard Six Have Novel Exhaust." *Motor Age*. April 9, 1914, p. 32.
"Lexington Gasoline Cars." *Cycle and Automobile Trade Journal*. March 1911, p. 179.
"Lexington Has New Six." *The Automobile*. December 31, 1914, p. 1243.
"Lexington in Two Six-Cylinder Chassis." *The Automobile*. October 12, 1916, pp. 612–613.
"Lexington Minute Man Six 1075." *Literary Digest*. December 25, 1915, p. 1485.
"Lexington Soon Will Be a Hoosier." *The Automobile*. Dec. 1909.

"Lexington This Very Moment You Are Reading." *The Automobile.* July 7, 1910, pp. 125–128.

"Lexington Thoroughbred Six." *The Horseless Age.* December 30, 1914, pp. 2–3.

"Lexington." *Life.* Oct. 25, 1917.

"The Majestic Setting of the Pikes Peak Hill Climb." *Motor Age.* September 23, 1920, p. 29.

"Map of States and Principal Cities Through Which the Tour Goes." *The Automobile.* June 16, 1910, p. 1076.

"Men of the Industry and What They Are Doing." *Automotive Industries.* January 21, 1926, p. 122.

"Motor Car Racing at Victoria Park Course, Sydney." *The Motor In Australia.* July 1, 1919, pp. 20–24.

"National Shows Issue Specification Number." *Motor Age.* January 7, 1926, p. 83.

"New Design in 1918 Lexington." *Motor Age.* September 27, 1917.

"New Home of Lexington." *The Hoosier Motorist.* April 1921, pp. 19–20.

"The New Howard "Six" and the Lexington "Four."" *Automobile Trade Journal.* May 1914, p. 218–222.

"Newcomer from the Blugrass Region." *The Automobile.* July 1, 1909, p. 32.

"Nine Days of Glidden Besmirched Records." *The Automobile.* June 23, 1910, p. 25.

"Nineteen Nineteen Touring Season to Be Record Breaker." *American Automobile Digest.* June 1919, p. 49.

Nolan, William E. "Ralph De Palma." *Automobile Quarterly.* Volume 2, Number 3, pp. 264–274.

"Open Cars for Five Passengers at $2400 to $3000." *The Automobile.* January 9, 1913, p. 83.

"Out of These Ten Big Factories." *The Saturday Evening Post.* August 12, 1916, p. 51.

"Passenger Prices and Weights." *Automobile Trade Journal.* February 1920, p. 399.

"Passing of Col. Kinzea Stone." *The Thoroughbred Record* (KY). March 1925, p. 304.

"Prices and Weights of Current Passenger Car Models." *Motor Age.* January 29, 1925, pp. 44–45.

"Railroads Recovering from the Flood." *Motor Age.* April 10, 1913, p. 19.

"The Rutenber 1909 Models." *The Automobile.* January 14, 1909. p. B-21.

"The Rutenber Motor." *The Horseless Age.* June 5, 1912.

"Sale of Lexington Ordered by Court." *Automotive Industries.* May 27, 1926, p. 908.

"The Six-cylinder Lexington Car." *The Autocar* (United Kingdom). July 10, 1915, p. 37.

"Six 1926 Show Cars Not in 1927 Exhibit." *Automotive Industries.* October 14, 1926, p. 672.

"6 Cylinder $2375 Fully Equipped." *Motor World.* April 9, 1914, p. 55.

"Some Points About the "U."" *Motor West.* March 15, 1922, p. 32.

"Specifications of Current Passenger Car Models." *Motor World.* May 3, 1922, p. 486.

"Standard Model-Price $1,775." *Motor.* June 1912, p. 17.

"A Summary of the Principal Factory Additions." *The Automobile.* Dec. 28, 1916, p. 1099.

"The Summing Up of the Tour." *The Automobile.* August 5, 1909, p. 209.

"This Advertisement Tells You Facts About a Greater Six-Cylinder Car." *The Automobile.* Nov. 26, 1914, pp. 82–83, August 5, 1909, p. 207.

"Turner—Record Master." *Wheels* (Australia). September 1954, pp. 39–40.

"Twenty-four of the 30 Contestants Finished the Run." *The Automobile.*

"Two New Lexington Ideas." *Motor West.* October 15, 1922, p. 32.

"We Say This to Dealers." *Motor.* October, 1914, p. 96.

"Worthy of Its Name." *Leslie's.* September 7, 1916, p. 1.

Correspondence and Unpublished Material

Adams, Jeff. Correspondence to Richard Stanley. July 12, 2005.

Bacon, Milton E. *Lexington Registry.* Connersville, IN. Richard Stanley (survey).

Bottom, David A. *Lexington Registry.* Connersville, IN. Richard Stanley (survey).

Ebert, Louis E. Correspondence to Richard Stanley. Oct. 26, 2003.

____. "Tentative Rutenber Motor Model List." Nov. 2000 (unpublished).

Gibbens, Mike. *Lexington Registry.* Connersville, Indiana: Richard Stanley (survey).

Gordon, Raymond D. Correspondence to Richard Stanley. February 15, 2004.

Goudeau, Todd. *Lexington Registry.* Connersville, IN. Richard Stanley (survey).

Heder, Mats. Correspondence to Richard Stanley. December 6, 2002.

Manson, David. "Aussie Lexingtons." December 3, 2002 (unpublished).

____. Correspondence to Richard Stanley. August 4, 2004.

Margello, Margaret, and Ron Margello. Correspondence to Richard Stanley. September 22 and September 26, 2004.

Mawhinney, John J. *Lexington Registry.* Connersville, IN. Richard Stanley (survey).

Olsson, Igamar, and Mats Heder. "Lexington in Sweden." March 18, 2004 (unpublished).

"Pikes Peak Home-Coming Celebration." Parody poem written to celebrate the Lexington win at Pikes Peak (unpublished).

St. Peter, Sturgis. *Lexington Registry.* Connersville, IN. Richard Stanley (survey).
Snyder, Robert H. Correspondence to Eric von-Grimmenstein. July 1, 1995.
Williams, R. Donald. Correspondence to Richard Stanley. Dec. 26, 2004.
Wolfson, Bernard. *Lexington Registry.* Connersville, IN: Richard Stanley (survey).

Interviews

Baker, Bill. Telephone interview, Dec. 14, 2004.
Bauer, Ruth, and Jerry Corbett (daughter and grandson of Otto Loesche). Interview, May 3, 2004.
Borufsen, Oscar. Telephone interview, Dec. 12, 2004.
Brown, Eldon. Personal interview, Sept. 30, 2004.
Estes, David. Telephone interview, Feb. 18, 2005.
Goudeau, Todd. Telephone interview, Jan. 25, 2005.
Goetz, Wayne. Personal interview, Feb. 2002.
Rigor, Pete. Personal interview, Jan. 8, 2004.
Schickli, Wesley. Telephone interview, Dec. 14, 2004.
Smith, Harry M. Personal interview, Feb. 20, 2004.
Tatman, George. Personal interview, Feb. 2004.
Vance, Thomas. Interview, April 11, 2005
vonGrimmenstein, Eric. Personal interview, Jan. 14, 2004.
Williams, Robert F. Telephone interview, July 1, 2004.

Lexington Literature*

A Wonderful New Lexington Series 22, 1922.
All About a New Light Six (Lexington-Howard Company), 1914.
Allied Companies (United States Automotive Corporation), 1920.
Announcing Series 4-KA The Minute Man Four (Lexington-Howard Co.), 1916.
Announcing the Lark, 1921.
At the Shows: Lexington Minute Man Six Closed Cars, 1926.
The Camp Chigger, July 4, 1920.
Information Book: the Lark and Series "ST" Models.
Lexington (Lexington-Howard Company), 1917.
Lexington: The Minute Man Six (Series "O"), 1918.
Lexington: The New Series 6–50 Minute Man Price List, 1926.
Lexington and the Ten Affiliated Factories Which Contribute to Its Success, 1920.
Lexington Information Book Series "T," 1921.
Lexington Minute Man Six—1917, 1917.
Lexington Minute Man Six Cars (The Seventy-Six Car), 1921.
Lexington Minute Man Six Models for 1924, 1924.
Lexington Minute Man Six Motor Cars, 1919.
Lexington Minute Man Six Series 23 Closed Cars, 1923.
Lexington Minute Man Six Series 23 Open Models, 1923.
Lexington Minute Man Six The Fashion Car for 1917 (Lexington-Howard Company), 1917.
Lexington Motor Cars New Series 6—50, 1926.
Lexington Series—Number 3, The Minute Man Four (Lexington-Howard Company), 1915.
Lexington Series—Number One, The Six Supreme (Lexington-Howard Company), 1915.
Lexington Series "T" Parts List, 1920.
Lexington Special Sedan Concord Model, 1925.
Lexington Thoroughbred Six (Lexington-Howard Company) 1917.
Lexingtons Win Race to Top of Pikes Peak in Blinding Blizzard, 1920.
The Miraculous Ansted Engine, 1922.
Moore Multiple Exhaust System: An Exclusive Feature of the Lexington. Connersville, IN.
The Motor Car Is the Magic Carpet of Modern Times, 1920.
The New Lexington Thoroughbred Six Series 6—N (Lexington-Howard Company), 1916.
The New Lexington Thoroughbred Six Series 6—N (Lexington-Howard Company), 1916.
Parts for Lexington Cars (Kokomo, IN: Ansted Engineering Company), 1927.
Parts Price List Lexington Series "R" Models, 1917.
The Revolutionary Car, 1921.
Series "S" Parts Book, July 1, 1920.
The Skylark: A New Lexington in a Class All Its Own, 1922.
Suggestions with Reference to the Operation and Maintenance of the Lexington Series "R" Models, 1918.
Suggestions with Reference to the Operation and Maintenance of the Series "S" Model, 1920.
Suggestions with Reference to the Operation and Maintenance of the Lexington Series 6-O-17 and 6-OO-17 (Lexington-Howard Company), 1917.
United States Automotive Corporation Stock as an Investment (Chicago: H. W. Dubiske & Company), 1920.

Books and Public Records

"Articles of Association." In *Fayette County Indiana Miscellaneous Records,* Book 6. Connersville, IN: January 16, 1913, pp. 436–437.
"Articles of Association of Howard Motor Car Company." In *Fayette County Indiana Miscellaneous Records,* Book 6. Connersville, IN: January 21, 1913, pp. 441–444.

Except where noted otherwise, all items issued by the Lexington Motor Company, Connersville, IN.

"Articles of Association of Lexington Motor Company." In *Fayette County Indiana Miscellaneous Records*, Book 7. Connersville, IN: August 29, 1917, pp. 472–475.

"Articles of Incorporation." *Fayette County Indiana Miscellaneous Records*, Book 6. Connersville, IN: December 23, 1913, pp. 524–525.

"Articles of Incorporation. The Lexington Motor Car Co." Lexington, KY, December 2, 1908.

"Articles of Incorporation. The Lexington Motor Car Co." Kentucky Secretary of State. Frankfort, KY, Dec. 15, 1908.

Barrows, Frederic I. *1917 History of Fayette County Indiana*. Indianapolis: D. F. Bowen & Company, Inc., 1917.

Blommel, Henry H. *Indiana's Little Detroit 1846–1964*. Connersville, IN, 1964.

"Bond for Deed." In *Fayette County Indiana Miscellaneous Records*, Book 7. Connersville, IN: May 9, 1917, pp. 416–417.

Burness, Tad, *Cars of the Early Twenties*. New York City: Galahad Books, 1968.

Clymer, Floyd. *Floyd Clymer's Historical Motor Scrapbook Number 3*. Los Angeles: Clymer Motors, 1946.

Crowell, Benedict. *America's Munitions*. Washington: Government Printing Office, 1919.

Fox, Jack C., Bob Mount and Donald Davidson. *The Illustrated History of the Indianapolis 500*. Speedway, IN: Carl Hungness & Associates, 1984.

Gould, Todd. *For Gold & Glory*. Bloomington, IN: Indiana University Press, 2002.

Gray, Ralph D. *Alloys and Automobiles*. Indianapolis: Indiana Historical Society, 1979.

Hubbard, Albert. *A Little Journey to Connersville*. East Aurora, NY: Roycrofters, 1914.

"Increase of Capital Stock." In *Fayette County Indiana Miscellaneous Records*, Book 9. Connersville, IN: December 16, 1922, pp. 140–142.

Kimes, Beverly Rae, and Henry Austin Clark, Jr. *Standard Catalog of American Cars 1805–1942*. Iola, WI: Krause Publications, Jan. 1985.

____. *Standard Catalog of American Cars 1805–1942*. 3rd Edition. Iola, WI: Krause Publications, 1996.

"Kinzea Stone." In *The Best of Scott County*. Vancouver, WA: Piedmont Publishing, 2000, p. 34.

"Lexington Howard Co. Increase Capital." In *Fayette County Miscellaneous Records*. Connersville, IN: April 26, 1916, pp. 229–231.

"The Lexington Howard Co. Resolution." Connersville, IN: June 28, 1916, pp. 263–265.

"Lexington Touring—6-P." *Handbook of Automobiles*. National Chamber of Commerce, pp. 144–145.

Meyers, Marjorie Teetor. *One Man's Vision*. Indianapolis: Guild Press of Indiana Inc., 1995.

"Moore, John." *Lexington City Directory* 1908, Volume IV. Lexington, KY: R. L. Polk & Co., 1908.

Nevins, Allan, and Frank E. Hill. *Ford Expansion and Challenge 1915–1933*. New York: Charles Scribner's Sons, 1957.

Rickert, Edwin L. *Record of the Transactions by Which the Properties of the Lexington Motor Co., and Ansted Engineering Co. Were Transferred to Auburn Automobile Co. August 26, 1926–May 27, 1927*. Connersville, IN: November 12, 1927.

Schlereth, Thomas. *U. S. 40: A Roadscape of the American Experience*. Indianapolis: Indiana Historical Society, 1985.

Walters, H. Max. *The Making of Connersville and Fayette County*, Vol. I. Baltimore: Gateway Press, Inc., 1989.

____. *The Making of Connersville and Fayette County*, Vol. II. Baltimore: Gateway Press, Inc., 1969.

Index

American Automobile Association 22, 46, 126, 139, 140
Anderson, Professor F. Paul 30
Ansted, Arthur A. 71, 148, 179
Ansted, Dale 72, 193, 200
Ansted, Edward W. (E.W.) 69, 70, 71, 75, 92, 99, 100, 160, 200
Ansted, Edward W., Jr. 71, 86
Ansted, Frank B. (F.B.) 45, 70, 71, 72, 75, 86, 92; as head of Lexington 100, 101, 103, 109, 111, 115, 117, 129, 131, 133, 137; ousted from Lexington 182, 189, 193, 199, 200; U.S.A.C. 148, 153, 156, 157, 162, 170, 176, 179, 180
Ansted, George W. 43, 71, 109, 148, 162, 179, 180, 182, 189
Ansted, Nellie 71, 200
Ansted, William B. (W.B.) 41, 148, 179, 180, 182, 217, 225, 226
Ansted automobile 193
Ansted engine 126, 128, 135, 139, 140, 145, 146, 151, 153, 154, 158, 159, 160, 162, 164, 165, 166, 167, 172, 174, 176, 179, 184, 185, 186, 189, 190, 192, 197, 198, 222, 225, 227, 229, 230, 232
Ansted Engine Works 100
Ansted Engineering Company 116, 148, 151, 162, 174, 177, 180, 182, 185, 189, 191; Kokomo 192, 193, 194, 197
Ansted Lexington automobile 166, 168, 169
Ansted Radiator Company 153
Ansted Special racecar 145 , 146
Ansted Spring and Axle Co. 40, 42, 70, 79, 82, 83, 100, 160, 162, 175, 198
Arbuckle, Samuel 148
Articles of Association or Incorporation 7, 68, 69, 100, 148
Atwater Kent 73, 75, 79, 83
Auburn Automobile Company 193, 195, 200
Auburn Cord Duesenberg Museum 219
Australia 100, 118, 125, 126
Auto-Light 67
Auto-Lighter 61
Automotive Industries 159, 160

Babcock, Guilford C. 69
Babcock, Howard 69, 70
Bacon, Milton 229

Baker, Bill 216, 223
Barbin, Ray 140, 142
Barnard, George M. 191, 192, 193
Barrows, B.M. 193
Barrows, Frederick I. 65, 66, 69, 75, 92, 94, 109, 148, 179, 182
Beaumont, C.H. 151, 189
Belknap, R.B. 180
Beneke, Henry 179
Bigger and Better Connersville Committee 193, 195, 196
Blackburn, Charles (Charley) 23, 24, 30
Blommel, Henry 2, 206, 216
Bosch Magneto 36, 54, 57, 73, 75, 83
Bottom, David 225
Bradley, Victor A. (V.A.) 7, 33
Broedlin, Herman 46
Brown, Ezra B. (E.B.) 78, 92, 103
Brush, Alanson 162
Bryan, Dr. Francis F. 7, 8, 10, 13, 14, 15, 17, 31, 33
Bryson, Thomas C. 69
Bullard, Clarence (Cuz) 140, 142
Burk, Catherine 71
Burk, John W. 69

California Top 179, 184, 185
Carlstrom, O.J. 126
Carter, George R. 41
Cassel, Charles C. 101
Central Car Company 69, 70, 75, 76
Central Manufacturing Company 1, 16, 40, 42, 71, 100, 113, 148, 151, 162, 175, 179, 195, 198
Clark, Ray 215, 219, 220
Clay, Herbert 140, 145, 182
Cline, Albert L. (Al) 98, 127, 128, 129, 130, 131, 135, 136, 137, 138, 140, 142, 145
Cline, Rose 135, 136
Coats, Fred N.: Connersville, IN 41, 43, 45, 52, 55, 56, 70; Lexington, KY 11, 13, 14, 15, 27, 30, 31, 33, 37
Coats, John 31
Connersville, Indiana 1, 13, 32, 33; factory move 34, 37, 40, 43, 45, 46, 53, 62, 86; Indy 500 Race 123; Lexington-Howard 97; Lexington Motor Co. 112, 117; Pike's Peak 128, 131, 132, 133, 143, 145; receivership 180, 195, 199, 201; USAC 154
Connersville Commercial Club 3, 41, 42, 43
Connersville Foundry Corporation 148, 198
Connersville Securities Corporation 65
Connersville ship 105
Connersville Wheel Works 42
Continental Discount Corporation 178, 182
Continental engine 72, 75, 78, 83, 93, 96, 97, 103, 149, 154, 163, 210, 215, 217, 219, 221
Corbin, Frank 10
Cord, Errett Lobban 193

Dana, C.A. 179, 180
Davis, Charles 179
Day, F.T. 86
Diamond, Harry 145
Dixon, Arthur 182, 191, 193
Dodge, Victor K. 7, 8, 23, 30, 33, 34, 46
Drach, Bob 121
Durant, William C. 5, 158, 162, 174, 177, 180, 182
Durant automobile 162, 174, 176, 182, 232

Eberhart, A.O. 179
Edsold, John A. 56
El Pomar Foundation 232
Engleka, Howard 149

Faught, J. Earl 160, 202
Fayette County, Indiana 1, 39, 45, 67, 103, 105
Fayette County, Kentucky 5, 7, 8, 39, 48
Fayette County Historical Museum 145, 146, 219, 223, 224, 225
Fayette Paint and Trim Company 162
Finney, Charles D. 203
Fowler, Ray 105
Freed, William H. 116
Frost, Hyatt 182, 193

General Parts Corporation 192
George R. Carter Leather Co. 40, 41, 42, 113
Georgetown, Kentucky 33, 118
Givens, Mike 207

251

Index

Glidden Tour, 1909 22, 23, 24, 25, 26, 27, 29, 30, 1910 46, 47, 48, 49, 50, 51, 53
GMC AA truck chassis 103, 109, 110, 113
Goetz, Henry 127
Goetz, Wayne 143
Gold and Glory Racing circuit 146
Goudeau, Todd 211
Gray and Davis starter 152

Hair, William 22
Hanch, Charles C 174
Hanson, LeRoy (L.A.) 86, 92, 148, 177
Hawkins, E.V. 43
Hayes, E.O. 46
Herod, William P. 140, 145, 182, 185, 191
Heron, Isabel 72
Heron, James M. 69, 148, 180
Hess, Elmer J. 148
Hess axle 79, 83
Himelick, Judge E. Ralph 101, 162, 182, 195
Hoosier Castings Company 71, 100
Hoosier Construction Company 92, 109, 202
Houk wheels 82
Howard automobile 69, 70, 72, 73, 74, 75, 76, 77, 78, 81
Howard-Jesco starter 75
Howard Motor Car Company 69, 70, 72, 76
Hull, Charles C. 148, 179, 195
Huston, Emery 70, 71, 90, 92, 127, 131, 133, 135, 137, 148, 182
Huston, Joseph E. 69, 75, 92
Huston, Robert T. 69
Huzell, Eskil 117, 126

Indiana Lamp Company 1, 40, 71, 100, 113, 148, 151, 193, 195, 198, 199
Indiana Piston Ring Company 162, 189
Indianapolis 500 Mile Race 62, 65, 112, 121, 123
Indianapolis Motor Speedway Museum 217, 225, 226, 230
Inland Motor Sales, Inc. 72, 87, 88, 90, 100, 101, 131, 133, 175
Irvin, Charles 175, 203

Jackson, J.P. 7
Jacquea Manufacturing Company 180
Jessup, Wilfred 180
Jiffy curtains 97
Johnson, Carl 156
Johnson, Harry 15, 46, 50
Johnson, H.D. 33
Johnston, Edgar D. (E.D.) 33, 34, 43

Kansas City hill climb 46
Karlstrom, Oskar 117
Keefe, William 30, 31
Keller, Charles 98

Knight, Harry 62, 121, 122, 123, 124
Knight, Jack 139

Lawton, Clarence 127, 140, 141, 142, 145
Leeds, Fred R. 127
Leiter, Arthur E. (A.E.) 33, 40, 41, 43
Lewis, Gerner 127
Lexington, Kentucky 32, 33, 37, 40, 46, 48, 201; Mammoth Skating Rink 9, 37, 38, 40, 45; West Main Street 9, 10, 14, 37, 38, 39, 45
Lexington automobile: Cable-Brake 149; Clubster 94, 96, 106; Concord 90, 184, 185, 186, 187, 188, 230; Convertible 96, 97, 98, 106, 118, 119, 120; gallery 207, 208, 209; Indiana produced 54, 56, 59, 62, 65, 76; Kentucky 11, 15, 17, 19, 21, 22, 23, 26, 27, 30, 31, 34, 36, 40, 46; Lark 158, 160, 167, 170, 171, 172, 179, 184, 190, 223, 224; Lex-Sedan 148, 157, 162; Lexigasifier 149, 166, 185; Lexington-Howard Co. 77, 80, 89, 90, 93, 95, 97; Lexington Motor Co. 101, 104, 105, 110, 111, 114, 115, 116, 117, 118, 123, 124, 125, 126; Minute Man 81, 84, 89, 90, 91, 94, 95, 99, 109, 118, 153, 158, 166, 184, 185, 186, 189, 190, 191, 203, 209, 211, 215, 219, 220, 223, 228, 229; Model A 20, 23, 34, 35, 36, 46, 53, 57; Model B 20, 35, 36, 53; Model C Roadster 20, 35, 36, 51, 53; Model D 35, 37, 46, 53, 67; Model D-F 53, 57, 60, 63; Model E, Standard 53, 57, 60, 63, 64; Model F, Master 53, 54, 57, 60, 61; Model G, Perfect Six 57, 63; Model G, Standard 67, 68, 69; Series H 75, 78, 79; Model K 56, 63, 81; Model L Thoroughbred, Light Six 81, 82, 83, 85; Model M Six Supreme, Big Six 81, 83; Model 6-N Thoroughbred 88, 94; Model O and OO 94, 96, 97, 102, 103, 106; Moore Multiple Exhaust 56, 60, 67, 78, 82, 83, 96 132, 102, 166, 185, 198; Number 6 132, 135, 137, 138, 203; Number 7 132, 135, 136, 137, 138, 139, 142, 145, 146, 203, 231; Number 103 46, 48, 49, 50, 53; Number 110 46, 48, 50; Number 114 24; One-Finger Emergency Brake 102, 104; Pike's Peak 127, 128, 129, 131, 132, 134, 135, 144; receivership 184, 186, 189, 191, 192, 194, 195, 198; Revolutionary Car 166; Series 4-KA 91; Series 6-P Thoroughbred 96, 99; Series 22 174, 175, 176; Series 23 179; Series R Minute Man 102, 103, 104, 105, 107, 108, 112, 118, 148; Series S 148, 149, 162, 211, 212, 213, 214, 216, 217, 218; Series Seventy-Six 90, 117, 165, 166, 221; Series T 151, 158, 163, 166, 170, 172, 224; Series U Ultimate 170, 173, 174, 225, 227; 6–50 190, 191, 192; Skylark 179, 183, 184, 190; Special 128, 139, 140, 142, 145; Supreme 172, 176, 226; Thorobred 128, 135, 139, 155, 160, 161, 162, 170, 217, 218, 219, 220; Thoroughbred 81, 89, 90, 120; Tourabout 119; Truck 28, 56; 2-Way Headlamps 148, 152, 153, 166; U.S.A.C. 149, 150, 153, 154, 155, 158, 160, 162, 166, 181
Lexington Commercial Club 9, 20, 33, 40
Lexington-Howard Motor Car Company 71, 72, 75, 77, 84, 89, 90, 91, 92, 98, 100
Lexington Motor Car Company: incorporated 5, 6, 7, 10, 11, 14, 33, 40; relocated 42, 43, 44, 53, 55, 67, 68, 69, 75, 76
Lexington Motor Company 100, 103, 105, 106, 109, 111, 113, 116, 119, 137; receivership 180, 182, 185, 192, 193, 194, 200, 202; U.S.A.C. 148, 149, 151, 158, 162, 167, 174, 176, 178, 179
Loesche, Carrie Lepple 131, 135, 136
Loesche, Otto (Ot) 127, 128, 129, 130, 131, 132, 133, 134, 135, 136, 137, 138, 139, 140, 142, 145, 146; U.S.A.C. 158, 184

Marion, Indiana 33, 41
Mawhinney, John J. 228
McClanahan, Gus 137, 140
McDuffee Automobile Company 70, 72
McFarlan, James E. (J.E.) 41
McFarlan, John B. (J.B.) 42
McFarlan Motor Car Company 179
McGraw, L.H. 7
McIlvain, Harold 184
Mekanisk Industri 117
Millard, Clarence I. 69
Milton, Tommy 174
Minute Man statue 176, 177, 203
Moore, John C. (J.C.): Indiana 41, 46, 50, 51, 56, 72, 82, 96, 102, 109, 127, 135, 137; Kentucky 5, 7, 11, 15, 23, 24, 25, 26, 27, 30; U.S.A.C. 148, 149, 172, 182, 186, 199, 200, 201
Moorish Tile Company 149
Morgan, Major Alexander G. 33
Mountain, Dr. J.R. 41

Neverleek one-man top 82
New Zealand 100

O'Neil, Charles 7
Osborn, John 7

Pantasote top 36, 38, 54
Patrick, Clinton (G.C.) 127, 137, 140, 142, 182, 201

Person, Per 117, 212
Picket Rope 99, 103
Pike's Peak National Hill Climb 126, 130, 135, 136, 137, 140, 145, 158, 176, 184, 186
Play Day celebration 113, 151, 199
Plenderlith, J.V. 145
Prest-O-Light 11, 54, 60
Prest-O-Start 61, 62, 67

Rayfield carburetor 96, 152
Rehberg, John 220
Rex Manufacturing Company 1, 97, 113
Rieman, Andrew H. 101
Rigor, Pete 198
Rudd, Bobby 140, 141, 142, 145
Rudd, Joe 140, 142, 145
Rune, Jan 214
Rutenber, Edwin A. 17
Rutenber engine 11, 16, 17, 15, 36, 37, 53, 56, 57, 60, 61, 67, 78, 123, 208
Ryan, Ellis 193

St. Peter, Sturgis 210, 211
Sample, Miss Ethelyn 105
Schebler carburetor 54, 58, 61, 79, 82, 83
Schwartz wheels 17, 36, 54
Service Clubs 132, 140, 143, 145, 193
Shearhod, G.E. 179
Smith, A.E. 109

Smith, I.I. 179
Snead Cushion Drive 163
Spencer Penrose Trophy (cup) 127, 129, 135, 139, 140, 144, 146, 147, 232
Springer, Raymond S. 69, 145
Standard Parts Company 113, 160
Stanley, Richard 221, 223
Stewart, Bob "Bud" 140, 142
Stewart vacuum system 82, 83
Stewart Warner 67, 162
Stone, Benjamin F. 7, 33
Stone, Kinzea 2, 7, 8, 9, 12, 17, 33, 118
Stoops, Thomas H. 42
Stromberg carburetor 72, 75, 83
Sullivan, Leonard 223, 224
Sweden 112, 117, 126, 211, 2112, 213, 214

Tatman, E.W. 90
Teetor, Charles 109
Teetor, Ralph 109
Teetor, Ray 109
Teetor-Hartley Motor Corporation 82, 86, 109, 116, 148, 162
Teetor T-head engine 82
Thiebaud, Benjamin F. 101
Timken axle 17, 83
Tractor-Train Company of Indiana 1, 199, 201
Turner, Albert Valentine (A.V.) 125
Tuttle, Harry 69, 70, 72

United Service Company 191
United States Automotive Corporation 137, 148, 149, 160, 170, 174, 180, 182, 196, 198, 203
Unser, Joe 145

vonGrimmenstein, Eric 202, 204, 205, 227

Wainwright, E. Pierre 160, 170, 176, 177, 178, 203
Wainwright, Harry 145
Walthall, William 146
Warner Gear Company 153
Warner-Toledo gearbox 75, 79
Western Motor Company 17
Westinghouse 82, 83
Wheeler and Schebler laboratory 78, 82
Wiles, Allen 69, 101
Williams, Bradley, McCaleb & Pierce law firm 162
Williams, G.H. 100
Williams, R. Donald 151
Williams, Robert F. (R.F.) 62, 199
Wills, Dr. N.G. 88, 185
Wilson, G.D. 7, 15, 33
Wolfson, Bernard 229
Woodruff, E.A. 86

Young, F.O. 7

www.ingramcontent.com/pod-product-compliance
Lightning Source LLC
Chambersburg PA
CBHW081548300426
44116CB00015B/2797